STRATEGY, VALUE AND RISK

Palgrave Macmillan Finance and Capital Markets Series
For information about other titles in this series please visit the website
http://www.palgrave.com/business/finance and capital markets.asp

Also by Jamie Rogers

STRATEGY, VALUE AND RISK – THE REAL OPTIONS APPROACH (2002)

Strategy, Value and Risk

The Real Options Approach

Jamie Rogers

Second Edition

First edition published 2002
Second edition published 2009 by
PALGRAVE MACMILLAN

Palgrave Macmillan in the UK is an imprint of Macmillan Publishers Limited,
registered in England, company number 785998, of Houndmills, Basingstoke,
Hampshire RG21 6XS.

Palgrave Macmillan in the US is a division of St Martin's Press LLC,
175 Fifth Avenue, New York, NY 10010.

Palgrave Macmillan is the global academic imprint of the above companies
and has companies and representatives throughout the world.

Palgrave® and Macmillan® are registered trademarks in the United States,
the United Kingdom, Europe and other countries.

ISBN: 978–0–230–57737–4   hardback

This book is printed on paper suitable for recycling and made from fully
managed and sustained forest sources. Logging, pulping and manufacturing
processes are expected to conform to the environmental regulations of the
country of origin.

A catalogue record for this book is available from the British Library.

A catalog record for this book is available from the Library of Congress.

10 9 8 7 6 5 4 3 2 1
18 17 16 15 14 13 12 11 10 09

Printed and bound in Great Britain by
CPI Antony Rowe, Chippenham and Eastbourne

Contents

List of Figures
and Tables

Figures

Tables

Preface

The objective of *Strategy, Value and Risk – the Real Options Approach* is to provide a background to the concept and method of real options. Real options analysis is a valuation, project management and strategic decision paradigm that applies financial option theory to real assets. The real options literature has produced many excellent books and academic papers since Stuart Myers first used the phrase in a 1984 article that discussed the gap between strategic planning and finance. This book surveys the development of real option theory and explores the relationships between strategy, value and risk, using concepts and methods that have been developed in response to an increasingly dynamic business environment, and the potential limitations with the status quo in dealing with this transformation. This book also explores the extension of traditional valuation methodologies in the context of seven case studies contrasting traditional valuation with a real options approach.

As a substantial part of value rests on corporate decisions, it is essential to bridge strategy and value-based management. Traditional value metrics, however, are becoming progressively more inadequate in capturing the value of strategic investments. Valuation approaches such as net present value (NPV) and return on investment (ROI) apply to a static world, and yet today's business environment is anything but static. The real options concept has the potential to capture the value of the flexibility to adapt and revise future management decisions with the benefit of better information. Real options can provide a framework for managing and creating value, and therefore provide a linkage between strategy and value-based management. The concept can be used to communicate management decisions to capital markets, align value and strategy, and demonstrate that risk can be influenced through managerial flexibility.

Real options applications can be found in industries such as natural resources, real estate, pharmaceuticals, high-tech valuation, e-business valuation, transportation industries, energy, telecommunications and information technology (IT).

Corporate finance and investment banking applications include areas such as initial public offerings, mergers and acquisitions, corporate restructuring, multimedia and intellectual property areas.

The real options material covers disciplines and functions as diverse as accounting, finance, economics, econometrics, financial mathematics and management science. These subjects have their own bodies of knowledge, and there are limitations on how much of the material can be covered in one text. The real options approach is a guide to strategy under uncertainty that is more or less quantifiable. As in other quantitative disciplines, much of the value of real options analysis is in the process of the analysis, as opposed to just producing an end number. With or without quantification, however, it is likely to produce different results to more conventional thinking about strategy and investment.

WHO SHOULD READ THIS BOOK

As we continue into the new millennium, it is likely that globalization and IT will continue to shape the business environment and provide the foundations of business opportunity. In this environment managers are now under pressure to develop a new set of capabilities. This requires not only an understanding of the market, customers, investors and the industry dynamics of the company, but also the operational drivers of success. Today it is essential for management to organize a company's resources so that there is a clear integration between a company's strategic objectives and competences and the changes that are occurring in the market. Developments in strategic concepts that include resources and capabilities, dynamic analysis and advanced financial analysis are providing frameworks to manage and cope with the external environment.

The role of the CFO is undergoing a transformation, expanding from a focus on external reporting and fiduciary duties to becoming a partner with other key business partners such as operations, marketing and executive management. This requires a strong strategic analysis on the business drivers of success and operational strategies that integrate finance into business and strategy. CFOs can enhance corporate value by promoting the use of a well-designed set of financial tools and guidelines to secure assets and maintain or even increase value. CFOs are also managers of the company's strategic resources through the organization of capital resources, and must ensure that they create value for the organization. By defining a new set of capabilities as a provider of strategic analysis and metrics, the CFO can increase the value-adding activity of the finance function.

Investment analysts and management consultants work in numerous areas that involve financial and economic concepts. These include projects of a strategic nature where the valuation of a corporation is critical. A successful analyst is required to see the larger economic setting and environment in which a company competes, assess a company's industry and its position within the industry, understand which projects best serve its broad strategic goals and recognize the company's strategic capabilities and options. In addition, the analyst must translate these broad insights into judgements about relative valuation of particular opportunities and communicate these to management and investors.

ORGANIZATION OF THE BOOK

The book is divided into four parts:

- *PART I* looks at the evolution of the major strategic and financial methods that emerged in the 1970s, 80s and 90s, and uses five case studies, an IT investment, an energy utility, a pharmaceutical company, firm growth and firm abandoment to illustrate these concepts. The case studies are idealized in the first two examples, while the third is an adaptation of a case study that appeared in the June 2000 *Financial Analysts Journal*.

- *PART II* discusses developments in strategy, followed by the real options framework and advances in risk management.

- The quantification of real options is outlined in *PART III*.

- In *PART IV* the five initial case studies are again analysed using a real options framework. In addition two further real options case studies explore the modularity concept and the sale of real estate assets. Finally the conclusions and practical applications are discussed.

Acknowledgements

The second edition of this book represents an accumulation of experience and feedback on the first edition from friends, colleagues, practitioners and academics.

I would like to thank Charles Alsdorf, Maria Barbera, Richard Baskin, Ian Clark, Satyajit Das, Roger Flather, David Kellogg, Richard LeBuhn, Greg Medcraft, Lloyd Spencer, Michael Stutchbury, Michael Thomas and Rob Thomsett. I also wish to thank and acknowledge Bill Birkett and Roger Flather Snr who are no longer with us.

My appreciation goes to Carliss Baldwin, Robert Geske, Stephen Penman and David Shimko for their contributions and advice. I thank Les Clewlow and Chris Strickland for their contribution and commitment to the quantitative sections of the book, Nicola Fusari and Andrea Gamba for the Modularity article, and David Friedman and Stephen L'Heureux for the Corporate Real Estate article. I also thank Lisa Von Fircks and Renée Takken at Palgrave for their commitment to the second edition and Mary Payne for copy-editing the book.

I dedicate this book to my mum and the memory of my dad and grandmother. I would also like to thank my wife Meg for her patience, guidance and support.

JAMIE ROGERS

List of Acronyms

ADF	Augmented Dickey-Fuller
AGLT	Adjusted Generalized Log-Transformed
ARCH	autoregressive conditional heteroskedasticity
BSM	Black–Scholes–Merton
BTU	British Thermal Unit
CAPM	capital asset pricing model
CCF	commercialization cash flow
CFAR	cash flow at risk
CI	capital invested
DA	decision analysis
DCF	discounted cash flow
EMM	equivalent martingale measure
EMV	expected monetary value
ENPV	expected net present value
EP	economic profit
EPS	earnings per share
FDA	Food and Drug Administration
GARCH	generalized autoregressive conditional heteroskedasticity
GBM	geometric Brownian motion
GOV	growth option value
IRR	internal rate of return
LSM	least-squares mean
MVA	market value added
MWh	megawatt hour
NME	new molecular entity
NPV	net present value
NOPAT	net operating profits after tax
PV	present value

PVCF	present value of expected operating cash flows
RE	residual earnings
ROE	return on equity
ROI	return on investment
SDE	stochastic differential equation
V (firm)	value
VAIP	value of assets in place
VAR	value at risk
VGO	value of growth opportunities
WACC	weighted average cost of capital

Introduction

THE BUSINESS ENVIRONMENT AND STRATEGY

Technology is defined as the processes by which an organization transforms labour, capital materials and information into products and services of greater value. All firms have technologies. *Innovation* refers to a change in one of these technologies. The wave of innovation in the late nineteenth century was so spectacular that the Commissioner of the United States Office of Patents recommended in 1899 that the office be abolished with the words 'Everything that can be invented has been invented'. History is scattered with such prophesies about technology, and with organizations that failed when confronted with changes in markets and technologies.

Over the last 20 years the surge of innovation in IT has reduced the cost of communications, which in turn has facilitated the globalization of production and capital markets. As a consequence globalization has spurred competition and hence innovation. These developments in technology in combination with the dereg- ulation of the transportation, financial services, energy and telecommunications sectors are redefining the business environment. New industries are being formed and the boundaries of existing ones being redrawn, creating a corporate envir- onment of intense change and competition. The instability of industry boundaries has been most evident in industries such as information technology and services, entertainment and communications, and also in historically relatively more stable environments such as energy, financial services and retail distribution.

The Austrian economist Joseph Schumpeter was the first to identify and study the dynamic relationship between industry structure and competition. Schumpeter saw innovation, a 'perennial gale of creative destruction' (cited in Grant, 1998 p. 71), as being fundamental to competition and the principal driver of the evolution of industry. A typically healthy economy as defined by Schumpeter is one that is continually disrupted by innovations in technology, and not one in equilibrium as described in classical economics, where the focus is on the optimization of resources within a stable environment. The role of the entrepreneur or innovator in the

Table 0.1 Surf's up: Schumpeter's waves accelerate

First wave: 1785 60 years	Second wave: 1845 55 years	Third wave: 1900 50 years	Fourth wave: 1950 40 years	Fifth wave: 1990 30 years
■ water power	■ steam	■ electricity	■ petrochemicals	■ digital networks
■ textiles	■ rail	■ chemicals	■ electronics	■ new media
■ iron	■ steel	■ the internal combustion engine	■ aviation	

Source: The Economist, 20 February 1999

creative destruction process is that of a catalyst, permitting the economy to invigorate and renew itself.

An issue is therefore whether established industry structures are a consistent guide to the competitive environment and industry performance. Schumpeter considered each *long wave* of economic activity created by disruption as unique, and determined by completely different industry clusters (see Table 0.1). Each wave starts with a boom, where the rise in the economic cycle is driven by new innovations that stimulate investment and economic growth. As the technologies mature and investors' returns decline, each long boom comes to an end and expansion slows. Eventually there is a decline in economic growth, followed by a new wave of innovations that bring old methods to an end and create the environment for a whole new cycle. The fourth cycle of Schumpeter's 'successive industrial revolutions', stimulated by electronics, oil and aviation is now rapidly running down, and a fifth wave, driven by software, semiconductors, fibreoptics, and genetics is not only in progress but also possibly reaching the end of the boom period.

The length of Schumpeter's long waves has also been decreasing. Governments and organizations began to search systematically for new technologies during the third wave in the early part of the twentieth century, which has increased the speed of industrial structural change. The overall implications are that many of today's organizations, even the biggest, can potentially fade and disappear, and be replaced by new organizations that are currently nothing more than the notion of some entrepreneur. Established dominant industry structures hold the seeds of their own destruction by providing incentives for organizations to strike through new methods in competing.

Creative destruction and discontinuity can, however, be leveraged by organizations to sustain competitive advantage. Organizations will need to transform rather than incrementally improve their strategies and processes, by creating new businesses, selling off or closing down businesses or divisions whose growth is slowing down, abandoning outdated, ingrown structures and rules, and adopting new decision-making processes and control systems. Most managers today however still focus on concepts based on continuous improvement, even though most organizations are realizing diminishing returns in their incremental improvement programs. In today's business environment it is the opportunities created by innovation that have the potential to create value and manage the unrelenting competition that is reducing margins in industry after industry.

VALUE AND RISK

Over the last 25 years there has been a broad transformation in the global financial markets. Developments such as deregulation, derivatives, securitization, structured products and risk management have improved access to the global financial markets for participants. Corporations now have the ability to go directly to financial markets rather than banks for finance. Consequently, the power of investment and commercial banks has shifted to shareholders, who now influence corporate boards and management through their fund managers. Shareholder value dominates the management agenda in much of the corporate world. The demands of shareholders and the threat of takeover have created strong pressure on management to maximize returns to shareholders, and have had an enormous impact on corporate strategies, management and performance.

While managers, therefore, believe they control corporate resources, in today's business environment it is the influence of investors that is determining how capital is allocated. Many strategic management decisions today, however, are made in environments where costs, prices, quantities, competitive behaviour, market size, share and growth, taxes, inflation and projects lifecycles are largely unknown, and introduce risk and uncertainty into the capital allocation process. Investor predictions are confounded by unexpected changes in macroeconomic indicators such as interest rates, and microeconomic factors such as unforeseen new firm-related competitors, and industry shocks in areas such as technology.

STRATEGY AND REAL OPTIONS

Managing innovation has two dimensions, the process of identifying, valuing and capturing opportunity, and managing resources in the context of the associated uncertainty. These two components will need to be embedded in the analysis of product development, forecasts, incentives, market structure, barriers to entry, valuations and financial structures. Financial metrics and strategic planning, however, emerged over the last 50 years as complementary but nevertheless unrelated systems for corporate decisions and investment. Most companies do not have any metrics that focus on innovation, and instead use metrics such as discounted cash flows, return on net assets and return on investment that focus on optimization. These metrics do not have the flexibility to take advantage of any future opportunities, or the potential to manage any downside risks, that are the consequence of an increasingly dynamic and volatile business environment. Strategic management decisions are based on static business cases that do not include any capabilities to respond and change strategy according to future contingencies.

Valuing these options considers the uncertainty or volatility associated with the business environment and capital allocation. Real options analysis is a valuation, project management and strategic decision paradigm that applies financial option theory to real assets. The concept has the potential to capture the value of the flexibility to adapt and revise management decisions made in the future with the benefit of better information. Real options can provide a framework for managing and creating value, and therefore provide an association between shareholder value, strategy and value-based management. The concept can also be used to communicate management decisions to financial markets, and also demonstrate that risk can be influenced through managerial flexibility. The real options approach is a guide to strategy under uncertainty that is more or less quantifiable. With or without quantification, however, it is likely to produce different results to more conventional thinking about strategy making and investment.

REFERENCES

Grant, R.M. *Contemporary Strategy Analysis*, Blackwell, 1998.

Hamel, G. *Leading The Revolution*, HBS Press, 2000.

Trigeorgis, L. *Real Options: Managerial Flexibility and Strategy in Resource Allocation*, MIT Press, 1996.

The Economist, A survey of the new economy, untangling e-economics, 23 September, 2000.

The Economist, Innovation in industry, 20 February, 1999.

PART I

The Evolution of Strategy, Value and Risk

CHAPTER 1

Strategy: From Corporate Planning to Shareholder Value

Strategy provides unity, consistency and guidance in an organization's decisions and activities and is fundamental to an organization's success. It is essentially about applying principles to various strategic situations. The development of business strategy over the last 50 years was initially driven more by business practicalities than theory. The business environment in the 1950s and 60s was a period of relative stability, and organizations focused on growth through diversification, vertical integration, mass marketing, efficiencies through scale and long-term investments. Corporate planning grew in popularity as a result of the increasing size and complexity of these organizations and the problems associated with management and control. Although financial budgeting offered some means for addressing these issues, the main strategic objective was the long-term planning of investments, which required a longer time horizon than that provided by annual budgets.

In the 1970s analytical concepts such as portfolio planning matrices became popular strategy and resource allocation frameworks. The matrix approach was designed to assess business unit performance and strategies, and the corporate portfolio's performance in general. Boston Consulting Group's growth/share matrix was an innovation in corporate strategy, and became a principal framework for resource allocation in diversified organizations. Strategic alternatives were based on the comparison, using industry appeal and competitive position as the criteria, of the strategic positioning of the various business units within the matrix. Figure 1.1 illustrates the Boston Consulting Group's growth/share matrix. The matrix consisted of four quadrants that showed cash flow patterns and potential strategies, and two dimensions that consisted of the market growth rate, which

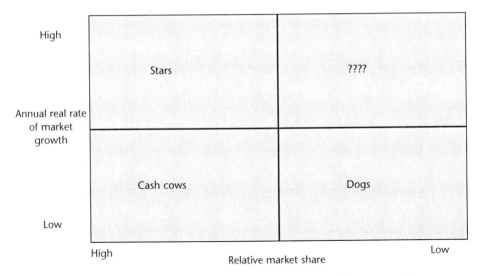

Figure 1.1 The Boston Consulting Group growth/share matrix

focused on capturing a business's potential use of cash, and relative market share, a proxy for competitive position and therefore a business's ability to generate cash. Examining the position of the business units as defined by their asset or revenue base within the matrix provided an analysis of the flow of financial resources within a diversified organization.

- *Cash Cows* were profitable businesses located in a slow growing industry that had relatively high market share, stable cash flows and that required little further investment. The strategy under these circumstances was to milk the cow.

- *Dogs* were businesses with low unstable earnings, a competitive disadvantage and slow industry growth. The best strategy in these cases was to divest or harvest.

- *Stars* were businesses with high growing earnings, whose dominant market position justified investment for growth.

- *Question marks* were businesses with low earnings and relative market share that required cash, with uncertain future performance and the potential to become either stars or dogs.

The matrix provided a framework for resource allocation, business unit strategy, business unit performance targets, and balancing of cash flows and growth. Management could allocate capital to business units, such as harvesting dogs, milking cash cows, investing in stars, or investing in any question marks with the potential to become stars, and rebalance the portfolio through the trading of business units. The decline in popularity of portfolio planning matrices during the 1980s was due to a number of factors. Only two variables, market share and market growth were used, and these were not particularly good surrogates for competitive advantage and profitability. The choice of metrics also blurred the positioning of businesses in the matrix, and furthermore the portfolio matrix ignored any interdependencies between businesses.

A number of events during the 1970s ended the post-war period of relative stability. The oil shocks, high interest rates and the increased international competition from Asia and Europe created an unstable environment in which diversification and planning no longer provided the expected synergies. As a result organizations moved towards more flexible strategic management methods that focused on competitiveness, with competitive advantage becoming the main strategic objective. This had a significant impact on strategic concepts at the beginning of the 1980s. One development pioneered by Michael Porter was the use of industrial organization economics in the analysis of profitability, which emphasized an organization's competition, market environment and industry structure. Capital market developments and the profit incentives in reviving non-performing corporations also created a fertile environment for the emergence of corporate raiders and leveraged buyout firms. The activities of these players exposed the vulnerability of many large diversified corporations which led to several takeovers.

As a result of these developments management became focused on the stock market valuations of their corporations. In the 1990s shareholders and the financial markets continued to pressure management to maximize shareholder returns, and as a result the shareholder value concept was included in all aspects of strategy. A variety of methods have been defined to measure shareholder value. One defines shareholder value as a return greater than the cost of capital employed to generate that return, and therefore distinguishes between accounting and economic profit. Another approach is to view an organization as a portfolio of assets, valued as the sum of the net present values (NPV) of each asset's cash flows. This concept can be extended by defining the value of a firm's equity as the NPV of the firm's cash flows that are accessible to shareholders. Shareholder value under this approach is therefore based on the discounted cash flow (DCF) method associated with investments.

REFERENCES

Collis, D.J. and Montgomery, C.A. *Corporate Strategy, A Resource Based Approach*, Irwin McGraw Hill, 1998.

Grant, R.M. *Contemporary Strategy Analysis*, Blackwell, 1998.

CHAPTER 2

Valuation

2.1 ACCOUNTING VALUATION

A business model provides a framework for identifying and creating value. Business models describe how the components of a business combine as a system. The phrase is widely used to describe the diverse features of a business, and its scope can include strategy, purpose, offerings, processes, operations, organizational aspects and trading practices. A good business model identifies the customer, what customers' value, and how value is created in a business. The ability to identify how a business model functions and creates value provides a foundation for valuation.

Financial statements provide a framework for identifying how firm value is generated for shareholders and other stakeholders. The attributes of a business model are translated into accounting metrics that provide a lens into how and where value is created. Accounting principles define how financial statements are organized and therefore how value is measured. Firms generally issue three primary financial statements, the balance sheet, the income statement and the cash flow statement. One additional report usually required is the statement of shareholder's equity.

The balance sheet itemizes a firm's assets, liabilities and shareholder equity. Assets are a firm's investments that are anticipated to generate future payoffs. Liabilities are claims to payoffs on the firm by non-owner claimants, while shareholders' equity is a claim on the firm by its owners. The balance sheet is therefore a statement of the firm's investments and the payoff claims on those investments. Assets and liabilities are also identified as being either current or long-term, where current defines those assets that produce cash or cash that is used to pay liabilities within one year. The balance sheet's three components are linked through the following accounting relationship:

shareholders equity = assets − liabilities

This accounting equation states that shareholder's equity is the equivalent to a firm's net assets, or the net difference between the firm's assets and liabilities. Shareholders' equity is therefore the residual claim on a firm's assets after liabilities have been subtracted.

The income statement gives an account of the increases or decreases in shareholders' equity that result from a firm's operations and activities. This value that is added to shareholder value is described by convention as the bottom line, net income, net profit or earnings. The income statement also itemizes the firm's revenues and expenses that are the foundation of net income. This is established through the following accounting relationship:

$$\text{net income} = \text{revenues} - \text{expenses}$$

The cash flow statement shows the cash generated and used by a firm over an accounting period. The various cash flows in the statement are identified as cash flows from operating activities, cash flows from investing activities and cash flows from financing activities. The total cash flows from the three definitions identify a firm's increase or decrease in cash activities:

$$\text{change in cash} = \text{cash from operations} + \text{cash from investment} \\ + \text{cash from financing}$$

The statement of shareholders' equity explains how a firm's equity changed over an accounting period:

$$\text{ending equity} = \text{beginning equity} + \text{total (comprehensive) income} \\ - \text{net payout to shareholders}$$

A firm's equity increases when value is added through operations as income and decreases on payouts to shareholders.

The financial statements are also described in terms of stocks and flows. The balance sheet describes the stock of value in a firm, while the income statement and cash flow statement account for flows, or changes, in the balance sheet. This concept can be extended to define value, with the balance sheet providing the shareholders' net worth as a stock, while flows are the value added through a firm's operations in the income statement, and in the cash flow statement as changes in cash. Therefore the value creation flowing to a firm's owners is the change in equity over an accounting year.

The value of a firm should always equal the value of the claims on the firm:

$$\text{firm value} = \text{value of debt} + \text{value of equity}$$

This relationship illustrates that total firm value is distributed to the various claimants on that value. Firm valuation can therefore be defined as either valuing the firm itself or valuing and summing the claims on the firm. The firm is also a portfolio of projects, with the value of the firm represented by the present value of the expected cash flows from operations, or free cash flows, from these projects. Firms seek continuity by investing in new projects while letting existing projects terminate. The cash generated from a firm's assets and operations flows to the claimants on the firm. Therefore the analysis of a firm's investments, financing activities and operations provides the foundation on how firm value is generated and the sustainability of that value creation.

2.2 DCF VALUATION

Studies of corporate investment practices (Seitz and Ellison, 1995) carried out over the past 40 years have shown that the payback and accounting rate of return approaches were the preferred decision methods in earlier years. By 1988, however, over 75% of companies were using the DCF approach to calculate the net present values (NPVs) of potential investment outlays and inflows.

There are two basic approaches to DCF methods, the NPV and the internal rate of return (IRR). The NPV is the difference between the present value of the net cash inflows generated by an investment, and the initial cash outlay. The IRR is the rate of return that equates the present value of the net cash inflows generated by an investment with its initial cash outlay. The IRR is the equivalent to interest rates quoted in financial markets. The NPV approach is the most popular, and has the following features:

■ NPV recognizes the time value of money.

■ NPV is a function of the future cash flows from an investment and reflects the opportunity cost of capital.

■ NPVs can be aggregated as they are measured in today's values.

The NPV of an investment is the sum of the present values of the expected benefits, generally in the form of cash flows, from which the present values of all expected cash outlays are subtracted. If I_0 is defined as the initial outlay of an investment, CF_t as the cash flow at period t, and k as the rate of return that can be earned on an alternative investment, the NPV is:

$$NPV = \frac{CF_1}{(1+k)^1} + \frac{CF_2}{(1+k)^2} + \dots + \frac{CF_n}{(1+k)^n} - I_0 \qquad (2.1)$$

$$= \sum_{t=1}^{n} \frac{CF_t}{(1+k)^t} - I_0$$

2.3 MANAGEMENT AND VALUATION

One essential function of general management is to ensure that an appropriate performance measurement framework is in place for issues such as strategy analysis and capital allocation. It is also essential that general management understand how investment analysts translate management behaviour into share prices. Management decisions based on valuation measures are made across such diverse areas as product development, finance, operations, restructuring, mergers and acquisitions and strategy. Different metrics, however, are used for these various valuations. Finance focuses on NPV for capital budgeting and investments and return on equity (ROE) for performance evaluation, marketing focuses on increasing market share, operations on the payback period, while general management advocates earnings per share (EPS) for investor communications. As the various functions use a diverse range of valuation metrics, aligning strategy across an organization can be a complicated exercise.

Most corporate managers continue to support an accounting perspective of a company, with earnings per share (EPS) being the main determinant of share prices. The goal of good corporate governance is therefore to maximize reported EPS. There is, however, a growing recognition that accounting metrics can give a distorted view of corporate value. Accounting metrics are essentially short term in nature, and are influenced by the interpretation of different standards for issues such as assets, liabilities, investments, research and development and taxation. Another problem is that accounting measures do not explicitly include a charge for the capital used by a business, and fail to describe the relative risk of an investment.

Shareholder value is only created when the return on capital exceeds the cost of capital. Value is therefore primarily determined by economic, and not accounting, cash flows. Accounting metrics such as EPS and ROE focus on a company's previous performance, whereas economic value is concerned with maximizing future cash flows over time. There are a number of valid approaches for quantifying corporate value, and all are based on some form of the DCF model. Economic profit and NPV are also closely linked, as the NPV is the present value of economic profit. The major difference is that economic value methods typically begin with accounting income as opposed to the net cash flows of NPV.

The shareholder value premise is that companies should be managed to maximize the worth of the owner's, that is, the shareholders, stake in the company. To maximize shareholder wealth management creates, evaluates and selects strategies that will increase the value of the company. The same principles used in the DCF method for valuing individual projects to companies can also be applied to strategy analysis. Maximizing shareholder value is consistent with maximizing the NPV in the analysis of investments, projects, organizational units and the firm generally. Different strategies are compared, and the strategy that results in the highest NPV is the one selected.

Managements' mandate is therefore to maximize shareholder value by accepting all investments with a positive NPV, based on a discount rate that reflects the return available from equivalent investment opportunities. A firm would select the port-folio of proposed investments that have a positive NPV, and reject those with a negative NPV. This is consistent with the premise of maximizing shareholder value, and also provides a focus on the management of a firm's capital. The value of the company is now defined as a function of the discounted future cash flows it is expected to generate for shareholders. As present values are additive, the value of the firm should equal the sum of the present values of all its subsidiaries, businesses and projects. The firm can therefore be thought of as a portfolio of projects or assets.

DCF strategy analysis does have some limitations despite the advantages. Accurate cash flow forecasts are required; however, incorrect estimates of future returns from an investment can easily invalidate the whole approach. Another lim-itation of DCF strategy analysis is the implied assumption that all investment proposals are independent. The independence assumption ignores the numerous interrelationships that typically exist across businesses and investments. Another problem is that the valuation of many long-dated assets is very difficult. The main advantages of economic value techniques also lie in improving the use of existing assets and investments, as opposed to developing long-term strategies.

2.4 INVESTORS AND VALUATION

Investment can be defined as the sacrifice of current dollars for future dollars (Sharpe et al., 1999). Understanding how investments are valued is important for investors, finance executives or management generally. Assets are only worth what someone is willing to pay for them, and as that person could be an analyst, a trader, a fund manager or a competitor, a background in the available valuation methods is essential. Investment valuation is used for a wide range of real and financial assets, including companies, bonds, stocks, real estate and derivatives. Although most investment valuation models are generalized rather than specific to particular markets, it is also probably one of the most difficult tasks in finance.

Many volatile factors can have an impact on the value of investments. Errors in forecasts can result from unforeseen changes in factors such as financial variables, markets, competitors and technology. Unexpected changes in asset values can also result from factors that are completely unrelated to a company, an industry or the economy generally. Another major influence today on the value of investments is the corporate emphasis on short-term results. A company will either be rewarded or penalized every quarter through its share price, depending on whether earnings satisfy investor expectations. A consequence often seen is the corporate behaviour of managing quarterly financial results to reduce share price volatility.

The basis for an investment will depend on the investment philosophy. Generally the value of an asset should be a function of the cash flows it is expected to produce. A wide variety of models are used for investment valuation with various levels of complexity, however there are some common features. Two common approaches are DCF valuation and relative valuation, which is similar to DCF in the sense that the value of an asset is derived from the cash flows of comparable assets. DCF analysis can be performed from either the viewpoint of equity holders, in which case the expected cash flows to equity are discounted, or by considering the firm from all perspectives and discounting the firm's expected cash flows.

REFERENCES

Brealey, R.A. and Myers, S.C. *Principles of Corporate Finance*, McGraw Hill, 1996.

Damodaran, A. *Investment Valuation*, Wiley, 1996.

Damodaran, A. *Applied Corporate Finance*, Wiley, 1999.

Hooke, J.C. *Security Analysis on Wall Street*, Wiley, 1998.

Magretta, J. *What Management Is*, The Free Press, 2002.

Morin, R.A. and Jarrell, S.L. *Driving Shareholder Value*, McGraw Hill, 2000.

Penman, S. *Financial Statement Analysis and Security Valuation*, McGraw Hill/Irwin, 2004.

Seitz, N. and Ellison, M. *Capital Budgeting and Long-Term Financing Decisions*, The Dryden Press, 1995.

Sharpe, W.F., Alexander, G.J. and Bailey, J.V. *Investments*, Prentice Hall, 1999.

CHAPTER 3

Investment Risk

Corporate management will typically develop strategies and allocate resources to increase shareholder value. Shareholders on the other hand will focus on the cash growth of their investments. As to whether there is value in any potential cash flow growth will depend on the risks associated with these investments. Investors will generally demand a higher rate of return from investments that are perceived to be relatively riskier. Corporate decisions are made in environments that are inherently risky and uncertain. The risks associated with corporate investments are found in variables such as prices, quantities, costs, competition, market share and project life-cycles. These variables can be unpredictable and result in cash flow volatility, which will therefore have an impact on any NPV calculations.

The risk appetite of investors should therefore be included in investment analysis. As a result the cash flows used in NPV estimates are modified by a discount rate that reflects both the time value of money and any related cash flow risks. Risk is therefore represented in the discount rate determined from the risk appetites of investors and the financial markets. The hurdle rate is the discount rate, that is, the minimum acceptable rate of return that a firm will accept for a project. A number of methods have been developed to determine the discount rate used in NPV calculations. These include the capital asset pricing model (CAPM) and risk-adjusted discount approach.

The foundations of quantifying risk can be found in Markowitz (1959), regarded as the origin of modern portfolio theory. Markowitz's solution was to assume that a portfolio could be structured as a function of the mean and the standard deviation of the portfolio return. His conclusions from this construct were that the risk of the portfolio will generally be less than the weighted average of the separate asset risks, and the lower the correlations between the component asset returns the lower the portfolio risk (the diversification principle). Each asset's risk therefore consists of two components; the diversifiable risk, which will disappear through the right combination of assets, and the non-diversifiable risk, which will always be carried by investors. The portfolio selection problem can therefore be defined as consisting of maximizing the return while minimizing the risk.

Sharpe, Linter and Mossin extended Markowitz's portfolio theory with the assumption of homogeneous expectations, where all investors concur on expected returns, standard deviations and correlations and therefore choose the same portfolio. This concept led to the CAPM. The CAPM is a general model for formulizing an asset's risk and return. The variance of the return is defined as the risk measure, with only the non-diversifiable, or systematic component of the variance being rewarded. The relevant risk in pricing an asset is that part of an asset's risk, or variance of the assets return, is correlated with the overall risk of a market, and not the overall risk of the asset. An asset's beta coefficent measures its systematic risk.

The CAPM model can be used to illustrate which businesses a firm should have operations in. Diversifying a corporation over a portfolio of independent businesses decreases the variance of the combined cash flows if the cash flows of the various businesses are not completely correlated. Reducing risk would therefore be consistent from the perspective of shareholders as they are typically adverse to risk. Shareholders can, however, reduce risk by maintaining diversified portfolios themselves. Individual shareholders can accomplish a broader diversification, typically at lower transaction costs, than that offered by the majority of firms diversifying through mergers and acquisitions. Creating shareholder value through diversification requires the existence of market imperfections that firms can exploit more efficiently than investors. As a firm can be described as a portfolio of assets and projects, the value of a new project would be conditional on the total risk of the firm, in which case NPV would not be additive. If, however, a project's risks are not correlated to existing assets or projects, NPV's will generally then be additive.

As the value of a firm can be considered as the value of all the firm's assets, the firm can therefore also be viewed as the value of all sources of financing. The weighted average cost of capital is a discount rate that represents the costs of the various sources of finance, which can consist of a firm's equity, debt and any hybrid securities. The cost of equity can be derived using a CAPM model, the cost of debt from interest rates and bond ratings, and the cost of hybrid securities through the characteristics of each of their components. The weighted cost of capital can be used in project-analysis decisions to determine which project NPV's do not change a firm's business risk, and also provide a hurdle rate for projects.

The objective of the risk-adjusted discount rate (RADR) method is to maximize a firm's market value by using discount rates from investments that have the similar risk characteristics as the investment projects under analysis. The NPV derived by discounting future cash flows at the RADR therefore reflects the opportunity cost of capital, or the rate of return required by the firm or investors for similar investments. The RADR includes the time value of money, the risk-free rate and the discount risk premium. Conventional projects that have similar risk characteristics as existing businesses should not influence the aggregate risk of a firm and would therefore be discounted at the opportunity cost of capital. The discount risk premium is adjusted upwards for projects with above-average risk, and down for projects with below-average risk. The return of an investment project can also be compared to a hurdle rate to determine whether the project should proceed.

REFERENCES

Barbera, M. and Coyte, R. *Shareholder Value Demystified*, UNSW Press, 1999.

Beckers, S. A survey of risk measurement theory and practice, in Alexander, C. (ed.) *The Handbook of Risk Management and Analysis*, Wiley, 1996.

Brealey, R.A. and Myers, S.C. *Principles of Corporate Finance*, McGraw Hill, 1996.

Damodaran, A. *Investment Valuation*, Wiley, 1996.

Grant, R.M. *Contemporary Strategy Analysis*, Blackwell, 1998.

Trigeorgis, L. *Real Options: Managerial Flexibility and Strategy in Resource Allocation*, MIT Press, 1996.

CHAPTER 4

Five Shareholder Value Case Studies

4.1 INTRODUCTION

The accounting approach and DCF principles are now applied to five case studies, an IT project, a power gas generator, a pharmaceutical company, a growth firm and a firm abandonment. The first two case studies are considered from a management viewpoint, while the remaining three are from an investor's perspective.

4.2 SOFTWARE DCF EXAMPLE

4.2.1 IT investments and value

Over the last decade investment in information technology (IT) has become a major component of the capital budget in many service and manufacturing organizations. Although IT investments can be highly risky, the corporate rewards can be enormous. Managing this expenditure in today's business environment raises a number of important issues for corporate decision makers, including how IT investments should be integrated with strategy, and the risk management implications of these investments. IT projects can be viewed as an activity where resources are allocated with the goal of maximizing shareholder value. Any software project is therefore managed with the goal of maximizing value, where value is defined in terms of the market value that is added to the firm. IT investments are not only costly, however, they are also often risky due to the uncertainty of the value of future payoffs.

The trend in placing IT on a cost recovery or profit centre basis introduced the return on investment (ROI) concept into IT project analysis. In a conventional discounted cash flow (DCF) valuation analysis, a forecast of the future cash flows is discounted at the risk-adjusted opportunity cost of capital to obtain the present value. Present values are derived for both costs and benefits. Taking the sum of the present value of the returns derives the net present value (NPV). If the resulting NPV is positive then the project is viable. The NPV of a feasible project corresponds to the change in value of a firm if it proceeds with the investment. If the NPV were positive the investment decision would be to proceed with the investment, as this would increase firm value by the NPV amount. Likewise if the NPV is negative the investment should not be made.

Valuing IT investments using cost/benefit or ROI analysis, however, has always been a problem in computation. It is typically a lot easier to calculate the costs/investment than it is to calculate the benefits/returns. However, there are concepts such as partitioning returns/benefit analysis into tangible and intangible benefits that can be used. The approach used in this case study is to ignore all intangible benefits and focus on tangible benefits, as most tangible benefits can be converted into measurable returns. The uncertainties associated with a firm's IT investments can also be defined as project- and market-related risks. Project-related risks are associated with the planning, implementation and management of a firm's IT project, such as the technology not delivering, cost overruns and project setbacks. Market-related risks are the factors that can influence the demand for a firm's products and services, such as customer approval and the behaviour of competitors. Even if a project meets management expectations, therefore, any capabilities created by the project may not be suitable for the existing market environment at the time of completion.

4.2.2 Software restructuring

The decision to restructure a software system is one confronted by many IT managers. Restructuring a system is often not only very costly but also risky, as the future payoffs are not only uncertain but also likely to be in numerous dimensions. If the focus is simply a payoff of reducing any costs that will be related to making future system alterations, for example, the future required changes might not materialize. Other uncertainties that can be associated with software restructuring projects include development costs, coding problems and subsequent operational failures, developments in future technology and standards, user acceptance and the possible costs associated with changes in processes.

IT managers cannot always predict how systems will need to be adapted to changing user requirements, market developments and developments in technology. The management objective, however, is still to design and implement IT investments that maximize firm value. Selecting a modular structure or architecture allows any future potential changes to be localized rather than system wide, and therefore can reduce any costs associated with software restructuring. The modular concept can be extended by considering the value of an information system as the sum of the values of each of the system's modules (Baldwin and Clark, 1999). The advantages of using this additive approach to value a system are its simplicity and the potential to provide a practical framework for managing systems that consist for the most part of independent components. Such an approach to managing software systems therefore would be consistent with maximizing value.

4.2.3 DCF analysis

A modular approach to software architecture has the potential to localize any required future software restructuring. Any payback from software modifications using a modular approach will therefore be in the form of reduced future costs. Under a DCF analysis based on using only tangible returns the IT manager would compare the present value of the future tangible benefits represented as a cash flow stream against the present value of the costs. The DCFs associated with the software restructuring appear in Table 4.1. The expected future tangible savings are $132,000 and associated costs are $100,000. A discount rate of 10% and a one-year time horizon (t) are used for illustration.

The NPV decision rule is to invest if the NPV is positive. As the static NPV of the investment is $20,000, which is positive, the decision under the NPV is to restructure immediately. The project would then be accepted immediately based on this analysis.

Table 4.1 IT software restructuring DCF analysis

Costs at t_0	=	(100,000)
Savings at t_1	=	132,000
Discount rate	=	10%

$$NPV = -100,000 + \frac{132,000}{1.10}$$
$$= 20,000$$

4.3 ENERGY

4.3.1 The global energy markets

The energy market is the largest market in the world after currencies. Over the last century world GDP grew by an average of 3% a year, sustained by an energy supply annual growth rate of 2%. Annual global energy consumption increased from the equivalent of 4 barrels of oil per person to 13 over the same period. Over the last decade the world's energy demand increased at 1.5% to 2% per annum. Today the world consumes 400 quads (quadrillion British thermal units – BTUs) of total energy per year, the equivalent to 200 million barrels of oil per day. This consumption is composed of 40% oil, 22% gas, 24% coal, 6% nuclear, and 8% for all other energy forms, which is mainly hydroelectric. Less than 0.5% of total consumption comes from renewable energy (statistics are from Economides and Oligney, 2000; Hamel, 2000).

Attempts at 20-year energy forecasts have been made in the past using annual growth rates to predict both total energy demand and the composition of the energy sources. Forecasts for the 1990s' energy consumption levels that were done in the 1970s have proved to be quite accurate. However forecasts of the market share of energy types have not had the same success, as political, economic and techno-logical events have influenced the various sources of energy. The challenge today in a world with a rapidly growing population is to meet the global energy require-ments with an approach that addresses both environmental concerns and the economics of sustainable development.

Georges Dupont-Roc, head of Royal Dutch/Shell energy planning group in the 1990s, analysed the long-term issues that might impact on the world's various sources of energy supply. His 1994 report, *The Evolution of the World's Energy Systems*, (see Hamel, 2000, p. 176) provides two potential scenarios for the next century:

- *sustained growth,* which assumes that energy use will maintain its historical growth rate, in which case an individual will be consuming the equivalent of 25 barrels of oil per capita by 2060.

- *dematerialization,* which assumes that energy growth would become detached from the growth in GDP as energy efficiency is improved through technologies and market trading. Under this scenario consumption per person will be the equivalent of only 15 barrels of oil a year by 2060.

Dupont-Roc's view is that the most likely alternative will be the continuation of *sustained growth,* where energy efficiency will continue to increase at 1% per annum as it has over the past century. Energy efficiency would have to grow at twice the historical rate for the dematerialization scenario to emerge, something that has not taken place for any sustained period of time. If dematerialization did occur it would have to start in the developed nations and then would take several decades to reach underdeveloped regions. Dupont-Roc's prediction was that as the world's popula-tion and environmental problems increased it is going to be impossible to avoid an energy shortage.

The development of a new energy market can take a long time if history is any precedent. As energy consumption increased in the past the energy markets divers-ified from coal to oil, natural gas and nuclear energies, although each of these markets took some time to develop. Global energy consumption in the twenty-first century will consist of energy types such as oil, natural gas, nuclear power, coal, renewable energies or other energy forms. While trend forecasts are likely to be reasonable based on Dupont-Roc's future growth scenario and the accuracy of past forecasts, the breakdown of total energy consumption into each energy type in terms of equivalent BTUs, however, will be much harder to predict. It is also impos-sible to foresee, as with any developing technology in its early stages, which new energy types will dominate in the twenty-first century. Uncertainty is assured as future political, economic and technology events develop, and therefore a strategy would be to pursue a portfolio approach to energy, where the goal would be to take options on a range of energy sources.

4.3.2 The power markets

For most of the twentieth century power companies existed as natural monopolies, dominating the industry's complex public, economic and technical structures while at the same time delivering ever-greater volumes of electricity at diminishing prices. Although state regulatory commissions were created to guarantee that the benefits from the monopoly flowed to customers, the regulatory environment gave utilities the protection needed to expand, develop alliances, and establish market power. In the 1970s things started to change, however, with the decline in productivity improvements from generating technologies and the effects of the 1970s energy crisis. Power companies could no longer continue to produce electricity at a diminishing cost, and their market power was beginning to be challenged by a developing environmental movement.

By the 1990s power companies began to lose their dominance over the utility system and no longer had the general support of stakeholders. When the structure for power markets was conceived initially in the twentieth century the consensus was for natural monopolies that were supervised by government. However it was evident by the 1990s that the original motivation for organizing the power markets as regulated monopolies no longer appeared to be valid. Support for the monopoly consensus had begun to erode among the various stakeholders as they began to see the opportunities in a new market structure based on deregulated markets.

As a result the power markets in the twenty-first century are likely to be entirely different to the protected market structures that emerged in the early twentieth century. The forces of deregulation, convergence through mergers and acquisitions, globalization and new technologies are now fundamental drivers in the energy markets. The trend to open markets is accelerating as governments separate and open to competition the traditional monopoly areas of power generation, transmission, and distribution. All these events have forced power companies to revaluate their strategies, organizational structures and asset profiles.

Power companies have responded to this new competitive environment through cutting costs, mergers and buying power companies in other countries. Another dominant trend in the energy industry is the convergence between gas and power business. Units of energy are becoming interchangeable, and companies are now exploring energy areas such as gas transmission, gas distribution, gas trading, wholesaling, power generation, electric utilities and electricity trading. At the same time small scale generation technologies are providing firms with the ability to produce electricity themselves, and therefore eliminating the need to purchase power from the utilities.

4.3.3 Power generator case study

Energy Corporation (EC) is an energy generator with a portfolio of electricity plants. An evaluation of the potential value of the Sparkie Power Station (SPS), a gas-fired power plant within the energy portfolio, was required by EC. EC's strategy is to use

SPS as a provider of high-peak power to maximize EC's gross margin, and also as a risk-management tool to cover plant failure events at its coal-fired power stations.

The industry standard for the valuation of power assets is the traditional dispatch model. This approach values plants by determining the marginal cost-based clearing price, and calculating cash flows that are based on the intrinsic spread, the spark spread, between the electricity price and the cost of fuel for generation. The dispatch model calculates the margin received, or the spark spread, over the life of the plant, and discounts it to the present. The discount rate used was based on EC's weighted average cost of capital.

Although electricity cannot be easily stored, the fuels used to generate the electricity can be stored, and the link between the two fuels implies that the forward curve for electricity should be related to the input fuels. An arbitrage pricing approach takes this into account by considering the conversion process. One of the key steps in the conversion process is the generation process itself and this depends on the efficiency of generation expressed as the *heat rate* – the number of BTUs required to generate one kWh of electricity.

A basic electricity forward curve can be obtained for the fuel forward curve via the following relationship:

$$Cost_{electricity} = Heat\ rate \times Price_{fuel} \tag{4.1}$$

A constant value of the heat rate implies that the shape of the electricity forward curve should resemble the forward curve of the input fuel. The cost of electricity can be converted into a forward price after taking into account costs associated with fixed assets, transmission and tolling charges and others such as fuel storage, and fuel transportation. These costs obviously change through time. Figures 4.1 and 4.2 illustrate SPS's power and natural gas curves respectively. Forward energy curves can be created as composite curves that consist of market data such as futures, forward prices and curve modelling. One feature exhibited by energy prices is the high level of seasonality, a repetitive cyclical pattern in the price over time. Seasonality in the energy markets is driven typically by demand caused by weather factors such as hot summer months.

The assumptions for the DCF analysis are:

- The plant output is 300 MWh

- It is assumed that SPS has a total remaining life of 15 years

- The 15-year power and natural gas forward price curves each consist of a series of one-month forward prices that represent the hourly average over each month

- The valuation cash flows are pretax

- The heat rate is 10,000. To derive the spark spread the heat rate is divided by 1,000

- The plant will run 16 hours per weekday, except in the summer months when it will run 24-hours per weekday

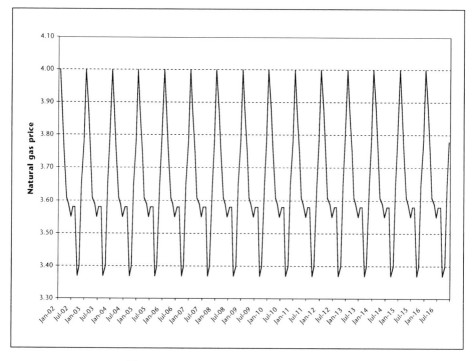

Figure 4.1 Power forward price curve

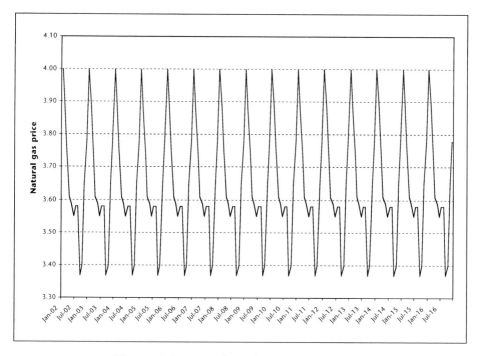

Figure 4.2 Natural gas forward price curve

Table 4.2 Discounted cash flow analysis (as at 31 December 2001)

Month	Jan 02	Feb 02	Mar 02	Apr 02	May 02	.....	Jul 16	Aug 16	Sep 16	Oct 16	Nov 16	Dec 16
Energy – MWh	300	300	300	300	300	.....	300	300	300	300	300	300
Power price	36.02	36.00	37.00	44.36	45.36	.....	62.93	61.93	59.40	39.98	38.57	37.88
Gas price	4.00	3.88	3.75	3.61	3.59	.....	3.58	3.58	3.37	3.40	3.65	3.78
Heat rate	10,000	10,000	10,000	10,000	10,000	.....	10,000	10,000	10,000	10,000	10,000	10,000
Spark spread – $/MWh	(3.98)	(2.80)	(0.50)	8.26	9.46	.....	27.13	26.13	25.70	5.98	2.07	0.08
Start-up costs	0.00	0.00	0.00	1.04	1.04	.....	0.16	0.15	0.12	1.04	1.04	1.04
Total operating hours	384	336	352	352	384	.....	528	552	552	352	368	368
Total revenue $	0	0	0	762,256	969,792	.....	4,272,392	4,302,128	4,235,920	521,488	113,528	0
O&M costs	1.50	1.50	1.50	1.50	1.50	.....	1.50	1.50	1.50	1.50	1.50	1.50
Total O & M costs $	172,800	151,200	158,400	158,400	172,800	.....	237,600	248,400	248,400	158,400	165,600	165,600
Net cash flows $	(172,800)	(151,200)	(158,400)	603,856	796,992	.....	4,034,792	4,053,728	3,987,520	363,088	(52,072)	(165,600)
Discount factor (6.5%)	0.9973	0.9923	0.9872	0.9820	0.9769	.....	0.4000	0.3979	0.3958	0.3937	0.3917	0.3896
Present value $	(172,339)	(150,031)	(156,377)	593,015	778,576	.....	1,613,998	1,612,923	1,578,253	142,955	(20,394)	(64,518)
NPV	=$136,874,152											

▨ The start-up cost is $5,000 per start-up. A MWh start-up cost was derived per month as the number of start-ups per month times $5,000, which is divided by the total operating hours per month times the number of MWs

▨ The operations and maintenance (O&M) costs are $1.50 per MWh

▨ The pretax discount rate is 6.50%. The maturity for each discount factor is the middle of each month

▨ The NPV of SPS is the sum of the present values of the net cash flows for each month.

4.4 THE PHARMACEUTICAL INDUSTRY

4.4.1 New drug development

The development of a new drug is risky business. Of the virtually infinite number of molecular compounds that may have pharmacological effects, drug companies must choose carefully the compounds in which to invest the millions of development dollars required before launching a new product on the market. The development process is composed of several stages, during which the drug company gathers evidence to convince government regulators that it can consistently manufacture a safe and efficacious form of the compound for the medical condition it is intended to treat. At the end of each stage the company uses the technological and market information revealed up to that point to decide whether to abandon or continue development.

Drugs that reach the market in the United States typically pass through the following stages:

1. *Discovery*: In this stage, chemists and biologists expend a significant amount of effort to develop concepts for synthesizing new molecular entities (NMEs). Many such entities are abandoned at this stage.

2. *Pre-clinical*: The NME is screened for pharmacological activity and toxicity in an artificial environment and then in animals. If the NME is a promising candidate for further development, the company files an investigational new drug application with the Food and Drug Administration (FDA). An approved investigational new drug application allows the company to continue development by testing the drug on humans in clinical trials.

3. *Clinical trials:* Clinical trials are generally broken down into three phases:
   ◆ *Phase 1:* Testing is conducted on a small number of (usually healthy) volunteers to obtain information on toxicity and safe dosing in humans. Data are also collected on the drug's absorption and distribution in the body, the drug's metabolic effects, and the rate and manner in which the drug is eliminated from the body.

- *Phase II:* The drug is administrated to a larger number of individuals selected from among patients for whom the drug is intended. Successful Phase II trials provide significant evidence of efficacy, and additional data on safety.
- Phase III: This final pre-marketing clinical development phase involves large-scale trials on patients to obtain additional evidence of efficacy. Larger sample sizes increase the likelihood that actual benefits will be found statistically significant, and that any adverse reactions that may occur infrequently in patient populations will be observed. Phase III trials are designed to closely approximate the manner in which the drug will be utilized after marketing approval.

4. *FDA filing and review:* After the clinical development phases have been completed and the company believes it has sufficient evidence for approval, it submits a new drug application (NDA) to the FDA for review. Marketing for approved uses may begin upon notification from the FDA.

5 *Post-approval:* While the firm receives revenues from the sale of its new drug, it conducts additional research to support the marketing efforts and to develop extensions of the product. Extensions include alternate formulations and dosages for subsets of patients such has children.

4.4.2 Agouron Pharmaceuticals

Agouron was founded in 1984 and became a public company in 1987. Until 1997, the company had no operating income from products and most of its efforts focused on the discovery of NMEs and clinical trials of them. Agouron also formed partnerships with large pharmaceutical companies to collaborate on the discovery, development and commercialization of drugs based on biotechnology.

Such partnerships are common in the pharmaceutical industry. For the biotech companies, the partnerships provide credibility, capital, additional technical expertise and the means to market their products in many areas of the world where the larger company has established operations. For the large pharmaceutical companies, the biotech companies provide additional sources of innovative ideas and become an extension of their research and development (R&D) groups. In a typical partnership the larger company acquires equity in the biotech company, and provides payments to the biotech company upon the initiation of the specified phase of development or governmental approval of a drug. The companies then share the resulting cash flows of the approved drug.

In July 1994, Agouron was conducting research on anti-cancer and anti-HIV compounds. It had two anti-cancer NMEs in Phase I clinical trials, and one anti-HIV NME in pre-clinical development. During the next four and a half years, Agouron made several major announcements about the progress of its research and development. On 26 January 1999, Agouron announced that it was being acquired by Warner Lambert Company for stock valued at $2.1 billion.

4.4.3 Assumptions

Because of the political environment regarding health care costs, much has been written recently about pharmaceutical R&D. For this study assumptions were made about development costs, probabilities of success, and profitability of new drugs based on the work of Myers and Howe (1997), the Office of Technology Assessment (1993), DiMasi et al. (1991) and Grabowski and Vernon (1994) to make assumptions about development costs, probabilities of success, and profitability of new drugs. All costs and revenues are stated in 1994 constant US dollars.

Following Myers and Howe it was assumed that a drug reaching the market would fall into one of five quality categories:

- dog

- below average

- average

- above average

- breakthrough.

A marketed drug has a 60% probability of being of average quality and a 10% probability of being in each of the other four categories. The revenues associated with each quality category are highly skewed, with the peak revenue for dog and below average drugs being no more that $7.4 million a year and that of breakthrough drugs being $1.3 billion a year. The assumed revenue for each category by year after launch is shown in Figure 4.3. Peak annual revenue by category is as follows (in millions):

Breakthrough	$1,323,920
Above average	661,960
Average	66,200
Below average	7,440
Dog	6,620

Table 4.3 shows, for each development stage, assuming successful completion of the prior stage(s), the assumed pretax cost, duration in years and probability of successful completion of that stage. For R&D stages of duration greater than one year, it was assumed that total cost was allocated equally to each year. For some approved drugs, it was assumed that post-approval clinical trials would be done. The purpose of these trials is to support the marketing effort for the drug. For example, the results of post-approval clinical trials are often cited in promotional literature presented to doctors by sales representatives. Without new information, getting the attention of a busy doctor is often difficult for a sales rep. For drugs with low sales (dog or below average drugs) it was assumed that revenues would be insufficient to warrant post-approval clinical trials.

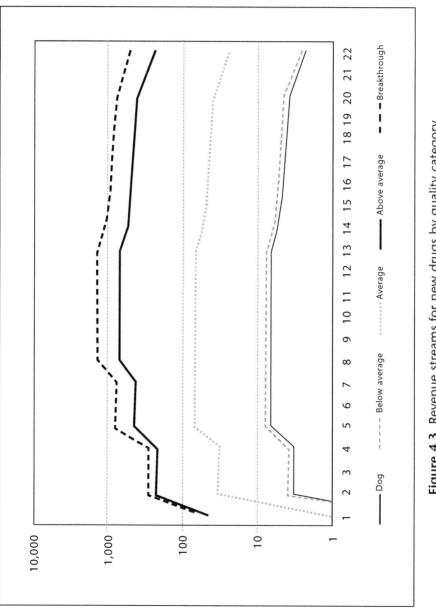

Figure 4.3 Revenue streams for new drugs by quality category
(Revenue $millions; log scale)

— Dog ----- Below average ········· Average — Above average – – Breakthrough

Source: Data for first 13 years from Myers and Howe; data for remaining years from US Congress, Office of Technology Assessment

Table 4.3 Pretax costs, durations and conditional probabilities of success for R&D stages

R&D stage	Total cost ($000)	Years in stage	Conditional success (probability)
Discovery	2,200	1	0.60
Pre-clinical	13,800	3	0.90
Clinical			
Phase I	2,800	1	0.75
Phase II	6,400	2	0.50
Phase III	18,100	3	0.85
FDA filing	3,300	3	0.75
Post-approval	31,200	9	1.00

Source: Myers and Howe (1997)

Table 4.4 Other cash flow assumptions

Item	Assumption	Source
Cost of revenue	25.5% of revenue	US Congress
Marketing expense		Myers and Howe
Year 1 after launch	100% of revenue	
Year 2 after launch	50% of revenue	
Year 3–4 after launch	25% of revenue	
Year 5–13 after launch	20% of revenue	
G&A*	11.1% of revenue	US Congress
Tax rate	35% of profit	Myers and Howe
Working capital	17% of revenue	US Congress

* General and administrative expenses

As are most products, drugs are subject to a product life cycle. The peak period of a drug's life cycle occurs just prior to patent expiration. After the patent expires, competitors may sell generic versions of the compound, and competition causes revenues to drop. Myers and Howe (1997) did not include revenues past the peak year, because the post-patent expiration years were not relevant to their analysis. The assumptions here regarding post-patent years were based on the Office of Technology Assessment report (US Congress). Table 4.4 provides details for other cash flow assumptions.

4.4.5 DCF valuation

The value of Agouron can be viewed as the sum of the values of its portfolio of projects. Each project's value can be derived using the DCF method. As at 30 June 1994 these projects consisted of the two anti-cancer NMEs in Phase I clinical trials, and Viracept, the anti-HIV NME in pre-clinical development. During the period 30 June 1994 to 23 December 1996 Agouron had other projects in the discovery, pre-clinical or Phase I clinical trials stages of development, but Viracept was the only NME to make it to approval during this period.

The assumptions for the biotechnology company's DCF analysis, based on the Kellogg and Charnes data, are:

- 100% of the cash flows for the development stage, that is, the projects make it through all the discovery stages to the approval, or the FDA filing stage.

- The constant 1994 USD revenue cash flows were inflated at 3.585% per annum for the revenue streams from year fourteen, when the revenue streams commence, to year thirty five. This inflation estimate is the average of the GDP deflator index over the five years prior to the date of the valuation.

- Real discount rates of 6.0% and 9.0% were used for the development cash flows and commercialization cash flows respectively. Adding the inflation estimate of 3.585% to the real discount rates provided the nominal discount rates of $r_d = 9.8\%$ for the development stage, and $r_c = 12.9\%$ for the commercialization stage.

Table 4.5 illustrates the cash flows for a drug at the discovery stage under the assumptions above.

The cash flow assumptions are:

- The present value of the R&D pre-commercialization costs is ($31,395), which assumes 100% of the cash flows for the development stage.

- The expected NPV of the commercialization stage. This is derived from:
  - The revenues for each drug quality from years fourteen to thirty five minus taxes, marketing costs, general and administration costs and other expenses.
  - The probabilities for each the five categories of a drug at the marketing stage.
  - The expected net present value of the commercialization cash flow is the sum of each drug quality at t_0 and scaled by the probability for that drug quality.

The NPV of a drug is therefore the present value of R&D pre-commercialization costs plus 12.9% (the product of the conditional probabilities from the discovery to the post-approval stages; see Table 4.3), times the expected NPV of the commercialization revenues:

$$(31,395,000) + 0.129*113,689,000$$
$$= (16,729,000)$$

Table 4.6 illustrates the calculation of the Agouron share price based on the NPV method. The Agouron portfolio consisted of two cancer drug projects, Viracept and seven drugs in research. It is assumed that there is a joint venture partner (to help fund development and bring the product to market) and that half of the value would accrue to the partner. The remaining proportion of the total expected NPV is

Table 4.5 NPV of a drug at the discovery stage (in 000s)

Phase	NPV
Discovery	(2,004)
Pre-clinical	(13,203)
Phase I	(15,223)
Phase II	(19,455)
Phase III	(29,810)
FDA filing	(31,395)

Quality of Drug:	Probability of drug quality	Commercialization NPV at t_0
Dog	10%	3,762
Below average	10%	4,230
Average	60%	33,011
Above average	10%	315,819
Breakthrough	10%	615,013
Expected NPV:		113,689

Table 4.6 DCF valuation of Agouron as at 30 June 1994 (in 000s)
(with approval probabilities)

	Cost of development	Probability of approval	Value of approval	Expected value
Cancer drug 1	22,968	23.90%	160,481	15,387
Cancer drug 2	22,968	23.90%	160,481	15,387
Viracept	31,155	21.50%	123,921	(4,512)
7 drugs in research	219,765	12.90%	795,823	(117,104)
Total				(90,842)
JV share				(45,421)
Shares			7,385,988	
Value per share				(6.15)

divided by the number of shares, which gives a share price based on the NPV method of ($6.15). The large negative value of (45,421,000) is due to seven projects that Agouron had in research which, based on the DCF method, produced a large negative value when combined together.

4.5 A GROWTH FIRM

4.5.1 Overview

One approach often used by investors is to develop a top-down framework to arrive at the decision to invest in a firm. The framework builds on a general outlook for the economy and capital markets, identifies industries expected to prosper within the framework, and then focuses on specific firms operating within those industries. Industry sectors are generally defined through the products they create or the services on offer. Industries are also identified by their response to economic and business cycles, typically defined as growth, defensive or cyclical. The industry life cycle considers an industry's viability over time, with the four stages of pioneer, growth, mature and decline indicating a phase in an industry's evolution.

The term growth as used in investment analysis has a range of interpretations. Growth is typically applied to sales, earnings and assets, generally, however, growth describes a capability to create value. A growth firm is able to grow sales and earnings regardless of its stage in the business cycle. A growth industry is typically identified with new technologies and products. Growth firms can have annual growth rates that exceed 12% to 15%, and while earnings will be typically steady or growing, these firms will generally consume cash, with investments exceeding cash generated internally.

Growth fundamentals are not the same for all firms. Three attributes can be identified that differentiate growth firms. The classic growth firm typically has innovative products or technologies in markets where demand is yet to be determined. The market share growth firm is located within a mature industry where growth is derived from increasing market share. A consolidating firm grows through acquisitions, typically in mature and fragmented industries, where cost synergies and valuations are the focus.

4.5.2 Growth valuation

The value of a firm is equal to the sum of the value of its debt and equity, or the value to all claimants on the firm. Summing the claims on the firm therefore represents the firm's value. The valuation of equity can be based on earnings, cash flow or assets. Earnings, or the income statement's net income, is the fundamental bottom-line metric for shareholder value. Growth is typically framed as a firm's capacity to grow earnings. The issue with growth in earnings for valuation however is that a firm can create growth in earnings though investment and accounting techniques that do not add value.

The valuation of equity based on the present value of future free cash flows focuses on the cash flow from operations with capital expenditure deducted. Cash flow from operations is the total cash flow derived from operations. Free cash flows will generally fluctuate over the life cycle of a product or firm, and are analysed in three life cycle phases. During the growth phase cash flow from operations is usually down while new products are being established and investments consume cash. The maturity phase will have positive free cash flow if the new venture is successful and investment requirements are reduced. Finally the decline stage is reached if product demand or cash flow from operations diminishes. Free cash flow at this point should continue however while investment decreases.

The cash flow life cycle illustrates why free cash flow is an imperfect metric for valuing a firm. Free cash flow does not measure the value added from operations over a period in time. Profitable firms can potentially have negative cash flows, while those with significant free cash flow can be barely profitable. A negative cash flow from investing more cash into operations than being received will give a negative NPV. This investment however could produce a return from cash flow from operations at some later stage. The three life cycle phases are also not consistent for all firms. Some firms can maintain growth consistently for extended periods, while others are unsuccessful at the initial phase. Firms have also been able to react to the risk of decline and continue in the mature phase.

A more appropriate metric for measuring growth is the residual earnings model. A firm's net assets quantify the book value of equity, which represents the total shareholder investment in the firm. The net assets are used in the firm's operations to generate shareholder value. The residual earnings measure captures the value in excess to book value over a cost of capital. Residual income models distinguish the excess earnings for a time period over an investor's required rate of return on equity. Residual earnings therefore represent the differential between earnings and investors' expected return on book value:

$$\text{residual earnings}_t\,(RE_t) = \text{earnings}_t - [(p_E - 1) \times \text{common shareholders equity}_{t-1}]$$

where t represents any year and $p_E - 1$ is the required return on equity. The added firm value to shareholders can therefore be defined in terms of the opportunity cost to investors.

4.5.3 Case study – fuel cells

Wave Nouveau Materials Inc. was founded in 1985 for the manufacturing of industrial materials. The firm focused on using science, engineering and chemistry to conceive, develop and commercialize new industrial products. Wave Nouveau also developed proprietary innovative processes for the manufacture of materials, equipment and various components. In addition the firm created an intensive R&D programme and partnered with commercial firms and government for the development of new technologies.

Over time Wave Nouveau developed markets worldwide, creating a reputation for performance and innovation with its products. The firm framed its growth strategy as leveraging its materials and manufacturing technologies to compete in the growing environmental and alternative energy markets. To take advantage of these trends the firm expanded its operations by adding a production facility for the development and production of fuel cells.

A fuel cell is an electrochemical conversion device that combines a fuel and an oxidant for the creation of electricity. The fuel is typically hydrogen and the oxidant is oxygen, while the by-products are heat and water. Fuel cells are modular, with sizes varying from a couple of watts up to around 250W, and have numerous power applications, including stationary and portable electricity generation, and transportation. The advantage of a fuel cell is that, while often compared to a battery, it does not lose power or need recharging. A fuel cell will continue to function as long as fuel is provided. The transformation of fuel into energy is also efficient, clean and quiet as no actual combustion process takes place.

The climate change and energy security issues that are driving alternative energy technologies have created a growth market for fuel cells. A fuel cell is actually a member of a group of technologies in various stages of development, with five classes defined by their electrolytes. Proton exchange membrane (PEMFC) are typically used in transportation, while alkaline (AFC) has its origins in the space programme of the 1960s and is currently used for smaller applications. Phosphoric acid (PAFC) and molten carbonate (MCFC) are applied to larger applications, while solid oxide (SOFC) fuel cells are suited to stationary small-scale power systems.

Wave Nouveau's strategy is to leverage its existing manufacturing and customer base, and use its new facility for the manufacturing of SOFC fuel cell types. Focusing on an existing commercialized product allows Wave Nouveau to cap research and development costs and facilitate access to capital. SOFC fuel cells are used widely in applications ranging from vehicles to stationary power generation, and although they currently operate at high temperatures the residual gases can be used as a secondary energy source. The materials used in manufacturing SOFCs, which include nickel and nickel oxide, are also available in large quantities.

The condensed financial statements for Wave Nouveau are illustrated in Table 4.7.

Table 4.7 Condensed financial statements for Wave Nouveau ($000)

Year	2005	2006	2007	2008
Balance Sheet:				
Assets	400,000	432,000	488,000	528,000
Liabilities	200,000	200,000	220,000	220,000
Shareholders' equity	200,000	232,000	268,000	308,000
Income Statement:				
Revenues	80,000	90,000	100,000	120,000
Expenses	48,000	54,000	60,000	72,000
Net income	32,000	36,000	40,000	48,000

The residual earnings with the required return on equity of 12% follows in Table 4.8:

Table 4.8 Residual earning trend for Wave Nouveau ($000)

Year	2005	2006	2007	2008
Earnings	32,000	36,000	40,000	48,000
Shareholders' equity	200,000	232,000	268,000	308,000
Cost of equity	24,000	27,840	32,160	36,960
Residual earnings	–	12,000	12,160	15,840

Wave Nouveau grew fixed assets by investing in plant and equipment for the manufacturing of fuel cells, and financed this expansion through debt in 2007. The firm also leveraged sales through its existing customer base, and therefore maintained the trend in sales and marketing costs. As a result expenses remained constant at 60% of revenues. As there were no dividends, the total earnings for each year flowed into shareholders' equity. The growth in residual earnings therefore can be attributed to the increased in revenues from fuel cell sales and maintaining the ratio of expenses to revenues.

4.6 FIRM ABANDONMENT

4.6.1 Overview

Many industries follow life cycles that are defined by convention as pioneer, growth, mature and decline. An industry in decline either has negative growth or is not expanding at a general economic growth rate. These industries are typically identified by extreme price competition, excess capacity, a lack of innovation, a dwindling number of competitors and buyouts of departing firms.

Firms within a declining industry can transition from the mature to the decline stage as a consequence of foreign competition, shifts in consumer behaviour and changes in technology and demographics. Declining revenues, margins, operating cash flows and earnings are all features of the final phase of a firm's existence. Other factors identified with declining firms include commoditized products, diminishing resources or substitutes appearing due to innovation.

Industry decline and falling market demand leads to uncertainty around the sustainability of product demand, which could either stabilize at some significantly lower level or in the worst case fade to where operations are no longer justified. Declining demand leads to industry-wide pressure to reduce capacity, as excess capacity diminishes profitability. Reducing capacity has significant costs, as both fixed and sunk costs can be a comparatively large percentage of an industry's total costs. These large sunk costs also, however, create high barriers to exit and prolonged excess capacity in the industry, which can lead to lengthy periods of industry downsizing. Firms in a declining industry are also motivated to reduce and stop investments in products when decreasing sale volumes reduce profitability. This leads to a fall in product quality and ultimately firms exiting the industry.

4.6.2 Strategies in declining industries

The conventional strategies in declining industries are either to maximize cash flows from existing investments with no further investment or to divest. These strategies can be extended to dominating the market through increased investment, staying at current investment levels, reducing investments, milking the cash cow or finally divesting.

Continuing to invest in the industry through research and development or marketing programmes has significant risks, and requires forecasts of declining product demand. In some cases a firm can be successful in a turnaround and return to the maturity phase, or reposition itself to take advantage of new market trends. Many firms in a declining industry will however ultimately face liquidation. If the future for a firm appears bleak then the best alternative may be divesting the business and selling assets before the industry decline gains momentum.

The market for a declining industry's assets is dynamic and can rapidly diminish. A firm would focus on resale asset values to establish potential realized proceeds, and try and maintain the flexibility to sell before asset values significantly decline. The firm also has value if the assets have the flexibility to switch to operations for other products. Both the industry and a firm's exit barriers are also factors that will influence a firm's decision on the timing of an exit.

4.6.3 The newspaper industry

The newspaper publishing industry in the United States is a $59 billion industry that employs an estimated 356,000. Circulation is the underlying driver of value in the newspaper industry, and makes up 15% to 20% of earnings for a typical newspaper and 85–90% of the advertising rate variance. The average newspaper with a circulation of 100,000 has an annualized 15.6% pre-tax profit margin.

The newspaper industry is inundated with problems. The peak of the industry was in the early 1920s, when the average household daily read 1.3 newspapers, and newspapers were highly profitable due to the (near) monopoly over retail customer access. By 2001 however nearly one out of two households were not reading a newspaper. Today four in ten Americans now read a newspaper daily whereas ten years ago one in two Americans read a newspaper daily. Consumers are switching to other media such as cable television, Internet news sites, Google, Yahoo! and blogs for news. Revenues from classifieds also declined from online classified sites. This has led to uncertainty in the industry's growth and future profit margins, with declines in the level of 15–20% of earnings. Many newspapers are shutting down operations and reducing staff, with approximately 2,800 permanent jobs to date disappearing this decade as a result.

Attempts at increasing revenue through newspaper price increases have a significant negative influence on circulation, and therefore the advertising charge rates that flow into revenue. There are growth areas in the newspaper industry however, which include the ethnic press, especially the Spanish language press, diversifying into niche newspaper distribution and investments in online media.

Newspapers are now offsetting losses from print editions with online editions. A critical issue is the offset on the loss on revenue from traditional print media with the gain in revenue when a consumer switches to the newspaper's online content. While newspaper online revenues are growing at more than 30% annually, expectations are that it will take until 2017 to 2018 before newspaper revenues return to previous levels, which assumes advertising rates stay constant and online media will continue to grow at 30%.

4.6.4 Case Study – *The Sunset Examiner*

Founded in 1857, *The Sunset Examiner* is a morning newspaper based in a provincial city with a daily circulation of 180,000 on weekdays and 225,000 for a weekend edition. The newspaper has won awards over the years, and is published from an editorial operations centre and printing plant in the provincial city. The publisher of *The Sunset Examiner*, Sunset Inc., is a single business newspaper firm. The circulation area covers the provincial city and surrounding counties. The firm has 1,500 employees and over 1,000 independent newspaper carriers. The firm operates on an 15% pre-tax profit margin.

The newspaper had enjoyed a monopoly on local news content for decades, with growth in circulation flowing into profit margins. In the late twentieth century, however, alternative sources of news became available, initially with cable news and then with Internet news sites. The newspaper's circulation started to decline as a result. While print advertising revenue had grown through to the end of the twentieth century, advertisers were aware of the declining circulation numbers and growth in advertising and classifieds revenue slowed considerably. By the start of the twenty-first century the newspaper's advertising revenues from the print edition were declining year on year.

Offsetting the decline in revenue was difficult as most of the firm's costs were fixed costs. In an attempt to reverse the declining circulation Sunset Inc. invested in marketing and redesigns to retain readers. These measures however were unsuccessful in reversing the decline in print circulation. Sunset Inc. was successful however in establishing an online edition strategy to offset the decline in print revenues.

A firm as a going-concern assumes that it will continue operations indefinitely, and firm value is based on this assumption. Managers and investors can however consider other values. A firm's liquidation also has value if the firm ceases operations and the assets are sold off. The firm as a going-concern is therefore one strategy while selling off the assets is another. Firm value is then either the maximum of the value as a going-concern or value in liquidation.

Sunset Inc.'s management and shareholders examined the value of the newspaper in liquidation while there was still a market for the newspaper's physical assets. The printing plant assets have the potential to be switched into alternative print media such as direct marketing and niche media markets.

A liquidation analysis involves valuing each asset in a sell off. Percentages for assets in liquidation founded on comparable firms are established. The sum of these asset values is netted against the liability redemptions and associated liquidation costs. A positive result provides a maximum value from which the investors' required return is deducted.

Table 4.9 illustrates Sunset Inc.'s liquidation analysis using balance sheet data. Percentages of asset value in liquidation were determined and the net liquidation value calculated. The investors' required rate of return would consider the range in the percentage estimates for the assets in liquidation, the rate at which the firm is consuming cash, and the probability of other firms also analysing the value in an acquisition.

Table 4.9 Sunset Inc. liquidation analysis ($000)

Assets		Liquidation (%)	Values
Cash	50,000	100%	50,000
Accounts receivable	22,000	72%	15,840
Inventory	2,000	55%	1,100
	74,000		66,940
Plant & equipment	125,000	54%	67,500
Goodwill	(1,000)	0%	–
	198,000		134,440
Liabilities & shareholder equity			
Short term debt	50,000	100%	(50,000)
Other liabilities	50,000	100%	(50,000)
	100,000		(100,000)
Shareholder equity	100,000	Cost of Shutdown	(5,000)
	200,000		(105,000)
		Net liquidation value	29,440
		Shares outstanding	3,000,000
		Value per share	9.81

The discount-to-book value of $29.4 million in liquidation value to the equity of $100 million reflects the value of the firm as a going-concern. The book value per share is $33, while the value to investors is $9.81 per share. If the assets take six months to liquidate then the present value at a 15% internal rate of return is $9.13.

REFERENCES

Baldwin, C. and Clark, K. *Design Rules: The Power of Modularity*, MIT Press, 1999.

Berger, P., Ofck, E. and Swary, I. Investor Valuation of the Abandonment Option, *Journal of Financial Economics* **42**: 257–87, 1996.

Challa, R. Discovering multiple interacting options, *Energy and Power Risk Management*, July 2000.

Clewlow, L. and Strickland, C. *Energy Derivatives, Pricing and Risk Management*, Lacima, 2000.

DiMasi, J., Hansen, R., Grabowski, H. and Lasagne, L. Cost of innovation in the pharmaceutical industry, *Journal of Health Economics*, **10**(2): 107–42, 1991.

Dupont-Roc, G. *The Evolution of the World's Energy Systems*, 1994.

Economides, M. and Oligney, R. *The Color of Oil*, Round Oak Publishing, 2000.

Grabowski, H.C. and Vernon, J.M. Returns to R&D on new drug introductions in the 1980s, *Journal of Health Economics*, **13**: 383–406, 1994.

Grant, R. *Contemporary Strategy Analysis*, Blackwell, 2006.

Hamel, G. *Leading the Revolution*, Harvard Business School Press, 2000.

Hirsh, R. *Power Loss*, MIT Press, 1999.

Hooke, J. *Security Analysis on Wall Street*, Wiley, 1998.

Jones, J. *What You Should Know about the Newspaper Industry*, Frontline, PBS.

Kellogg, D. and Charnes, J.M. Real options valuation for a biotechnology company, *Financial Analysts Journal*, May/June, 2000.

Kohut, A., Doherty, C., Dimock, M. and Keeter, S. *Online Papers Modestly Boost Newspaper Readership*, The Pew Reseach Center, 2006.

Kulatilaka, N., Balasubramanian, P. and Storck, J. Using real options to frame the IT investment problem, in Trigeorgis, L. (ed.) *Real Options and Business Strategy*, Risk Books, 1999.

Myers, S. and Howe, C.A. *Life Cycle Financial Model of the Pharmaceutical R&D Program on the Pharmaceutical Industry*, Massachusetts Institute of Technology, 1997.

Myers, S. and Shyam-Sunder, L. Measuring pharmaceutical industry risk and the cost of capital, in Helms, R.B. (ed.) *Competitive Strategies in the Pharmaceutical Industry*, Washington, DC, American Enterprise Institute Press, 1996.

Penman, S. *Financial Statement Analysis and Security Valuation*, McGraw Hill/Irwin, 2004.

Rose, R. *A Comprehensive Strategy for Federal Investment in Fuel Cell Technology and Fuel Infrastructure*, Breakthrough Technologies Institute, Inc., 2003.

Rudie Harrigan K., *Declining Demand, Divestiture, and Corporate Strategy*, Beard, 2005.

Stowe J.D., Robinson, T.R., Pinto, J.E. and McLeavey, D.W. *Equity Asset Valuation*, Wiley, 2007.

Sullivan, K., Chalasani, P., Jha, S. and Sazawal, V. Software design as an investment activity: a real options perspective, in Trigeorgis, L. (ed.) *Real Options and Business Strategy*, Risk Books, 1999.

Thomsett, R. *Third Wave Project Management*, Prentice Hall – Yourdon Press, 1993.

US Congress, Office of Technology Assessment, *Pharmaceutical R&D: Costs, Risks and Rewards*, OTA-M-522, Washington DC: US Government Printing Office (February), 1993.

PART II

Developments in Strategy, Value and Risk

CHAPTER 5

Developments in Strategy

Strategy is defined as the process by which a firm deploys its resources and capabilities within its business environment in order to achieve its goals. Corporate strategy is concerned with *where* a firm competes; business strategy is concerned with *how* a firm competes. There are essentially two schools of thought in regards to strategy, the *design* school and the *process* school (Grant, 1998). The design school views strategy as a rational process where the organization, its external environment and performance are analysed and evaluated. The subsequent strategy is then conveyed and implemented throughout the organization. Although normative in approach, in practice the design method is typically less regimented. The process school focuses on the practicalities of how strategies materialize, focusing on the strategic decision processes. The goal is to uncover the factors that determine the managerial development of successful performance enhancing strategies.

A strategy that cannot be implemented has no value. Strategy development, however, has to include rational analysis, perceptions and experience. Therefore the analysis and implementation of strategy cannot be separated, as in practice strategy is constantly being modified and revised as new information and knowledge becomes available. The advantage of analytical frameworks is that they provide a method for systematically assessing the enormous amount of information available on both the internal and external environment. Strategic analysis provides a framework where the value lies not so much in providing answers, but rather in the guidance of decision making, the comparison and evaluation of alternatives, and studying the source of business successes and failures.

The objective of all organizations is the creation of value. Value, however, has different meanings to different stakeholders. Organizations create value by managing resources through their capabilities to deliver products or services that offer customer value, by maintaining relations with resource providers and customers, and by organizing activities through management systems, processes and governance. To do this an organization has to create an equitable balance between stakeholders such as management, customers, employees, financiers, unions, suppliers, shareholders, government and society in general. Although value has to be established and maintained by organizations in order to offer incentives to various stakeholders, a premium is associated with value creation for customers and shareholders. The creation of value for other stakeholders is dependent on the success of creating value for customers and the incentives offered to shareholders, the residual stakeholders. Offering unsuitable incentives to stakeholders, however, is likely to lead to the destruction of shareholder value (Birkett, 2001).

The increasing international competition and deregulation of markets are intensifying competitive pressure, and most business environments are facing rigorous price competition. Innovations and changes in demand patterns are causing many industry barriers to break down, making sustainable competitive advantage an increasingly difficult proposition. This is introducing a number of issues in organizations. How can value be created and managed in an increasingly dynamic environment? How can organizations improve their capabilities to respond and adapt to these continuous and multidimensional changes in their environment and markets? How do organizations manage the effect of competition on industry structures? How can organizations create internal environments that create and manage innovation?

In response to these issues a number of concepts have had an impact and influence on organizations in recent years. These include the role of resources and capabilities, the dynamic analysis of industry and competition, and real options analysis. Seeking sustainable competitive advantage by defining the organization in terms of matching resources and capabilities, or competences, focuses on an organization's internal environment. The economic disciplines of Schumpeterian analysis and game theory focus on the instability of industry boundaries and the competitive environment. Real options analysis provides a framework that links value to risk and uncertainty, and a metric for managing flexibility and long-term strategic opportunities.

5.1 CREATIVE DESTRUCTION

The organizations of the twentieth century were managed with the assumption of continuity, which was reinforced with techniques that focused on sources of efficiency such as economies of scale, labour specialization, cost controls and vertical integration. This static regime of incremental change lasted for more than 70 years. This assumption of continuity, however, is no longer valid. Organizations are now confronting the deconstruction of markets and industries. This trend is likely to broaden and therefore ultimately influence all sources of competitive advantage, and raises issues that are likely to heavily influence strategic management in the future. The first development is the increasing commoditization of corporate assets, and the second is the difficulty that management will have in sustaining any competitive advantage.

In their book *Creative Destruction*, Richard Foster and Sarah Kaplan analysed the continuity of organizations over the twentieth century, using business publications, market indices and corporate performance data. The focus of the analysis was the limitations of long-term corporate performance that result from the inevitable changes in the business environment, which Foster and Kaplan call 'discontinuities'. A comparison of ranked US companies illustrates these discontinuities. In 1917 Forbes published their first list of the 100 largest American companies, which were ranked by assets. Forbes revisited its initial 100 list in 1987 and compared it to its then current list of top organizations. Sixty-one of the original 100 companies had survived, with 18 of the remaining 39 companies managing to stay in the top 100. These 18 companies, however, earned an investment return that was 20% less than the total market between 1917 and 1987.

The same result is found for Standard & Poor's (S&P) 500. After the S&P 90 index was initially started in the 1920s, changes in the index were relatively slow for the first 20 years, with an average turnover in companies of 1.5% per year. A firm that was included in the index during this period would remain there for an average of more than 65 years. By 1998 the rate of change in the S&P, however, had shifted dramatically, increasing to nearly 10%. The time a firm spent in the index over the last 70-plus years had decreased from an average of 65 years to 10 years. Over the last 40 years only 74 of the original 500 firms that comprised the S&P 500 in 1957 still remained on the index in 1997. Only 12 of these 74 firms outperformed the S&P index over the period from 1957 to 1998.

The results of this analysis raise the question as to why do indices such as the S&P 500 perform better in the long run than nearly all of the major corporations of the twentieth century. Foster and Kaplan conclude that the capital markets and their benchmark indices support the formation of firms and allow their continuation if they remain competitive. The capital markets will, however, eliminate any firms that fail in their capacity to perform, a process Schumpeter referred to as 'the gales of creative destruction'. Organizations that are managed with the notion of continuity have not been able to transform themselves and therefore create value at the pace of the markets.

There are some fundamental drivers of this regime of discontinuity. Capital markets have become increasingly efficient, flexible and transparent due to financial innovation and the increasing amount and accuracy of corporate information. Barriers to entry are being eroded through competition that is the result of improved capital markets, globalization, political transformations and the developments in communications and information. The inevitable end result of these developments is that *economic profits are becoming less sustainable*, and it is therefore becoming almost impossible to develop a long-term strategy based on management philosophies entrenched in the notion of continuity.

5.2 INNOVATION

In recent years innovation has become a corporate religion, with organizations considering it the foundation for managing and increasing value. The search for excess returns to create shareholder value has placed an enormous pressure on managers to innovate with new technologies. What exactly innovation is and represents, however, is not only difficult to define but even harder to measure. Most innovators create value by taking advantage of some type of new transformation in areas such as technologies, demographics, markets or regulatory environments to either create new markets or further develop existing markets. Seeking innovations that challenge incumbent markets and participants is an entirely different approach from that where the focus is on incremental improvements to an organization's product offerings. Although incremental improvements are important, they do not create new markets or ensure continuity, and value can quickly be destroyed in an environment of continuous new product innovation, shorter product life cycles, additional capacity and lower product costs.

The term 'innovation' was defined by Schumpeter as:

> the commercialisation of all new combinations based upon the application of new materials and components, the introduction of new processes, the opening of new markets, and the introduction of new organisational forms. (quoted in Jansen, 2000)

Invention is the creation of new products and processes that is made possible through the development of new knowledge, or more typically from new combinations or permutations of existing knowledge. Innovation is the initial commercialization of invention, either through the production and marketing of a new product or service, or through the use of a new production method (Grant, 1998). Bringing new products and processes to market therefore not only requires invention, but also the resources and capabilities needed to finance, produce and market the innovation.

Innovation can provide the primary basis for competitive advantage and serve as a principal driver of industry change. It can not only maintain sustainable competitive advantage, but also provide a source for overturning the competitive advantage of other firms. Schumpeter's view of the competitive process as a 'gale of creative destruction' involved the erosion of market leadership through innovation and not imitation. Not all inventions, however, progress into innovations. Many firms have portfolios that contain numerous inventions that have never been commercialized. Managers will require a venture capital approach to innovation, undertaking several projects and knowing how and when to exit a project at an early stage. A culture of innovation, therefore, is not a guarantee of success in today's business environment. Firms known for their capacity to innovate and execute can also lose market leadership when confronted with market and technological change.

Christensen (2000) proposes three reasons why good management can lead to corporate failure:

▨ The distinction between *sustaining* and *disruptive* technologies: most new advances in technologies will lead to product improvement, which Christensen terms sustaining technologies. While sustaining technologies can be either discontinuous or incremental, they all typically lead to improved performance in established products, within the scope that conventional customers previously valued. Now and then, however, disruptive technologies will emerge, innovations that bring to markets a very different value proposition than previously available. Products based on disruptive technologies are typically cheaper, simpler, smaller and frequently more convenient to use, and therefore open new markets. As the developers of disruptive technologies improve their product's performance with experience and sufficient investment, they are eventually able to take over the mature markets.

▨ The speed of technology development can and often does surpass market requirements. The relevance and competitiveness of different technologies can change with respect to different markets over time. As a result, organizations, in their pursuit to offer better products to customers than competitors to increase margins, provide more than customers need or are prepared to pay for.

▨ Established organizations typically do not invest in disruptive technologies. This rationale is based on three foundations:
  ◆ Although disruptive technologies are often relatively simpler and cheaper, they normally offer lower margins.
  ◆ Disruptive technologies typically are initially introduced into minor or emerging markets.
  ◆ The most profitable customers of a major organization typically do not need products sourced from disruptive technologies. Initially the least profitable customers within a market will typically adopt a disruptive technology. Most organizations with a culture of listening to their best customers and pursuing new products that promise greater margins and growth are usually unable to put together a case for investing in disruptive technologies until it is too late.

An organization's resource allocation process determines which projects are funded and which are not. Innovation and the allocation of resources are interrelated in that only those projects that receive sufficient funding and resources have any chance of success. Innovation within an organization will therefore be ultimately reflected in how resources are allocated. However, while management may believe they control the allocation of resource within their organizations, in today's environment it is ultimately the customers and the capital markets that determine how capital is allocated. Organizations depend on customers and the capital markets for resources in order to survive, and therefore provide the products, services and returns that they demand. Organizations that make investments that do not satisfy customers and investors are unlikely to last. As a result, organizations have developed cultures and systems for eliminating ideas that customers and investors do not want. It is therefore difficult for these organizations to allocate adequate resources to opportunities, or disruptive technologies, that are initially not required by customers. When demand takes off for these opportunities, however, it is usually too late. Most organizations have well-developed processes for managing sustaining technologies that are seen as vital to servicing and keeping existing customers. Few organizations, however, have systems and processes in place to identify and manage potentially disruptive technologies.

5.3 RESOURCES AND CAPABILITIES

Focusing an organization's strategy on the markets in which it competes may not provide the stability for long-term survival as these markets become increasingly volatile. This has increased interest in the role of an organization's *resources* and *capabilities* as a foundation for strategy and profitability. Creating sustainable competitive advantage by identifying the organization with its internal environment in terms of resources and capabilities can provide a more stable foundation on which to define its uniqueness in volatile external environments.

> An organisation's strategies define how it proposes to create value for customers, and therefore for other stakeholders, in terms of the scope and scale of its service offerings over an immediate period and the opportunities it seeks to make or find over a longer term. (Birkett, 2001)

An organization's success in achieving its strategies depends on its capabilities to execute them over the short and the long term. An organization's *strategic portfolio* defines the extent of an organization's products or services through the identification of customers, competitors, assets, investors, competitive environments, value creation and any associated risks. Although identified the portfolio is also dynamic. In the short term the portfolio is sustained through the efficiency of operations and incremental improvements. In the long term, however, lies a range of opportunities that are yet to be understood, created and realized. Organizations operate under the assumption of continuity while markets operate under a notion of discontinuity, and so the current portfolio probably cannot exist in its current familiar form.

Destruction is a mechanism that maintains innovation through the elimination of those elements in the market that are no longer required, and as such is an unavoidable and essential feature of capitalism. Securing an identified strategic portfolio in a regime of discontinuity depends on an organization's ability to establish and take advantage of opportunities as they materialize. An organization can recognize and define these options by establishing capabilities to search for the potential value in opportunities that lie in the future. Strategy will therefore need to focus on an organization's *portfolio of real options* and the associated value in opportunities that can be maintained within the portfolio. An organization's strategy will therefore consist of two components. The first is the customer value provided through the organization's strategic portfolio, while the second is the value opportunities created by the organization's real options portfolio. These two portfolios have to be maintained simultaneously, and so an organization will need the capabilities to manage both the known and the unknown as it positions itself for the future.

The capabilities to manage the real options portfolio, and therefore future value opportunities, are likely to be included in the capabilities necessary to sustain the current strategic portfolio. The combined strategic capabilities are even more likely to encompass the *core competences* of an organization. These core competences will provide the foundation for managing an organization's dynamic range and size of products and services and the transformations necessary to take advantage of opportunities that lie in the future. An organization is therefore likely to move from being an efficient operator of assets to becoming the creator, operator and trader of a portfolio of assets, based on these core competences, that will provide the foundation for managing value from the present into the future. Managing value in both the short and long run will require the management and governance capabilities to steer strategy, innovation, resource allocation and the restructuring of organizations and processes through an external environment of continuous and accelerating change.

5.4 GAME THEORY

A substantial amount of economic theory focuses on the conditions under which individuals or organizations maximize benefits or minimize costs. There are many situations, however, where economic decisions are made under conditions of conflict, in which the action of one party will provoke a response from others. In volatile markets an organization not only confronts known competitors, but other uncertainties such as entry from new unforeseen competitors, product substitutes or new technologies, all of which can transform the competitive landscape.

Game theory is the study of the optimal strategies that can maximize payoffs, given the risks associated with assessing the reaction of rivals, and the conditions under which there lies a unique solution. Games can be categorized as zero sum games, where one player's gain is another's loss, non-zero games, where a decision by one player may benefit all players, cooperative games, where collusion is feasible, and non-cooperative games when it is not (Bannock et al., 1987).

There are two areas where game theory has made important contributions to strategic management. Game theory's first contribution is that it has provided a framework for strategic decisions by defining the game in terms of the players, the player's options, the payoffs from every option combination and the decision sequences. The second is that the insights into bargaining and competition gained from game theory can be used to forecast the equilibrium results of competitive conditions, and the impact of the strategic repositioning by another player.

While game theory has provided insights and background into competitive situations, it has however been less effective in forecasting outcomes and in strategic planning. Game theory relies on constructs based on assumptions that can use few external variables, and can have problems in establishing whether an organization should compete or cooperate, the sequences of competitive moves, and the role of threats, assurances and commitments. The value from using game theory is less in the analysis of competitive responses and other issues associated with the game, and more in transforming competitive games by establishing sustainable competitive advantage.

Concepts from game theory are now making a contribution to the analysis of real options. The opportunities within real options may be influenced by competitive actions, which can be included in an analysis by combining concepts from both game theory and real options. While academic research on the relationship between option pricing and game theory may still be in its early stages, the combination has the potential to offer solutions to many strategic questions and improve an organization's strategic positioning in competitive and dynamic environments.

5.5 MODULARITY

The waves of innovation since the start of the Industrial Revolution have created an economic system that is increasingly sophisticated and complex. This economic system consists of objects that result from human intelligence and endeavour. These objects, or artifacts, include physical activities such as technologies and products, and intangible objects such as systems of law, organizations, strategies, science and designs.

Artifacts develop and evolve over time, as do the firms and markets that create and support these objects. These markets, technologies, products and firms evolve interactively to produce adaptive complex systems that ultimately become industries. An artifact is described by its design, and this designing of artifacts is a continuing process that accumulates at all levels to transform industries and economies.

Modularity is a theory of complex adaptive systems, design and industrial evolution that describes the creation of complex products and processes from smaller subsystems or modules that, although independent in their design, nonetheless function together as a complete system. The modularity concept facilitates the management of complex systems by dividing them into smaller more manageable components. This is achieved by creating a particular design structure with a set of design principles that separate the knowledge and tasks required for complex designs and artifacts.

The modularity concept can be found in numerous applications, which include production scale and scope, mass customization and organizational theory. An example can be found in computers, an artifact that has grown in complexity over the twentieth century. In the 1970s the computer business evolved from a highly concentrated industry to modular clusters which manufactured components of larger computer systems. New designs created the opportunity for the emergence of new firms, which focused on manufacturing specialized components, or modules, that were linked by design rules for the creation of computer systems.

At the start of a modular design process mandatory design rules are established for all stages of design and production. These design rules allow pieces of a modular system to be changed without the need to change the system as a whole. This capability creates the flexibility for design to evolve at the module level, and therefore creates options for designers. These options provide opportunities for innovation and capabilities for firms to compete in today's environment.

At the start of the twenty-first century the dynamics of global commerce continue to accelerate. The new technologies, markets, products and competitors that emerge from this process present both risks and rewards. In this context modularity can address three issues, it increases the ability to manage complexity, it facilitates various components of a design to be worked on simultaneously, and it accommodates uncertainty. Modularity offers therefore the capabilities to manage the complexities and uncertainties in this environment, and provide a framework for creating value, growth and innovation.

5.6 STRATEGY AND REAL OPTIONS

Advances in strategy have largely been determined by changes in the competitive environment and the subsequent reaction to these changes by organizations. A number of developments in today's environment have been discussed as being likely to heavily influence an organization's strategy. These include the speed at which products and services are becoming commoditized, the breakdown of industry barriers, the management of disruptive technologies, changes in demographics and demand patterns, and the increasing dynamics and instability of markets generally. Sustaining competitive advantage and value creation using management processes based on the notion of continuity and incremental improvement is becoming a difficult proposition. Static long-term strategies based on these management values will become increasingly hard to execute.

Value creation will require the strategic capabilities both to manage the current portfolio and manoeuvre an organization through an increasingly dynamic environment. Few organizations have methods, systems and processes to identify and manage discontinuity and disruptive technologies. Transforming an organization so as to be able to create sustainable competitive advantage and value will require new capabilities in strategy, innovation, resource allocation, organizational form and processes. An organization's strategy will focus on maintaining its strategic portfolio through managing both the known and the uncertain as it positions itself for the future. This will require the capabilities to manage both sustainable technologies, incremental improvements to the existing portfolio, and innovation as value opportunities, the disruptive technologies that are options on the future. An organization's strategy will therefore need the capabilities to manage a portfolio of real options to sustain value creation. A real options framework has the potential to link value analysis to the problems of uncertainty, discontinuity, resource allocation, management flexibility, managing innovation, and communicating strategy to stakeholders and financial markets.

REFERENCES

Baldwin, C. Y. and Clark, K. B. *Design Rules: The Power of Modularity*. MIT Press, 2000.

Bannock, G,. Baxter, R. and Davis, E. *Dictionary Of Economics*, 4th edn, Penguin, 1987.

Barbera, M. and Coyte, R. *Shareholder Value Demystified*, UNSW Press, 1999.

Birkett, W. Value creation, UNSW unpublished White Paper, 2001.

Brandenburger, A. and Nalebuff, B. The right game: use game theory to shape strategy, *Harvard Business Review*, July–August, 1995.

Christensen, C. *The Innovator's Dilemma*, Harper Business, 2000.

Garten, J. *The Mind of the CEO*, Basic Books, 2001.

Grant, R.M. *Contemporary Strategy Analysis*, Blackwell, 1998.

Hamel, G. *Leading the Revolution*, Harvard Business School Press, 2000.

Jansen, F. *The Age of Innovation*, Prentice Hall, 2000.

Foster, R. and Kaplan, S. *Creative Destruction*, Doubleday, 2001.

The Economist, Innovation in industry, 20 February, 1999.

Trigeorgis, L. (ed.) *Real Options and Business Strategy, Applications to Decision Making*, Risk Publications, 1999.

CHAPTER 6

Real Options

6.1 THE NET PRESENT VALUE RULE

The net present value rule is to accept investments that have positive net present values, that is, when the present value of the investment's cash inflows are at least as large as the present value of the cost outlays. There are some implicit assumptions underlying the NPV method (Dixit and Pindyck, 1994):

- the investment can be reversed or unwound and any outlays recovered if circumstances prove to be less than expected, or

- the choice is either a now or never decision, even if the investment cannot be reversed. If the investment is not made immediately then it cannot be made in the future.

Most investments actually do not meet these requirements. Instead the majority of investment decisions have three central features that interact at various levels:

- The investment cannot be reversed, if not totally then as least to some degree, in which case the initial investment is to some extent a sunk cost, or a cost that cannot be recovered;

- The investment's future payoffs have an associated uncertainty;

- There is some flexibility in the investment timing. There is an opportunity to delay a decision until further information becomes available.

The opportunity to delay and the inability to reverse an investment decision are significant features found in most investments. NPV valuations, however, compare investing immediately with never investing, and reflect a static value derived from assumptions that only consider a single scenario. A NPV analysis does not recognize any flexibility management has to assess and react to future circumstances that were not initially anticipated. The NPV approach assumes a static commitment to a static strategy. Any business case based on NPV analysis will therefore ignore management's potential to modify a decision alternative in the future.

Although the NPV approach assumes a predetermined path no matter how events materialise, the business environment today is anything but static. NPV techniques are not designed to capitalize on future opportunities when they arise, or to manage any potential downside risks. NPV valuation methods do not include the value of the opportunity to wait and act in the future as more information becomes available. NPV valuations also imply that risk is a single dimension that reduces value. All uncertainties and decisions are reduced to one single scenario that is adjusted for risk through the level of a discount rate.

6.2 REAL OPTIONS

Strategic flexibility has become a critical management issue in the dynamic business environment that exists today. Management concepts and methods will need therefore to be able to identify and include opportunities that may develop, and losses that may result from adverse market developments. Expanding a strategic analysis so that it includes the value of potential upside gains and downside losses will enhance management's capabilities to adapt to future market conditions. A better strategic framework would consider a range of opportunities, opportunities defined as options, rights but not obligations to some particular action in the future. Corporate strategy should therefore include in any analysis the concept of a portfolio of options, rather than just a portfolio of predetermined cash flows.

Real options analysis is a valuation and strategic decision paradigm that applies financial option theory to real assets. Stewart Myers (1987) first referred to the term in a discussion about the gap between strategic planning and finance theory. DCF analysis, developed from finance theory, made sense when applied to businesses such as 'cash cows'. However the discontinuities associated with today's business environment is putting limitations on the life of businesses such as these and therefore the DCF techniques used to analyse them. Risk can also be leveraged to create rather than suppress value. Hedges can protect investments from downside risks while an exposure is maintained to any upside potential. Real options offer a framework and the metrics for managing strategy, value and risk in today's business environment.

Organizations will typically invest in projects that generate a return greater than a hurdle rate. Hurdle rates can, however, often be observed at three to four times the cost of capital (Dixit and Pindyck, 1994). One explanation is the implied option value, or opportunity cost associated with a capital investment. Rather than the investment decision being that (discounted) cash inflows must equal or exceed (discounted) cash outflows as per the NPV rule, the investment's cash inflows must exceed the cash outflows by the value of keeping open any optionality in the investment. If a decision is made to proceed with an irreversible investment the opportunity to delay the investment is forfeited, and so the rights to any option implied in the investment are exercised. This opportunity cost should therefore be included in the valuation of an investment.

The NPV rule should therefore be revised by subtracting the opportunity cost of exercising any options, and then invest if the modified NPV is positive. The alternative is to keep the conventional NPV and the option value distinct. The investment framework can therefore include two identified value components, the NPV and the real option value. A strategic NPV can therefore be defined as (Trigeorgis, 1996):

> Strategic NPV = standard NPV + option premium

The modified NPV rule is now to invest if the strategic NPV is greater than zero.

6.3 VALUING REAL OPTIONS

Financial options are asymmetric relationships, where the option holder has a right but not the obligation to transact at a contracted price (the exercise price) on or before a predetermined date (the exercise or maturity date). A call option is the right to buy, and a put option the right to sell the underlying instrument at the exercise price. A European option can only be exercised at the end of its life, while an American option can be exercised at any time during its life. In the case of a real option it is the right but not the obligation to act, such as deferring, expanding, contracting, or abandoning a project or investment at a predetermined cost (the exercise price) for a predetermined period of time (Trigeorgis, 1996; Copeland and Antikarov, 2001). Value is created in a financial option from the volatility in an underlying financial asset, and the same concept is applied to real options, where value is derived from the uncertainty or the volatility associated with a real asset. Table 6.1 compares the variables found in a financial option with the real option equivalents.

A relatively simple argument has been developed in financial economics to price an option under the assumption that no arbitrage opportunities exist. An economy exists that has an abundant set of traded assets from which a portfolio can be created. This portfolio consists of buying a specific number of shares of a stock,

Table 6.1 Comparison between a call option on a stock and a real option on a project

Call option on stock	Real option on project
Current value of stock	(Gross) PV of expected cash flows
Exercise price	Investment cost
Time to expiration	Time until opportunity disappears
Stock value uncertainty	Project value uncertainty
Riskless interest rate	Riskless interest rate

Source: Trigeorgis (1996)

against which a certain amount is borrowed at a risk-free rate such that the portfolio replicates an option's returns in any state of nature. In the absence of any arbitrage opportunities, or risk-free profits, the option and the corresponding portfolio must sell for the same price, as they provide the same future return. Therefore the price of the option is the equivalent to the cost of setting up the replicating portfolio.

The no-arbitrage replicating portfolio concept used to price options can be applied to real options by employing the assumptions used in deriving the NPV of an asset or project. The discount rate used in DCF analysis typically estimated using the CAPM is based on the price of traded twin security with the same risk characteristics as the investment or project being analysed. Therefore the same traded twin security can be used to replicate the real option's returns. This leads to an important assumption in valuing real options, that existing assets in the economy span the risks in the asset or project being valued. Capital markets must be adequately complete so that an asset exists such that its price is perfectly correlated with the asset underlying the real option. Real options can, however, have risks that are not priced or spanned in the financial markets. These risks that cannot be represented by the price of a traded security are known as private risks.

Incomplete markets can be found in all real asset markets, and even in financial markets. Incomplete markets are likely to remain in regards to a specific risk if the costs exceed the benefits of creating the securities required to span a specific risk, or if there are problems associated with making such securities legitimate. Other market imperfections include intermittent trading, sporadic price discovery and a lack of liquidity. Robert Merton (1998) presented a framework in his 1997 Nobel Prize lecture for determining the value and risk of a non-traded asset by using a portfolio of traded securities. There are two aspects that can be drawn from Merton's address. The first is that it is probable that some kind of tracking of the risks in a corporate investment can be established through a portfolio of traded securities, in spite of market imperfections. The second is the rigorous definition Merton offers of private risk. Merton defines and measures private risk as the size of the tracking error between the portfolio of traded securities and the value of the underlying asset. Private risk can therefore be identified through the data rather than through subjective breakdowns of market and private risks.

Other techniques that can be used when spanning does not hold are decision analysis and dynamic programming. Decision analysis is a structured quantitative approach for the evaluation of decisions that have complex alternatives, competing objectives and major sources of uncertainty. The origins of decision analysis began at Harvard Business School in the early 1960s as a continuation of the quantitative advances in operations research and management science. Decision analysis combines systems analysis, which considers the interactions and dynamic behaviour of complex situations, and statistical decision theory, which focuses on logic in simple uncertain situations. Merging these two concepts into decision analysis provided a focus on logic in uncertain and complex dynamic situations.

Real options and decision analysis both have the common goal of modelling the decisions and uncertainties associated with investments. Where there is a distinction between the real options and decision analysis method is in the definition of valuing risky cash flows. Valuation in decision analysis is derived from the values and preferences of an individual or organization, whereas valuation in real options is derived from prices in traded markets. As value in real options is based on markets, risk-neutral probabilities and risk-free discount rates, the utility functions and risk adjustments to discount rates as used in decision analysis are unnecessary.

The holder of a financial option has an exclusive right over exercising that option. The same however is not always the case in real options. Some real options will be exclusive or proprietary, and therefore the holder of the real option will have sole exercise rights without the threat of competitors. Other investment opportunities however will have shared real options and may also be available to competitors or other potential participants. Other possible situations are where shared real options have no value as they collectively belong to a whole industry, or where they are a public good.

In option markets the best strategy for the holder of a non-dividend paying American call option on a stock is typically to delay the exercise until the option maturity. There is no benefit or opportunity cost associated with waiting to exercise the option, and therefore the holder of the call option would rationally wait as long as possible before exercising that option. If a stock does pay a dividend, however, its value will typically fall after the dividend payout, and so reduce the payoff for a dividend paying American call option if it is exercised immediately after the dividend payout.

Therefore there is an associated opportunity cost in waiting to exercise if a stock option does pays a dividend, in which case early exercise would be a better strategy. In a similar sense, if there were no opportunity costs associated with delaying an investment, the holder of a real option would wait until its maturity before exercising. In circumstances where competitors can enter a market, however, the real option holder would forgo any potential value from waiting to exercise so as to pre-empt competitors. Competitors entering a market can reduce the value of the cash flows from an investment made in that market, and therefore the value of any investment opportunities.

While there are many issues associated with identifying and valuing real options, in the final analysis the critical issue is to be able to think in terms of real options. Projects and investments can be conceptualized as portfolios of assets that have opportunities, option portfolios that can be managed dynamically as the future unfolds, uncertainty is resolved and new information becomes available. Real options analysis draws on a range of techniques that include market values, quantitative methods, and also qualitative assessment. Even if objective market-based valuations are not always obtainable, a qualitative interpretation of real options is essential, as a real options framework provides management with a structure for decisions that have to be made in any case.

6.4 TYPES OF REAL OPTIONS

Real options can exist in almost every business decision, although they are not always easily identified. Many types of real options have been recognized and analysed (Dixit and Pindyck, 1994; Trigeorgis, 1996), and the following is a summary of common categories:

- *Option to defer:* The opportunity to invest can be more valuable than investing immediately, as it provides management with the flexibility to defer the investment until conditions become more favourable, or to cancel completely if they become unsatisfactory. The opportunity to defer is the equivalent to a call option on the value of a project. These investment opportunities can still be beneficial even though the investment may have a negative NPV.

- *Option to expand or contract:* Options can exist in projects and operations to expand, to contract, and to shut down and restart. Management can expand production or increase resource deployment if the market environment develops more favourably than expected. This is the equivalent to a call option. On the other hand, operation scale can be reduced if market developments are less than initial expectations, which is the equivalent to a put option.

- *Option to abandon:* Management can abandon an operation if market conditions deteriorate, and liquidate any capital and other assets. The option to abandon is the equivalent to a put option. If the value of the asset or project falls below its liquidation value, the owners or holder of the option can exercise the put.

- *Option to switch:* Management can change a project or an operation by restarting an operation that has been shut down, the equivalent to a call option, or shut the operation down, the equivalent to a put option. The cost of starting up or shutting down is the equivalent to the strike of the call or put.

- *Growth options:* Investments such as R&D, undeveloped land, oil and gas reserves and acquisitions and information networks connect a chain of interrelated projects, and can create future growth opportunities such as new products or processes and new markets.

- *Compound options:* Projects frequently involve a collection of options, with combinations of upward value and downward protection options present. The combined value of interacting options can differ from the sum of the separate parts due to their interaction. Some real options are relatively simple as their value if exercised is limited to the value of the underlying project. Other real options, however, can lead to further investment opportunities when exercised. These are *options on options*, or *compound options*, where the option payoff is another option.

- *Rainbow options:* These are options that have multiple sources of uncertainty. Options that have payoffs that depend on two or more assets are usually called rainbow options. In the financial world rainbow options can refer to the maximum or minimum of two or more assets, or other options, for example where the payoff depends on the spread between two assets, the better of two assets and cash, portfolio options and dual strike options. In the case of real options, numerous sources of uncertainty can exist in forms such as prices, quantities, technologies, regulation and interest rates.

REFERENCES

Amram, M. and Kulatilaka, N. *Strategy and Shareholder Value Creation, The Real Option Frontier*, Harvard Business School Press, 1999.

Briys, E., Bellalah, M., Minh Mai, H. and De Varenne, F. *Options, Futures and Exotic Derivatives*, Wiley, 1998.

Copeland, T. and Antikarov, V. *Real Options*, Texere, 2001.

Damodaran, A. *Applied Corporate Finance*, Wiley, 1999.

Dixit, A. and Pindyck, R. *Investment Under Uncertainty*, Princeton University Press, 1994.

Howard, R.A. and Matheson, J.E. *The Principles and Applications of Decision Analysis*, SDG, 1989.

Luehrman, T. Investment opportunities as real options: getting started on the numbers, *Harvard Business Review*, July–August, 1998.

Luehrman, T. Strategy as a portfolio of real options, *Harvard Business Review*, September–October, 1998.

Merton, R. Applications of option-pricing theory: Twenty five years later, *The American Economic Review*, June, 1998.

Myers, S. Financial theory and financial strategy, *Midland Corporate Finance Journal*, 1987.

Smith, J. *Much Ado About Options?* Fuqua School of Business, Duke University, July, 1999, http://www.real-options.com.

Trigeorgis, L. *Real Options: Managerial Flexibility and Strategy in Resource Allocation*, MIT Press, 1996.

CHAPTER 7

Firm Value

7.1 OVERVIEW

Corporate finance has the objective of optimizing firm value while minimizing the associated risks. This encompasses the management of real assets that create firm value, minimizing the costs associated with the financing of these investments, and maintaining the firm's working capital.

Corporate finance is also framed within short- and long-term domains. The short-term domain focuses on a firm's working capital, defined as the net of current assets and current liabilities, and includes cash management, inventory and short-term lending and borrowing. The goal of working capital management is to optimize a firm's liquid assets. The long-term domain focuses on the capital investment decisions that involve a firm's fixed assets and capital structure. These decisions involve capital expenditure, the balance sheet debt and equity financing choices and dividend decisions. Capital investment decisions consist of an investment, a financing, and a dividend decision, and are usually framed with the goal of maximizing firm value by investing in projects with a positive NPV.

Firm value is equivalent to the firm's total capitalization, which is equivalent to the market value aggregate of the firm's equity, bonds and any other claims, or the present value of all the claims on the firm. The value of the firm is therefore the present value of all free cash flows created from the firm's business model that are available for claimants on the firm. The concepts behind the analysis of real asset investments are equivalent for either the value for specific projects, or the firm itself, as the firm represents a collection of projects.

Capital structure is defined as the way in which a firm finances its balance sheet through the weighting of equity, debt and other security types. A firm's leverage is the ratio of firm debt to total financing. The goal of defining a firm's capital structure is to finance the assets so as to maximize firm value.

7.2 THEORIES OF FIRM VALUE

Initial theories of firm value were proposed by Miller and Modigliani, who examined the associations between a firm's operations in the real economy and its financing decisions in the financial economy. Miller and Modigliani showed that under an assumption of no taxes firm value is the same regardless of whether it is financed through equity or debt. The only impact that the type of financing made was on the distribution of a firm's value between its investor types.

Miller and Modigliani also suggested that establishing firm value enabled the valuation of the firm's stock, bonds and other claims on the firm. A firm is represented by the present value of the firm's free cash flows discounted at a risk adjusted interest rate, with the assumption that financing, the ratio of equity and debt, had no influence on the firm's operating cash flows and therefore on firm value. Once the value of the firm is established the market value of debt is deducted to arrive at the firm's capitalization.

A firm's capital structure defines the manner in which it finances its assets or structures its liabilities that include equity, debt and other claims. The Miller and Modigliani theory provides a foundation for the analysis of capital structure. Using the assumptions of perfect markets, no taxes, a universal borrowing interest rate, no bankruptcy or transaction costs and financing decisions not affecting investments, Modigliani and Miller drew two conclusions on capital structure. The first, defined as their first proposition, was that a firm's value is not influenced by capital structure. Their second proposition was that a leveraged firm's cost of equity is the same as that of a firm with no leverage. Miller and Modigliani later revised some of the assumptions, in particular taxes.

The Modigliani–Miller theory provides a framework to examine how a firm's value is influenced by capital structure decisions and determining optimal capital structures. The Modigliani–Miller representation is defined as the primitive firm, for which its value is represented by the sum of the expected free cash flows discounted by the weighted average cost of capital. The primitive firm represents the DCF model of the firm, and provides a foundation for the analysis of a firm's financial structure through the financial options on the primitive firm.

Black, Scholes and Merton were the first to formalize the association between a firm's equity and debt. The insight from these researchers is that equity can be defined as an option on a firm's assets, with the value of debt being equivalent to the residual of the value of assets over the value of equity. The Black and Scholes theory of the firm considered equity as a call option with a strike equalling the notional value of zero coupon debt on the value of the primitive firm. Merton also considered equity as an option on a firm's assets to define the firm's debt value and credit risk. The model developed by Merton uses the value and volatility of the firm's assets and the notional value of debt.

Geske extended the Black and Scholes model by specifying the stock itself underlying a call option as an option of the firm's assets, or the equivalent to a compound option. Whereas the Black and Scholes model assumes that the volatility of a stock price is constant, the Geske model recognizes that volatility is not constant.

The compound option model identifies volatility as a function of the level of the firm's stock price, or more fundamentally on firm value. To achieve this the Geske model adds an additional variable, the firm's notional debt, to the Black and Scholes model, as it is financial leverage that influences the volatility or risk of a firm's equity.

The next development in defining firm value focused on the actual firm as the underlying asset. Myers proposed that a firm's investments can be represented as options. Firm value had been defined as the primitive model, or a pool of projects that represents the present value of free cash flows. Investing in product markets can however produce cash flows from an initial investment and also value from growth options if a product market continues to expand. A firm's initial investments therefore provide a base for a sequence of potential follow-on investment decisions.

The identification of this time series of investments is an extension of the primitive firm, and these discretionary future investments were defined by Myers as real options, or options on real assets. Real options identify the investment decisions within a firm as a right without an obligation, or as state contingent decisions on real assets. A firm has the choice in the future whether or not to exercise the option on follow-on investments.

7.3 DEVELOPMENTS IN THE THEORIES OF FIRM VALUE

7.3.1 Overview

The theories of the primitive firm, financial options and real options can be combined to provide a framework for firm value that provides the flexibility required by a firm to adapt to its external environment. Copeland defines the combination as a 'three layer cake', with the primitive firm as the foundation, real options consisting of a portfolio of growth options and a firm abandonment option, and a portfolio of financial options. The three layer framework identifies the relationships between a firm's real and financial options. A firm has both an optimal real options investment structure and an optimal capital structure, and there is a trade-off between the two. Therefore the firm's operating and financial decisions are not unrelated as per the Modigliani and Miller theory.

The following illustrates the components of the three layers which, when combined, offers a framework to manage firm value in an increasingly dynamic environment where operating and financial flexibility is critical.

7.3.2 Primitive firm valuation

The primitive firm is defined as an underlying security that represents the firm's business risks. The firm's value, market capitalization, debt and other claims are defined as contingent claims on this underlying security, the primitive firm itself. The valuation of the underlying security is represented by the expected free cash flows to the firm, $E(FCF_t)$ discounted at the weighted average cost of capital w with the assumption that systematic risk is the only risk factor. It is also assumed that the firm has no debt or other claims and is financed only with equity, and that the firm pays no taxes to segregate the tax issues from business risks. The value of the primitive firm V therefore is equal to V_0, the expected present value at $t = 0$:

$$E(V_0) = \sum_{t=0}^{N} \frac{E(FCF_t)}{(1 + w)^{-t}} \qquad\qquad t = 0, 1, ...N. \qquad\qquad (7.1)$$

The assumptions underlying the primitive firm are naive, as firms will delay investments until uncertainty is reduced or divest. These investment alternatives can be reduced to growth and expansion, defined as a European call option, or abandonment, or the equivalent to an American put option.

The DCF case studies illustrate the primitive firm concept.

7.3.3 Growth options

Given that is possible to define the notion of a capital structure, it is also possible to define a firm's investment structure that includes its real options portfolio. This investment structure can be optimized to provide a firm the flexibility to adapt to its environment, and includes growth options, an abandonment option, and also a trade-off between scale and modularity.

The discretion a firm has on exercising its future investment opportunities is identified as call options on real assets. These options are growth options, and can be defined as a sequence of growth opportunities embedded in a firm's investments that have an impact on a firm's value.

Refer to the case study in Section 13.5 for an illustration of growth options.

7.3.4 Modularity

A firm's operational capacity is also a fundamental component of its investment structure. The firm has the option to expand capacity to meet increased demand, or not to expand if it has excess capacity. A firm's operating leverage is defined as the ratio of its fixed to variable costs. A high operating leverage is associated with less flexibility to adapt to change. Flexibility is therefore a function of a firm's operating leverage, and the capability to invest in modules has an impact on the firm's operating leverage.

The term modularity is defined as a specific design structure where within each unit or module the parameters and tasks are mutually dependent, whereas across each module they are independent. Modularity is a concept that can define a firm's operating leverage, or the degree to which the firm lacks flexibility due to its fixed costs. A firm's excess capacity is the variation between the firm's output capacity and expected output. The trade-off between modularity and economies of scale has an impact on a firm's excess capacity, and therefore its investment and capital structure. Firm value can be optimized through its investments in growth, abandonment and also modularity.

Refer to the case study in section 13.7 for an illustration of modularity.

7.3.5 The abandonment option

A firm has value in the decision to discontinue operations and liquidate the firm's assets. This liquidation value is the equivalent to an option to abandon the firm to the firm's investors, with the exit value equal to the firm's total collateral or the total cash proceeds from liquidation. This option is an American put option, with the value of the option increasing as the value of the firm's total collateral or exit value increases.

Refer to the case study in Section 13.6 for an illustration of the abandonment option.

7.3.6 Financial options

A firm's capital structure is defined by the financial options on the primitive firm as in the theories of Merton, Black and Scholes and Geske. The only decision variable in this case is the firm's debt policy, a choice that does not have an effect on primitive firm value. Under these assumptions the same value will be generated by a marginal investment no matter what debt policy is selected.

7.4 OPTIMIZING THE FIRM STRUCTURE

An optimal firm structure that provides the flexibility and capabilities to adapt to its external environment consists of the primitive firm, an optimal investment structure, modularity, and an optimal capital structure. The optimal investment structure includes the real options in the European call option growth portfolio and the American put option to abandon the firm. A firm therefore has three layers that consist of the primitive firm, the real options portfolio and a capital structure consisting of debt and equity that is represented by financial options.

The variables of interest in an investment policy are:

- Capital structure, which is influenced by the trade-off between a firm's real options portfolio and debt ratio, and the tax benefits of leverage on equity. Copland presents a model for an optimal capital structure using the variables described here.

- Modularity, which can have a function in establishing a firm's investment structure. Flexibility in a firm's capacity provides the ability to adapt to changing markets and industries.

- Volatility, which creates value in real options along with a firm's ability to exercise these options. Volatility and flexibility also influence a firm's level of cash.

The variables of interest in an optimal financial structure are:

- The abandonment or collateral value, which has a positive relationship with firm value.

▓ A firm's debt policy, or leverage, which has an influence on growth and abandonment.

▓ Taxes, which will raise the value of the firm's equity if the balance sheet has debt due to tax benefits. This upside will however start to roll off or fall beyond a leverage threshold and ultimately goes to zero if the firm is abandoned.

▓ Cash and cash management, which are related to flexibility. Firms with large cash reserves are able to react quickly to market and industry conditions, and exercise real options when compared to firms with higher debt ratios and external funding requirements. Growth through expansion and abandonment are both influenced by the level of a firm's debt, or its leverage.

▓ Volatility, which also has an influence on the firm's financial option values. Increases in volatility will influence the firm's debt costs and therefore the firm's capital structure.

A firm's investment and capital structure is ultimately a function of the industry in which it operates, its external environment and the firm's strategy. The interactions between a firm's investment structure, modularity versus economies of scale and capital structure create trade-offs in framing the firm's structure. Leverage will have an impact on the firm's equity when viewed as a call option on the firm's assets, and therefore its growth and abandonment options. The use of tax to optimize a firm's capital structure will influence the flexibility of its operations. A firm's overall structure should therefore consider a range of variables and trade-offs when defining its capabilities to adapt to its environment.

REFERENCES

Baldwin, C. and Clark, K. *Design Rules*, MIT, 2000.

Black, F. and Scholes, M. The pricing of options and corporate liabilities, *Journal of Political Economy*, 1973.

Copeland, T. *The Firm as a Three-Layer Cake – Optimal Investment and Financial Structure*, MIT Sloan School of Business.

Clayman, M., Fridson, M. and Troughton, G. *Corporate Finance – A Practical Approach*, 2008. J. Wiley & Sons.

Geske, R. The valuation of compound options, *Journal of Financial Economics*, 1978.

Ho, T. and Lee, S. *The Oxford Guide to Financial Modeling*, Oxford, 2004.

Merton, R. On the pricing of corporate debt: the risk structure of interest rates, *Journal of Finance*, 1973.

Miller, M. and Modigliani, F. Dividend policy, growth and the valuation of shares, *Journal of Business*, 1961.

Myers, S. The determinants of corporate borrowing, *Journal of Financial Economics*, 1977.

The Economist, Corporate finance, 27 January 2001.

CHAPTER 8

Risk Management

8.1 WHY MANAGE RISK?

Risk can be viewed as either a threat or an opportunity. Value is not created without risk, and innovation without risk is a contradiction. Attempting to entirely eliminate risk is not a practical exercise because of the associated costs, and so there has to be a trade-off between any benefits from reducing risk and the costs of doing so. Business risks are those that an organization willingly assumes to create a competitive advantage and add value. The motivation for organizations to better understand and measure risk is being driven by:

- The increasing awareness that earnings volatility can significantly affect stock price valuation and shareholder value;
- The increasing size and types of interrelated risk exposures organizations are facing due to the globalization of markets and increased international trade;
- Organizational requirements for improved exposure and risk-related information to define management's risk appetite and improve decision-making.

Business risk management is a process where risk exposures are identified, measured, and managed where possible within the context of corporate finance and strategy, and is essentially a core competency of all business activity. The focus in risk management is moving from individual price exposures to the management of an organization's exposure as a portfolio of interrelated risks. An effective risk management framework can address issues such as:

- organizations requiring more transparent risk management methods to manage the external factors that can influence performance;
- risk management practices being increasingly scrutinized by analysts, investors and rating agencies;

- evaluating the potential impact of adverse market movements on a firm's capital;

- defining risk and return targets for businesses and projects;

- the use of risk-adjusted measures to influence management decisions; and

- whether the rewards are adequate for a given level of performance.

8.2 DEFINING AND MEASURING RISK

Before defining, identifying and quantifying risk it is important to distinguish between definitions and measures of risk. Defining risk under the concept of diversifiable risk, non-diversifiable risk and the CAPM has been discussed in Chapter 3. Event definitions of risk differentiate risk types by the nature of the event that can cause a loss. Market risk is defined within an event risk framework as the changes in prices of assets, liabilities or financial variables that impact on cash flows. Risk factors are any market price, value or index that can have an influence on cash flows.

Financial theory defines risk as a dispersion of unexpected outcomes due to movements in market values or risk factors. Positive and negative deviations are both viewed as sources of risk. Changes can be expressed as either absolute or relative returns, and probabilities can be derived for the distributions of these returns. Risk can therefore be evaluated and measured in a probability context, where risk is conceptualized as the probability that an event will occur rather than in terms of the consequences of that event. Measures of risk can now be defined as the volatility of unexpected outcomes, such as the variance or volatility of an asset's returns.

8.3 STRATEGY, VALUE AND RISK MANAGEMENT

To continue to establish and maintain value in an increasingly competitive and dynamic environment, organizations will need to identify and manage sustainable competitive advantage. This requires the ability to select markets that match an organization's capabilities, and abandon markets where the organization is at a competitive disadvantage. In this environment value is created through the planning and management of an organization's strategic portfolio and its real options portfolio, where real options that have value are identified and exercised, and those that do not are abandoned. An organization's capabilities will therefore include the ability to both manage and direct its strategic portfolio, and to effectively identify, value and manage its real options portfolio.

Strategy includes not only identifying opportunities but also attaching some estimate of risk to the alternatives. Financial risk can be defined within the dimensions of an organization's value, cash flows and/or earnings. An organization's value is a stock at a point in time, representing the discounted present value of all of the organization's future cash flows and option values of future opportunities. Cash flows and earnings are flows that occur over a period of time. Any one or a combination of risk factors can impact on value, and so what is at risk in an environment of discontinuity is the likelihood that organizations will be unable to sustain value creation.

Two risk measures that are based on volatility, value at risk (VAR) and cash flow at risk (CFAR) have become increasingly popular. These measures of market risk use probabilities to interpret risk exposures as a potential loss. VAR summarises the expected maximum loss over a target horizon within some confidence interval. However VAR is not always a suitable risk measure for many organizations, as it focuses on the potential loss in the market value of assets and liabilities over a short horizon. Many organizations have physical assets, brand names, and intangible assets such as capitalized research and development, for which market or liquidation values are only relevant for a small portion of the balance sheet. In these situations an alternative risk measure is CFAR, where an aggregate risk exposure is derived from the variability of projected cash inflows and outflows over a multiyear planning horizon.

VAR and CFAR focus on the risk of a potential loss in a portfolio of assets based on the volatility of those assets, whereas real options derive value from the volatility of the underlying real assets. Option-like exposures in an organization can be viewed as either sources of risk or sources of opportunity. A key distinguishing characteristic in the future will be found in those organizations with a risk management process that aims at value enhancement, where risk exposures are identified and managed in the context of strategy, investments and revenue optimization rather than just pure risk control. While an organization's real assets are a significant component of its risk profile, its real options can make a significant contribution to value. An organization can therefore enhance its capabilities by integrating real options analysis into its risk management as well as its corporate finance and strategic management processes.

REFERENCES

Birkett, W. Value creation, UNSW, unpublished White Paper, 2001.

Culp, C.L. *The Risk Management Process*, Wiley, 2001.

Dembo, R.S. *Seeing Tomorrow: Rewriting the Rules of Risk*, Wiley, 1998.

Jorion, P. *Value at Risk*, Irwin, 2000.

Shimko, D. VAR for corporates, *Risk*, September 1995.

PART III

Quantifying
Real Options

THE SOLUTION METHODS

To establish a real options framework some background in option valuation theories, decision sciences and model estimation is required. Real options analysis of strategic investments applies option and decision theory to managing real assets. Financial options and real options differ, however, in regard to traded markets and the sources of uncertainty, with real options being more complex. The trade-off in a real options framework is the value of including flexibility in the analysis versus the complexities of doing so. The value lies in combining economic, financial and mathematical principles to identify the implications of any uncertainty in resource allocation and planning decisions. The difficulty lies in the computations, data requirements and analytical and technical background that are required. There are numerous ways to calculate the value of an option. If the real options are properly structured, all the methods should give the same result, and therefore the solution method should not influence the results.

CHAPTER 9

Derivatives

9.1 FUTURES, FORWARDS AND OPTIONS

A derivative is a financial instrument whose payoff depends on the values of other more basic variables. The variables underlying derivatives are often the prices of traded securities. Derivatives separate market and credit risks from the underlying assets and liabilities, and offer the ability to reduce a risk exposure through its transfer to a party that is prepared to take on and manage those risks. Derivative securities are also known as contingent claims, and can be contingent on almost any variable, from the price of a commodity to weather outcomes. There are two basic types of derivatives, futures/forwards and options.

Forward and futures contracts are agreements to buy or sell an underlying asset at a predetermined time in the future for a specified price. Futures are exchange-standardized contracts, whereas forward contracts are direct agreements between two parties. The cash flows of the two contracts also occur at different times. Futures are daily marked to market with cash flows passing between the long and the short position to reflect the daily futures price change, whereas forwards are settled once at maturity. If future interest rates are known with certainty then futures and forwards can be treated as the same for pricing purposes.

There are two sides to every forward contract. The party who agrees to buy the asset holds a long forward position, while the seller holds a short forward position. At the maturity of the contract (the 'forward date') the short position delivers the asset to the long position in return for the cash amount agreed in the contract, often called the delivery price. Figure 9.1 shows the profit and loss profile to the long forward position at the maturity of the contract. If T represents the contract maturity date, a long forward payoff is expressed as $S_T - K$, where S_T represents the asset price at time T, and K represents the agreed delivery price. The payoff can be positive or negative, depending on the relative values of S_T and K. The short position has the opposite payoff to the long position, that is, $S_T + K$, as every time the long

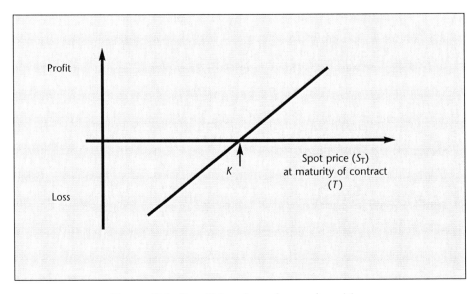

Figure 9.1 Payoff to a long forward position

position makes a profit the short incurs a loss and vice versa. As the holder of a long forward contract is guaranteed to pay a known fixed price for the spot asset, futures and forwards can be seen as insurance contracts providing protection against the price uncertainty in the spot markets.

For an arbitrage relationship to exist the forward price has to equal the cost of financing the purchase of the spot asset today and holding it until the forward maturity date. Let F represent a forward contract price on a spot asset that is currently trading at S, T the maturity date of the contract, c the cost of holding the spot asset (which includes the borrowing costs for the initial purchase and any storage costs) and δ the continuous dividend yield paid out by the underlying asset. The price of a forward contract at time t and the spot instrument on which it is written are related via the 'cost of carry' formula:

$$F = Se^{(c-\delta)(T-t)} \tag{9.1}$$

where $T - t$ represents years. The continuous dividend yield can be interpreted as the yield on an index for index futures, as the foreign interest rate in foreign exchange futures contracts, and as the convenience yield for various energy contracts.

Options contracts are the second foundation to derivatives markets. Options are asymmetrical relationships where the option holder has a right, but not an obligation, to transact at a contracted price, called the exercise price. There are two basic types of options. A call option gives the holder the right, but not the obligation, to buy the spot asset on or before a predetermined date (the maturity date) at a certain price (the strike price), which is agreed today. A put option is the right to sell, at the

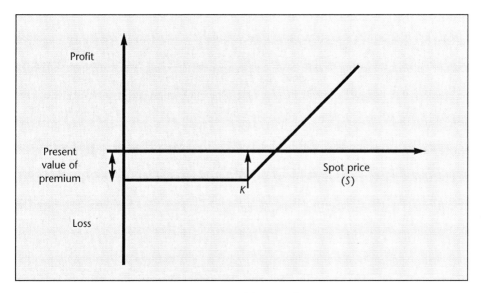

Figure 9.2 Payoff for a call option

exercise price. Option sellers, or writers, are obliged to commit to the purchaser's decision. Figure 9.2 shows the payoff to the holder of a call option.

Options differ from forward and futures contracts in that a payment, or the option price or premium, must be made by the buyer, usually at the time the contract is entered into. If the spot asset price is below the agreed strike or exercise price K at the maturity or expiration date, the holder lets the option expire worthless, forfeits the premium and buys the asset in the spot market. For asset prices greater than K, the holder exercises the option, buying the asset at K and has the ability to immediately make a profit equal to the difference between the two prices (less the initial premium). The holder of the call option therefore essentially has the same positive payoff as the long forward contract without the downside risk.

The payoff to a call option can be defined as:

$$Max(S - K, 0) \tag{9.2}$$

The second basic type of option, a put option, gives the holder the right, but not the obligation, to sell the asset on or before the maturity date at the strike price.

The payoff for a put option can be written as:

$$Max(K - S, 0) \tag{9.3}$$

Figure 9.3 shows the payoff to the holder of a put option.

As with forwards, there are two sides to every option contract. One party buys the option and has the long position, while the other party writes (or sells) the option and takes a short position. Figure 9.4 shows the four possible combinations of

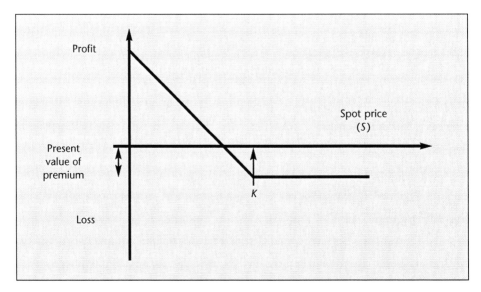

Figure 9.3 Payoff for a put option

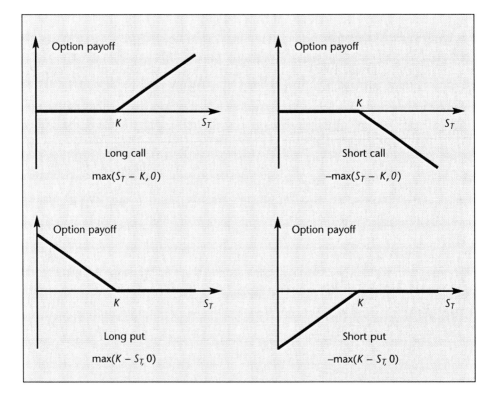

Figure 9.4 Payoffs for European options

payoffs for long and short positions in European call and put options at the maturity date T. Options are also classified with respect to their exercise conventions. European options can only be exercised on the maturity date itself, whereas American-style options can be exercised at any time up to and including the expiration date. While early exercise of an American option is generally not optimal, there are exceptions to the rule. One example is where the underlying asset pays dividends, therefore reducing the value of the asset and any call options on that asset, in which case the call option may be exercised before maturity.

Forwards and options are also the key building blocks of more complex derivatives, and these building blocks are themselves interdependent. The decomposition of derivatives into their components assists in identifying a derivative's risk characteristics, which promotes more accurate pricing and better risk management strategies. The basic futures and options described are the building blocks of all derivative securities and the principles are consistent across all underlying markets. In some markets, however, derivative structures exhibit a number of important differences from other underlying markets. These differences arise because of the complex contract types that exist in these industries, as well as the complex characteristics of the relevant prices. Both the type of derivatives and the associated modelling need to capture the evolution of prices to reflect these differences.

9.2 THE REPLICATING PORTFOLIO AND RISK-NEUTRAL VALUATION

The modern theory of option pricing is possibly one of the most important contributions to financial economics. The breakthrough came in the early 1970s with work by Fisher Black, Myron Scholes and Robert Merton (Black and Scholes 1973; Merton 1973). The Black–Scholes–Merton (BSM) modelling approach proved not only important for providing a computationally efficient and relatively easy way of pricing an option, but also demonstrated the principal of no-arbitrage risk-neutral valuation. Their analysis showed that the payoff to an option could be perfectly replicated with a continuously adjusted holding in an underlying asset and a risk-free bond. As the risk of writing an option can be completely eliminated, the risk preferences of market participants are irrelevant to the valuation problem, and it can be assumed that they are risk-neutral. In this construct all assets earn the risk-free rate of interest, and therefore the actual expected return on the asset does not appear in the Black–Scholes formula.

Options can be valued by deriving the cost of creating the replicating portfolio such that both the option and the portfolio provide the same future returns, and therefore must sell at the same price to avoid arbitrage opportunities. The portfolio consists of Δ units of an underlying asset S and an amount B borrowed against Δ units at the risk-free rate r. This combination of the borrowing and the underlying asset creates the same cash flows or returns as an option. A binomial model can be used to illustrate the replicating portfolio. The binomial model assumes that the

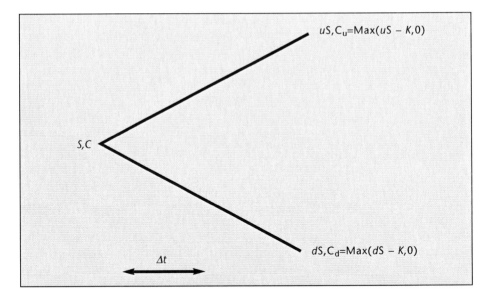

Figure 9.5 Binomial model of an asset price and call option

underlying asset price follows a binomial process, where at any time the asset price S at t_0 can only change to one of two possible values over the time period Δt, either up to uS or down to dS at time t_1. Figure 9.5 is a binomial model for a one-period process, in which a risk-free portfolio consisting of the underlying asset and the call option is illustrated.

The call option has been defined as:

$$C \approx (\Delta S - B)$$

The value of the portfolio is the same regardless of whether the asset price moves up or down over the period Δt:

$$C_u = \Delta uS - (1 + r)B$$

and

$$C_d = \Delta dS - (1 + r)B$$

which after rearranging becomes:

$$-C_u + \Delta uS = -C_d + \Delta dS \tag{9.4}$$

This is the equivalent to:

$$\Delta = \frac{C_u - C_d}{(u - d)S} \tag{9.5}$$

The portfolio must earn the continuously compounded risk-free rate of interest as it is risk-free:

$$(-C + \Delta uS) = e^{r\Delta t}(-C + \Delta S) \tag{9.6}$$

Substituting into equation (9.6) for ΔS, using equation (9.5) and rearranging for the call price at t_0 obtains:

$$C = e^{-r\Delta t}\left(\frac{e^{r\Delta t} - d}{u - d}C_u + \frac{u - e^{r\Delta t}}{u - d}C_d\right) \tag{9.7}$$

The actual probabilities of the asset moving up or down have not been used in deriving the option price, and therefore the option price is independent of the risk preferences of investors. Equation (9.7) can be interpreted as taking discounted expectations of future payoffs under the risk-neutral probabilities. This provides a means to derive the risk-neutral probabilities directly from the asset price:

$$uSp + dS(1 - p) = Se^{r\Delta t} \tag{9.8}$$

for which the return can now be assumed as being the risk-free rate. Rearranging gives:

$$p = \frac{e^{r\Delta t} - d}{u - d} \tag{9.9}$$

Equation (9.7) can now be written as:

$$C = e^{-r\Delta t}(pC_u + (1 - p)C_d)$$

This is the price of the call option with one period to maturity.

Note: This chapter has largely been adapted from Clewlow and Strickland (1998, 2000).

REFERENCES

Black, F. and Scholes, M. The pricing options and corporate liabilities, *Journal of Political Economy*, **81**: 637–59, 1973.

Clewlow, L. and Strickland, C. *Implementing Derivative Models*, Wiley, 1998.

Clewlow, L. and Strickland, C. *Energy Derivatives, Pricing and Risk Management*, Lacima, 2000.

Hull, J.C. *Options, Futures and Other Derivatives*, Prentice Hall, 2000.

Merton, R. Theory of rational option pricing, *Bell Journal of Economics and Management Science*, **4**: 41–183, 1973.

Trigeorgis, L. *Real Options: Managerial Flexibility and Strategy in Resource Allocation*, MIT Press, 1996.

CHAPTER 10

Data Analysis

10.1 DATA AND INFORMATION

One fundamental change in today's business environment is the gradual replacement of the industrial society with the information society. Information has become one of the most powerful commodities in the world today. Information systems management is increasingly becoming integrated into corporate and business strategy, with data integrity and availability improving as a result. This process is providing a rich source of financial and business data, much of which is proprietary to an organization, which managers and investors can utilize for the analysis of strategic decisions. Statistical analysis can provide inferences about the properties of the behaviour of economic, financial and business data. These properties can include price processes, trends, seasonality, and distributions, which are important considerations in the modelling and analysis of data.

10.2 TIME SERIES ANALYSIS

The econometric analysis of economic, financial and business time series has become an integral part in the research and application of quantitative descriptions of the real world. A time series typically consists of a set of observations of some observational unit or variable, y, which is taken at equally spaced intervals over time (Harvey, 1993). A time series can be considered from two aspects, analysis and modelling. The objective of a time series analysis is to identify and summarize its properties and describe its prominent characteristics. The analysis can be framed in either the time domain or the frequency domain. In the time domain the focus is on the relationship between observations at various points in time, whereas in the frequency domain the analysis focuses on the cyclical movements of a series.

Economic, business and financial time series will have at least one of the following key features:

- *Trends:* are one of the main features of many time series. Trends can have any number of attributes, such as upward or downward with relatively different slopes, and linear, exponential or other functional forms.

- *Seasonality:* time series can often display a seasonal pattern. Seasonality is a cyclical pattern that occurs on a regular calendar basis.

- *Irregular observations:* there can be periods or samples within a time series that are inconsistent with other periods, and therefore the series is subject to regime changes.

- *Conditional heteroskedasticity:* is a time series condition where there is variation (as opposed to constancy) in the variance or volatility, where patterns emerge in clusters, that is, high volatility is followed by high volatility, and low volatility is followed by low volatility.

- *Non-linearity:* generally a time series can be described as non-linear when the impact of a shock to the series depends if it is positive or negative and is not proportional to its size.

A stochastic time series is generated by a stochastic process, that is, each value of y in a series is a random draw from a probability distribution. Inferences can be made about the probabilities of possible future values of the series by describing the characteristics of the series randomness. Much of the research in time series has focused on investigating the hypothesis as to whether a series is a random walk or reverts back to a trend after a shock. The simplest random walk process assumes that each successive change in y_t is drawn from a probability distribution with zero mean:

$$y_t = y_{t-1} + \varepsilon_t \tag{10.1}$$

where ε_t is an error term which has a zero mean and whose values are independent of each other. The price change $\Delta y_t = y_t - y_{t-1}$ is therefore the error ε_t and is independent of price changes.

The question of whether economic variables follow random walks or tend to revert back to a long-run trend after a shock is an important issue for modelling. Most financial models of futures, options and other instruments tied to an underlying asset are based on the assumption that the spot price follows a random walk. In some markets, however, the prices of such assets as energies and commodities are tied in the long run to their marginal production cost. Although the price of an energy or commodity may be subject to sharp short-run fluctuations, it typically tends to return to a mean level based on cost.

A number of methods exist to test hypotheses about the properties of a time series. One technique is to examine its *autocorrelation* properties. Time series can be characterized by a set of autocorrelations, which can provide insights into possible models to describe the time series. A *correlogram* displays the autocorrelation and partial autocorrelation functions up to the specified order of lags. These functions characterize the pattern of temporal dependence in time series data. Another method for testing the hypothesis that the process is a random walk against the alternative that it is stationary, that is, the stochastic process in fixed time, is the unit root test introduced by Dickey and Fuller. Formally stated, the simplest model tested is:

$$y_t = \phi y_{t-1} + \varepsilon_t \qquad\qquad t = 2,.......T \qquad\qquad (10.2)$$

where the null hypothesis is that $\phi = 1$ and the alternative hypothesis is $\phi < 1$. The generalization of the test for a unit root is known as the augmented Dickey–Fuller (ADF) test (1979, 1981).

Most statistical tools are designed to model the conditional mean of a random variable. Autoregressive conditional heteroskedasticity (ARCH) models are specifically designed to model and forecast *conditional variances*. ARCH models were introduced by Engle (1982) and generalized as GARCH (generalized ARCH) by Bollerslev (1986). These models are widely used in econometrics, especially in financial time series analysis. The modelling of variance or volatility can be used, for example, in the analysis of the risk of holding an asset or in the valuation of an option. In a GARCH model there are two separate specifications, one for the conditional mean and one for the conditional variance. The standard GARCH(1,1) specification is:

$$y_t = \alpha_0 + \sigma_t \varepsilon_t \qquad\qquad\qquad (10.3)$$

$$\sigma_t^2 = \varpi + \alpha_1 \varepsilon_{t-1}^2 + \beta \sigma_{t-1}^2 \qquad\qquad\qquad (10.4)$$

where y_t is the log return of a series, and the mean equation in (10.3) is written as a function of exogenous variables with an error term. As σ_t^2 is the one-period ahead forecast variance based on past information, it is called the conditional variance. The conditional variance equation specified in (10.4) is a function of three terms, the mean, news about volatility from the previous period, measured as the lag of the squared residual from the mean equation (the ARCH term), and last period's forecast variance (the GARCH term).

10.3 VOLATILITY

Volatility, defined as the annualized standard deviation of price returns, is one of the critical concepts in option pricing and risk management. A percentage is derived as:

$$r_t = \frac{S_t}{S_{t-1}} - 1 \qquad\qquad\qquad (10.5)$$

where S_t is the spot price at the time t. Price returns are typically calculated by taking the natural logarithms of the price ratios:

$$r_t = \ln\left(\frac{S_t}{S_{t-1}}\right)$$

(10.6)

which is an approximation of the percentage change. Log returns are usually used to calculate volatility, as the natural log of S_t/S_{t-1} is equivalent to the natural log of $1 + r$, which is approximately equal to r. Another advantage is the log of a product is equal to the sum of the logs, and therefore a log return over a time period can be calculated as the sum of log returns for the sub-periods. Figure 10.1 illustrates the S&P index during the second half of the twentieth century, and Figure 10.2 the S&P returns for the same period.

Volatility, rather than standard deviations or variances, is used as a measure of uncertainty so that any comparisons of distributions are equivalent. Normalizing a price return's standard deviation into a volatility measure creates a consistent measure of magnitude of random behaviour, and therefore facilitates the comparison of various markets and models. The volatility of a price process also measures the annualized distribution of price returns, whereas standard deviations can measure the width of any distribution. The probability of exceeding an option's exercise price increases as a result of the volatility of the underlying asset, which is why volatility increases the value of options. Typically the greater the volatility associated with an underlying asset the greater the value of an option on that asset.

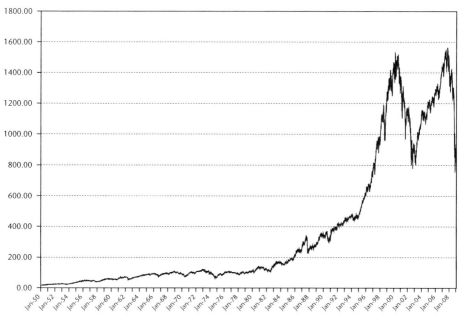

Figure 10.1 S&P 500 – 3 January 1950 to 30 January 2009

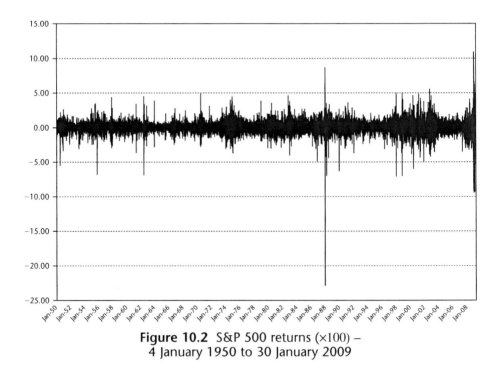

Figure 10.2 S&P 500 returns (×100) –
4 January 1950 to 30 January 2009

Volatility can be estimated from historical data or implied from option market prices. If there is a reasonably liquid market for traded options, then the implied volatility can be derived through an iteration process using an analytical pricing formula, such as the Black–Scholes model, the option price, and the known variables such as the interest rate, time to maturity and exercise price. The result is a forecast of the volatility implied in the quoted price of the option, with the forecast horizon being the maturity or expiry of the option. Volatility can also be derived from historical data by annualizing the standard deviation of the log returns through a scaling factor defined as the square root of time. The annualization factor depends on the price data frequency. If the data is monthly, the factor is $\sqrt{12}$, for weekly data, $\sqrt{52}$, and for the daily data for each calendar day it is $\sqrt{365}$. If the data is available for trading days only, the relevant number may vary from $\sqrt{250}$ to $\sqrt{260}$, according to public holidays.

While volatility provides a comparative risk parameter, other test statistics can provide insights as to how well the assumptions capture the behaviour of a time series. The properties of a time series can be depicted by its descriptive statistics. The mean and standard deviation are descriptive measures of the properties of a time series. Other descriptive measures can be illustrated using a histogram, which displays the frequency distribution of a series. A histogram divides the range between the maximum and minimum values of a series into a number of equal length intervals or bins, and exhibits the number of observations within each bin. Figure 10.3 illustrates the histogram of the S&P 500 index log returns from January 1997 to December 2001.

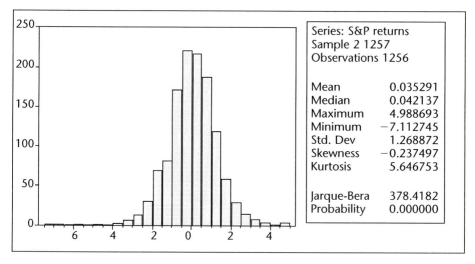

Figure 10.3 Histogram of the S&P 500
returns (×100) – 3 January 1997 to 31 December 2001

The descriptive statistics of the S&P returns sample are:

- The *mean* is the average value of the series sample, derived by adding up the series sample and dividing by the number of observations.

- The *median* is a measure of central tendency, or the middle value (or average of the two middle values) of a series sample sequenced from the smallest to the largest. The median is a more robust measure of the centre of the distribution than the mean, as it is less sensitive to outliers.

- The *maximum* and *minimum* values of the series sample.

- The *standard deviation* is a measure of dispersion or spread in the series.

- *Skewness* is a measure of the asymmetry of a series distribution around its mean. The skewness of the normal distribution, which is symmetric, is zero. Positive skewness implies that a distribution has a long right tail, while negative skewness indicates a long left tail.

- *Kurtosis* measures the peakness or flatness in the distribution of a series. A normal distribution has a kurtosis of three. If the kurtosis exceeds three, the distribution is leptokurtic or relatively peaked to the normal distribution, while if the kurtosis is less than three, the distribution is platykurtic or relatively flat to the normal distribution.

- *Jarque-Bera* is a test statistic for testing whether the series approximates the normal distribution. The test statistic measures the differences of the skewness and kurtosis of the series with those from the normal distribution. The null hypothesis is that a series has a normal distribution.

The annualized volatility for the S&P 500 index sample period is 20.06%, which is 1.268872, the standard deviation, times √250. The histogram in Figure 10.3 also illustrates the presence of fat tails in the distribution of the S&P 500 index returns. Fat tails refers to the probability of extreme outcomes in an observed series exceeding the assumed theoretical probability distribution. Distributions displaying fat tails are described as leptokurtic and are measured by kurtosis, which in this case is 5.646753 and therefore greater than three. The skewness, which is zero in a normal distribution, is negative in this case, and is typical of many financial assets such as stock prices.

10.4 THE LOGNORMAL DISTRIBUTION

A variable has a *lognormal distribution* if the natural logarithm of the variable is normally distributed. Figures 10.4 and 10.5 illustrate the distributions of a simulated series and its natural log equivalent respectively. A lognormal variable can have any value between zero and infinity. As a result the lognormal distribution has a positive skew and so is unlike the normal distribution, as indicated by the skewness and kurtosis statistics. The log series, however, has a skewness close to zero and a kurtosis that is approximately three, and therefore can be described as being normally distributed.

The use of the log of financial variables is popular in derivative modelling as the price can never become negative, and the return is the relative change in the level of the log price. Figure 10.6 illustrates the distribution of the log returns of the simulated series. The returns can also be described as being normally distributed. The

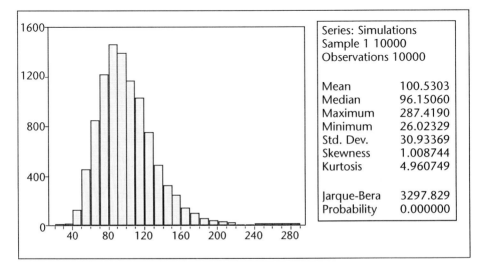

Series: Simulations	
Sample 1 10000	
Observations 10000	
Mean	100.5303
Median	96.15060
Maximum	287.4190
Minimum	26.02329
Std. Dev.	30.93369
Skewness	1.008744
Kurtosis	4.960749
Jarque-Bera	3297.829
Probability	0.000000

Figure 10.4 The simulated series

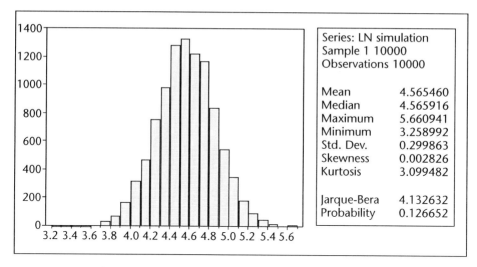

Figure 10.5 The natural log of the simulated series

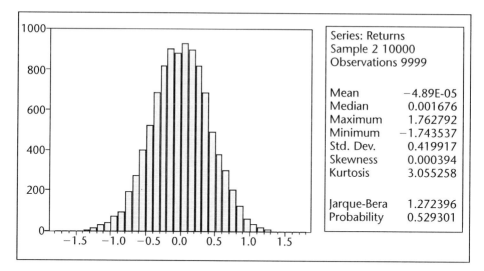

Figure 10.6 The simulated log returns

lognormal property of asset prices also can be used to describe a price process and its probability distribution. If an asset price follows geometric Brownian motion, then the natural log of an asset price follows a process called a generalized Weiner process. This implies that given an asset's price today the price at T is lognormally distributed. The standard deviation of the logarithm of an asset is $\sigma\sqrt{T}$, that is, it is proportional to the square root of the length of time into the future. This stochastic process is the basis for the Black–Scholes option pricing model.

10.5 WHICH VOLATILITY?

The volatility of a project, asset or firm is not necessarily the same as the volatility of one of its components. One example is the difference between the volatility of a firm's market value and the volatility of its equity. A firm's capital structure is the mixture of debt, equity and other liabilities that the firm uses to finance its assets. Merton (1974) defined the value of a firm's equity as a call option on the assets of the firm, where the strike is the book value of the firm's liabilities, and the underlying asset is the total value of the firm's assets. Merton's approach illustrated the link between the market value of the firm's assets and the market value of its equity, and provided a framework for determining the value of a firm's equity by reference to the underlying market value of the firm.

The analysis can be reversed to estimate a firm's value and volatility from the market value of its equity, the volatility of its equity, and the book value of its liabilities. KMV Corporation extended Merton's approach to estimate probabilities of default for credit analysis. If the market price of equity is available, the market value and volatility of assets can be determined directly using an options pricing based approach, which recognizes equity as a call option on the underlying assets of the firm. The limited liability of equity provides equity holders with the right but not the obligation to pay off the debt holders and acquire a firm's remaining assets. A call option on the underlying assets has the same properties. The holder of a call option on a firm's assets has a claim on those assets after fulfilling the option's strike value, which in this case is equal to the book value of the firm's liabilities. If the value of the assets is not sufficient to meet the firm's liabilities, the shareholders, the holders of the call option, will not exercise the option and will abandon the firm to its creditors. KMV utilize the optional nature of equity to derive the market value and volatility of a firm's underlying assets implied by its equity market value by solving backwards for the implied asset value and asset volatility.

REFERENCES

Bollerslev, T. Generalized autoregressive conditional heteroskedasticity, *Journal of Ecometrics*, 31: 307–27, 1986.

Clewlow, L. and Strickland, C. *Implementing Derivative Models*, Wiley, 1998.

Clewlow, L. and Strickland, C. *Energy Derivatives, Pricing and Risk Management*, Lacima, 2000.

Copeland, T. and Antikarov, V. *Real Options*, Texere, 2001.

Culp C.L. *The Risk Management Process*, Wiley, 2001.

Dickey, D.A. and Fuller, W.A. Distribution of the estimators for autoregressive time series with a unit root, *Journal of the American Statistical Association*, **74**, 1979.

Dickey, D.A. and Fuller, W.A. Likelihood ratio statistics for autoregressive time series with a unit root, *Econometrica*, **49**: 1057–72, 1981.

Engle, R.F. Autoregressive conditional heteroskedasticity with estimates of the variance of UK inflation, *Econometrica*, **50**: 987–1008, 1982.

Franses, P.H. *Time Series for Business and Economic Forecasting*, Cambridge University Press, 1998.

Harvey, A.C. *Time Series Models*, Harvester Wheatsheaf, 1993.

Hull, J.C. *Options, Futures and Other Derivatives*, Prentice Hall, 2000.

Merton, R. On the pricing of corporate debt: the risk structure of interest rates, Journal of Finance, 29: 449–70, 1974.

Mills, T.C. *The Econometric Modelling of Financial Time Series*, Cambridge University Press, 1999.

Pindyck, R. and Rubenfield, D. *Econometric Models and Economic Forecasts*, McGraw Hill, 1998.

Taylor, S.J. *Modelling Financial Time Series*, Wiley, 1986.

CHAPTER 11

Option Pricing Methods

11.1 A MODEL FOR ASSET PRICES

The evolution of uncertainty over time can be conceptualized and modelled as a mathematical expression, known as a stochastic process, which describes the evolution of a random variable over time. Models of asset price behaviour for pricing derivatives are formulated in a continuous time framework by assuming a stochastic differential equation (SDE) describing the stochastic process followed by the asset price. The most well-known assumption made about asset price behaviour, which was made by Black and Scholes (1973) is geometric Brownian motion (GBM).

The GBM assumption in the Black–Scholes model is the mathematical description of how asset prices evolve through time. In the GBM assumption proportional changes in the asset price, denoted by S, are assumed to have constant instantaneous drift, μ, and volatility, σ. A non-dividend paying asset S following GBM is represented by the following stochastic differential equation:

$$dS = \mu S dt + \sigma S dz \tag{11.1}$$

dS represents the increment in the asset price process during a (infinitesimally) small interval of time dt, and dz is the underlying uncertainty driving the model, representing an increment in a Weiner process during dt. The risk-neutral assumption implies that the drift can be replaced by the risk-free rate of interest (that is, $\mu = r$). Any process describing the stochastic behaviour of the asset price will lead to a characterization of the distribution of future asset values. An assumption in equation (11.1) is that future asset prices are lognormally distributed, or that the returns to the asset are normally distributed. Dividing through by S gives:

$$\frac{dS}{S} = \mu dt + \sigma dz \tag{11.2}$$

In equation (11.2) the percentage change or return in the asset price dS/S has two components. The first is that during the small interval of time dt the average return on the asset is $\mu\,dt$, which is deterministic. The parameter μ is known as the drift. Added to this drift is the random component made up of the change dz, in a random variable z, and a parameter σ, which is generally referred to as the volatility of the asset. The random variable z or equivalently the change dz is called a Weiner process. A Weiner process is defined by two key properties. The first is that dz is normally distributed with mean zero and variance dt or the standard deviation of the square root of dt. The second is that the values of dz over two different non-overlapping increments of time are independent. Equations (11.1) and (11.2) are examples of an Itô process, as the drift and volatility only depend on the current value of the variable (the asset price) and time. In general the stochastic differential equation for a variable S following an Itô process is:

$$dS = \mu(S,t)dt + \sigma(S,t)dz \tag{11.3}$$

where the functions $\mu(S,t)$ and $\sigma(S,t)$ are general functions for the drift and volatility. Many models for the behaviour of asset prices assume that the future evolution of the asset price depends only on its present level and not on the path taken to reach that level. A stochastic process possessing this property is known as Markovian.

The stochastic process followed by any derivative can be inferred from the assumption of the behaviour of the asset price, on which the derivative's payoff is dependent. It follows that, using the Black–Scholes concept of constructing a riskless portfolio, a partial differential equation can be derived that governs the price of the derivative security.

11.2 THE BLACK–SCHOLES FORMULA

The stochastic differential equation for the asset price S is the starting point for any derivative model. As the process for the asset and the process for the derivative have the same source of uncertainty, it is possible to combine the two securities in a portfolio in such a way as to eliminate that uncertainty. A portfolio consisting of a short position in the option and a long position in the underlying asset can be constructed such that the change in its value over an infinitesimal increment of time is independent of the source of randomness, and is therefore risk-free. This relationship leads to the Black–Scholes partial differential equation. The Black–Scholes formulae for standard European call and put options are the result of solving this partial differential equation.

As the expected return on the underlying asset does not appear in the Black–Scholes partial differential equation, the value of the derivative is independent of the risk preferences of investors. The implication of this risk-neutral pricing is that the present value of any future random cash flow, for example the payoff for an option, is given by the expected value of the random future value discounted at the riskless rate. By replacing the expectation with the integral and solving obtains the Black–Scholes equation.

The Black–Scholes formula for a European call option on a non-dividend paying stock is:

$$c = S_0 N(d_1) - Ke^{-r(T-t)}N(d_2)$$

(11.4)

where:

$$d_1 = \frac{\ln\left(\dfrac{S_0}{K}\right) + \left(r + \dfrac{1}{2}\sigma^2\right)(T-t)}{\sigma\sqrt{T-t}}$$

$$d_2 = d_1 - \sigma\sqrt{T-t}$$

The corresponding equation for the European put is:

$$p = Ke^{-r(T-t)}N(-d_2) - S_0 N(-d_1)$$

(11.5)

where the parameters are:

S_0 = the value of S at time zero
K = the strike price of the option
r = the risk-free interest rate
t = a point in time
T = Time at maturity of a derivative

One of the qualities that has led to the enduring success of the Black–Scholes model is its simplicity. The inputs of the model are defined by the contract being priced or are directly observable from the market. The only exception to this is the volatility parameter and there is now a vast amount of published material in the finance literature for deriving estimates of this figure either from historical data or as implied by the market prices of options.

One widely used relaxation of the original formula takes into account assets that pay a constant proportional dividend. Assets of this kind are handled by reducing the expected growth rate of the asset by the amount of the dividend yield. If the asset pays a constant proportional dividend at a rate δ, over the life of the option, then the original Black–Scholes call formula (11.4) can be used with the adjustment where the parameter S is replaced by the term $Se^{-\delta(T-t)}$. This adjustment has been applied to value options on broad-based equity indices, options on foreign exchange rates, and real options that allow for competition, where the fall in value due to competition is the equivalent to the dividend yield.

The intuition of the replicating portfolio concept can be illustrated with the Black–Scholes formula. The Black–Scholes formula can be defined as a combination of two binary options, a cash-or-nothing call and an asset-or-nothing call:

asset-or-nothing call:

$$Se^{-\delta(T-t)}N(d_1) \qquad (11.6)$$

cash-or-nothing call:

$$Ke^{-r(T-t)}N(d_2) \qquad (11.7)$$

A European call option represents a long position in an asset-or-nothing call and a short position in a cash-or-nothing call, where the cash payoff on the cash-or-nothing call is the equivalent to the strike price. A European put is a long position in a cash-or-nothing put and a short position in an asset-or-nothing put, where the strike price represents the cash payoff on the cash-or-nothing put. $N(d_1)$, the option delta, is the number of units of the underlying required to form the portfolio, and the cash or nothing term is the number of bonds each paying \$1 at expiration.

Although it is possible to obtain closed-form solutions such as equation (11.4) for certain derivative pricing problems, there are many situations when analytical solutions are not obtainable and therefore numerical techniques need to be applied. Examples include American options and other options where there are early exercise opportunities, 'path-dependent' options with discrete observation frequencies, models that incorporate jumps and models dependent on multiple random factors. The description of two of these techniques is the subject of the next section.

11.3 NUMERICAL TECHNIQUES

Two numerical techniques which are most commonly used by practitioners to value derivatives in the absence of closed-form solutions are (binomial and trinomial) trees and Monte Carlo simulation. Practitioners also use other techniques such as finite difference schemes, numerical integration, finite element methods and others. However, these methods require more advanced expertise in numerical techniques. It is possible to price not only derivatives with complicated payoff functions dependent on the final price using trees and Monte Carlo simulation techniques, but also derivatives whose payoff is determined also by the path the underlying price follows during its life.

11.3.1 Monte Carlo simulation

Monte Carlo simulation provides a simple and flexible method for valuing complex derivatives for which analytical formulae are not possible. The method can easily deal with multiple random factors, can also be used to value complex path dependent options, and also allows the inclusion of price processes such as price jumps. In general the present value of an option is the expectation of its discounted payoff.

Monte Carlo simulation derives an estimate of this expectation by simulating a large number of possible paths for the asset price from time zero to the option maturity and computing the average of the discounted payoffs.

Geometric Brownian motion (GBM) for non-dividend spot prices with constant expected return μ and volatility σ is represented by the SDE in equation (11.1). The Black–Scholes perfect replication argument leads to the risk-neutral process in which the actual drift of the spot price μ is replaced by the interest rate r:

$$dS = rSdt + \sigma Sdz \tag{11.8}$$

If the asset pays a constant continuous dividend yield δ then the risk-neutral process becomes:

$$dS = (r - \delta)Sdt + \sigma Sdz \tag{11.9}$$

Transforming the spot price to the natural log of the spot price $x = 1n(S)$, gives the following process for x:

$$dx = vdt + \sigma dz \tag{11.10}$$

where $v = r - \delta - \frac{1}{2}\sigma^2$. The transformed GBM process represented in equation (11.10) can be discretized in the following way:

$$x_{t+\Delta t} = x_t + (v\Delta t + \sigma(z_{t+\Delta t} - z_t)) \tag{11.11}$$

In terms of the original asset price the discrete form is:

$$S_{t+\Delta t} = S_t \exp(v\Delta t + \sigma(z_{t+\Delta t} - z_t)) \tag{11.12}$$

Equations (11.11) or (11.12) can be used to simulate the evolution of the spot price through time. The change in the random Brownian motion, $z_{t+\Delta t} - z_t$, has a mean of zero and a variance of Δt. It can therefore be simulated using random samples from a standard normal multiplied by $\sqrt{\Delta t}$, that is, $\sqrt{\Delta t}\varepsilon$ where $\varepsilon \sim N(0,1)$. In order to simulate the spot price the time period $[0,T]$ is divided into N intervals such that $\Delta t = T/N$, $t_i = i\Delta t$, $i = 1, \ldots, N$. Using, for example, equation (11.12) gives:

$$S_{t_i} = S_{t_{i-1}} \exp(v\Delta t + \sigma\sqrt{\Delta t}\varepsilon_i) \tag{11.13}$$

As the drift and volatility terms do not depend on the variables S and t, the discretization is correct for any chosen time step. Therefore the option can be simulated straight to the maturity date in a single time step if the payoff is only a function of the terminal asset value and does not depend on the asset's path during the life of the option. Repeating this process N times, choosing ε_i randomly each time, leads to one possible path for the spot price.

At the end of each simulated path the terminal value of the option (C_T) is evaluated. Let $C_{T,j}$ represent the payoff to the contingent claim under the jth simulation. For example a standard European call option terminal value is given by:

$$C_{T,j} = \max(S_{T,j} - K, 0) \tag{11.14}$$

Each payoff is discounted using the simulated short-term interest rate sequence:

$$C_{0,j} = \exp\left(-\int_0^T r_u du\right) C_{T,j} \tag{11.15}$$

In the case of constant or deterministic interest rates equation (11.15) simplifies to:

$$C_{0,j} = P(0,T) C_{T,j} \tag{11.16}$$

This value represents the value of the option along one possible path that the asset can follow. The simulations are repeated M times and the average of all the outcomes is taken to compute the expectation, and hence the option price:

$$\hat{C}_0 = \frac{1}{M} \sum_{j=1}^{M} C_{0,j} \tag{11.17}$$

Therefore $\hat{C}_0$ is an estimate of the true value of the option, C0, but with an error due to the fact that it is an average of randomly generated samples and so is itself random. In order to obtain a measure of the error, the standard error SE(.) is estimated as the sample standard deviation, SD(.), of Ct,j divided by the square root of the number of samples:

$$SE(\hat{C}_0) = \frac{SD(C_{0,j})}{\sqrt{M}} \tag{11.18}$$

where $SD(C_{0,j})$ is the standard deviation of C_0:

$$SD(C_{0,j}) = \sqrt{\frac{1}{M-1} \sum_{j=1}^{M} \left(C_{0,j} - \hat{C}_0\right)^2} \tag{11.19}$$

For many American-style options early exercise can be optimal, depending on the level of the underlying price. It is rare to find closed-form solutions for prices and risk parameters of these options, so numerical procedures must be applied. Using Monte Carlo simulation for pricing American-style options, however, is difficult. The problem arises because simulation methods generate trajectories of state variables forward in time, whereas a backward dynamic programming approach is required to efficiently determine optimal exercise decisions for pricing American options. Therefore practitioners usually use binomial and trinomial trees for the pricing of American options.

11.3.2 The binomial and trinomial method

The binomial model of Cox et al. (1979) is a well-known alternative discrete time representation of the behaviour of asset prices to GBM. This model is important in several ways. First, the continuous time limit of the proportional binomial process is exactly the GBM process. Second, and perhaps most importantly, the binomial model is the basis of the dynamic programming solution to the valuation of American options. Section 8.2 discussed a one-step binomial tree as part of the overview of the replicating portfolio. To price options with more than one period to maturity, the binomial tree is extended outwards for the required number of periods to the maturity date of the option. Figure 11.1 illustrates a binomial tree for an option that expires in four periods of time.

A state in the tree is referred to as a node, and is labelled as node (i,j), where i indicates the number of time steps from time zero and j indicates the number of upward movements the asset price has made since time zero. Therefore the level of the asset price at node (i,j) is $S_{i,j} = Su^j d^{i-j}$ and the option price will be $C_{i,j}$. At the lowest node at every time step $j = 0$, and j will remain the same when moving from one node to another via a downward branch, as the number of upward moves that have occurred have not changed. It is generally assumed that there are N time steps in total, where the Nth time step corresponds to the maturity date of the option. As is the case with the one period example, the value of a call option at the maturity date is the payoff:

$$C_{N,j} = \max(S_{N,j} - K,\ 0) \tag{11.20}$$

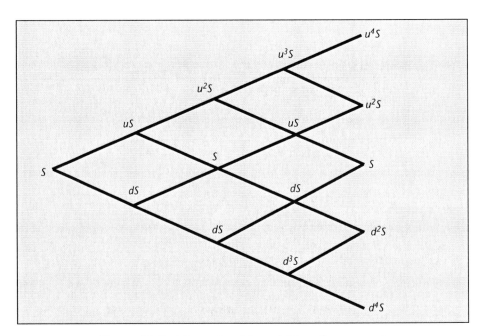

Figure 11.1 A four-step binomial tree for an asset

As the value of the option at any node in the tree is its discounted expected value, at any node in the tree before maturity:

$$C_{i,j} = e^{-r\Delta t}\left(pC_{i+1,j+1} + (1-p)C_{i+1,j}\right) \tag{11.21}$$

Using equations (11.20) and (11.21) the value of the option can be computed at every node for time step $N-1$. Equation (11.21) can then be reapplied at every node for every time step, working backwards through the tree to compute the value of the option at every node in the tree. The value of a European option can be derived using this procedure. To derive the value of an American option, the value of the option if it is exercised is compared at every node to the option value if it is not exercised, and the value at that node set to the greater of the two.

Although binomial trees are used by many practitioners for pricing American-style options, trinomial trees offer a number of advantages over the binomial tree. As there are three possible future movements over each time period, rather than the two of the binomial approach, the trinomial tree provides a better approximation to a continuous price process than the binomial tree for the same number of time steps. The trinomial tree is also easier to work with because of its more regular grid and is more flexible, allowing it to be fitted more easily to market prices of forwards and standard options, an important practical consideration. A discussion of trinomial rees as a possible numerical technique follows.

In the following it is more convenient to work in terms of the natural logarithm of the spot price as defined in equation (11.10). Consider a trinomial model of the asset price in which, over a small time interval Δt, the asset price can increase by Δx (the space step), stay the same or decrease by Δx, with probabilities p_u, p_m, and p_d respectively. This is depicted in terms of x in Figure 11.2.

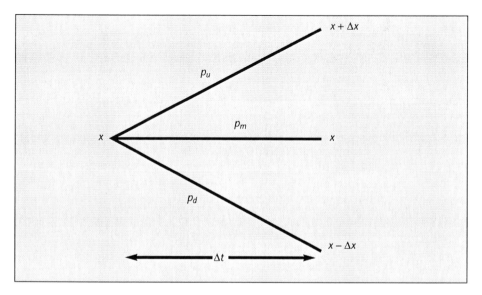

Figure 11.2 Trinomial model of an asset price

The drift and volatility parameters of the asset price are now captured in this simplified discrete process by Δx, p_u, p_m, and p_d. It can be shown that the space step cannot be chosen independently of the time step, and that a good choice is $\Delta x = \sigma\sqrt{3\Delta t}$. The relationship between the parameters of the continuous time process and the trinomial process is obtained by equating the mean and variance over the time interval Δt and requiring that the probabilities sum to one, that is:

$$E[\Delta x] = p_u(\Delta x) + p_m(0) + p_d(-\Delta x) = v\Delta t \tag{11.22}$$

$$E[\Delta x^2] = p_u(\Delta x^2) + p_m(0) + p_d(\Delta x^2) = \sigma^2\Delta t + v^2\Delta t^2 \tag{11.23}$$

$$p_u + p_m + p_d = 1 \tag{11.24}$$

Solving equations (11.22) to (11.24) yields the following explicit expressions for the transitional probabilities:

$$p_u = \frac{1}{2}\left(\frac{\sigma^2\Delta t + v^2\Delta t^2}{\Delta x^2} + \frac{v\Delta t}{\Delta x}\right) \tag{11.25}$$

$$p_m = 1 - \frac{\sigma^2\Delta t + v^2\Delta t^2}{\Delta x^2} \tag{11.26}$$

$$p_d = \frac{1}{2}\left(\frac{\sigma^2\Delta t + v^2\Delta t^2}{\Delta x^2} - \frac{v\Delta t}{\Delta x}\right) \tag{11.27}$$

The single period trinomial process in Figure 11.1 can be extended to form a trinomial tree. Figure 11.3 depicts such a tree.

Let i denote the number of the time step and j the level of the asset price relative to the initial asset price in the tree. If $S_{i,j}$ denotes the level of the asset price at node (i, j) then $t = t_i = i\Delta t$, and an asset price level of $S\exp(j\Delta x)$. Once the tree has been constructed the spot price is known at every time and every state of the world consistent with the original assumptions about its behaviour process, and the tree can be used to derive prices for a wide range of derivatives.

The procedure is illustrated with reference to pricing a European and American call option with strike price K on the spot price. The value of an option is represented at node (i,j) by $C_{i,j}$. In order to value an option the tree is constructed as representing the evolution of the spot price from the current date out to the maturity date of the option. Let time step N correspond to the maturity date in terms of the number of time steps in the tree, that is, $T = N\Delta t$. The values of the option at maturity are determined by the values of the spot price in the tree at time step N and the strike price of the option:

$$C_{N,j} = \max(S_{N,j} - K, 0) \quad ; j = -N, \dots, N \tag{11.28}$$

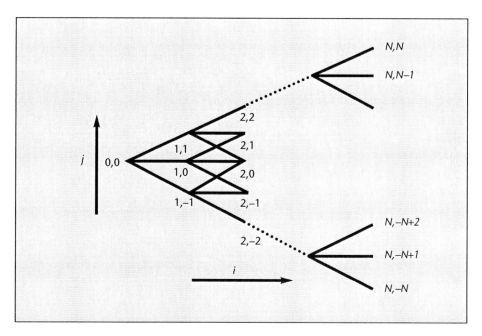

Figure 11.3 A trinomial tree model of an asset price

It can be shown that option values can be computed as discounted expectations in a risk-neutral world, and therefore the values of the option at earlier nodes can be computed as discounted expectations of the values at the following three nodes to which the asset price could jump:

$$C_{i,j} = e^{-r\Delta t}(p_u C_{i+1,j+1} + p_m C_{i+1,j} + p_d C_{i+1,j-1}) \tag{11.29}$$

where $e^{-r\Delta t}$ is the single period discount factor. This procedure is often referred to as 'backwards induction' as it links the option value at time i to known values at time $i+1$. The attraction of this method is the ease with which American option values can be evaluated. During the inductive stage the immediate exercise value of the option is compared with the value if not exercised as computed from equation (11.29). If the immediate exercise value is greater, then this value is stored at the node, that is:

$$C_{i,j} = \max\left\{e^{-r\Delta t}(p_u C_{i+1,j+1} + p_m C_{i+1,j} + p_d C_{i+1,j-1}), S_{i,j} - K\right\} \tag{11.30}$$

This method also provides the optimal exercise strategy for the American option, since for every possible future state of the world, that is, every node in the tree, it can be determined whether to exercise the option or not. The value of the option today is given by the value in the tree at node $(0,0)$, $C_{0,0}$.

REFERENCES

Black, F. and Scholes, M. The pricing options and corporate liabilities, *Journal of Political Economy*, **81**: 637–59, 1973.

Clewlow, L. and Strickland, C. *Energy Derivatives, Pricing and Risk Management*, Lacima, 2000.

Clewlow, L. and Strickland, C. *Implementing Derivative Models*, Wiley, 1998.

Cox, J.S., Ross, S. and Rubinstein, M. Option pricing: a simplified approach, *Journal of Financial Economics*, **7** (September): 229–63, 1979.

Hull, J.C. *Options, Futures and Other Derivatives*, Prentice Hall, 2000.

CHAPTER 12

Implementing Real Options

12.1 SPOT PRICE MODELS

The Black–Scholes GBM model can be generalized to other models that are more realistic for particular markets. The various simple extensions to the Black–Scholes model assume constant parameters for ease of calculation. In reality the properties of time series such as volatility, mean reversion, long-term levels and jump behaviour will at the very least vary through time with reasonably predictable patterns. These characteristics can be included in spot models.

12.1.1 Geometric Brownian motion models

The GBM assumption defined in equation (10.1) as a process that describes the dynamics of the prices of financial instruments is an approximation of the behaviour observed in real markets. GBM models are frequently used for security prices, interest rates, commodities and other economic and financial variables, and follow what has been defined as a random walk. The Weiner process is the continuous limit of a discrete time random walk. A generalized Weiner process introduces the concept of expected drift rate. The drift rate is the average increase in a stochastic variable for each unit of time. In models for financial variables the expected drift rate is replaced with a constant drift rate. Another issue in GBM models is that the uncertainty associated with the price path is greater the longer the time horizon. As the variance of the Weiner process increases linearly as the time horizon increases, the standard deviation grows as the square root of the time horizon. This is the equivalent to the definition of volatility, where scaling the standard deviation by the square root of T annualizes the volatility σ.

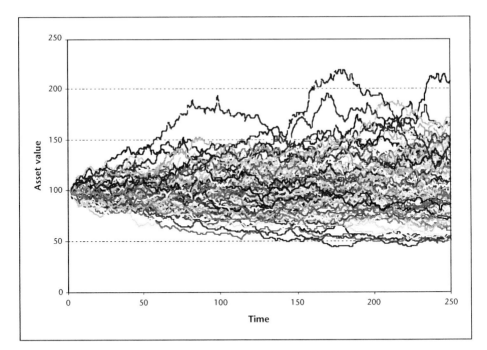

Figure 12.1 Illustration of 100 simulated GBM paths

The GBM process represented in equation (10.9) was discretized in equations (10.11) and (10.12) for the simulation of a spot price. Figure 12.1 illustrates a GBM process simulated 100 times with the parameters $S = 100$, $r-\delta = 0.05$, $\sigma = 0.30$, and $\Delta t = 1/250$. In this example $r - \delta$ is the drift, and $\sigma\varepsilon\sqrt{\Delta t}$, is the stochastic component. One observation is that the sample paths in Figure 12.1 tend to wander from the initial starting point of $S = 100$. While this may be realistic for some variables, and can be verified in tests for random walks, it may however not be suitable for other financial and economic time series.

12.1.2 Mean reversion

The usual assumption made for asset price evolution in many markets is the GBM model assumption. This model, however, allows prices to wander off to unrealistic levels when applied to markets such as energy and commodities. Mean reversion was first described by Vasicek (1977) for modelling interest rate dynamics and has subsequently been widely adapted. Mean reversion can be understood by looking at a simple model of a mean reverting spot price (Schwartz, 1997), represented by the following equation:

$$dS = \alpha(\mu - \ln S)Sdt + \sigma Sdz \qquad (12.1)$$

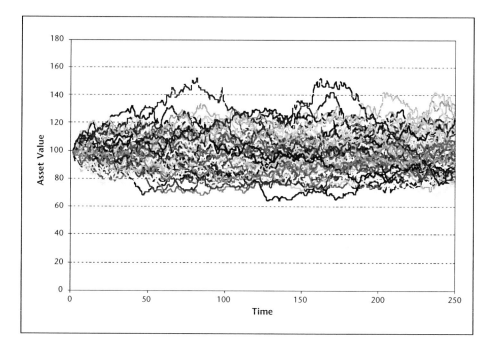

Figure 12.2 Illustration of 100 simulated mean reversion paths

Figure 12.2 illustrates the log form of a mean reverting process simulated 100 times with the parameters $S = 100$, $\alpha = 3$, $\bar{S} = 100$, $\sigma = 0.30$, and $\Delta t = 1/250$. In this model the spot price mean reverts to the long-term level $\bar{S} = e^{\mu}$ at a speed given by the mean reversion rate, α, that is taken to be strictly positive. If the spot price is above the long-term level $\bar{S}$, then the drift of the spot price will be negative and the price will tend to revert back towards the long-term level. Similarly, if the spot price is below the long-term level, then the drift will be positive and the price will tend to move back towards $\bar{S}$. Note that, at any point in time, the spot price will not necessarily move back towards the long-term level as the random change in the spot price may be of the opposite sign and greater in magnitude than the drift component. This formulation of the mean reversion process represents one of a number of possible equations that capture the same type of market evolution of prices over time. In reality the spot price does not mean revert to a constant long-term level. Information on the level to which the spot price mean reverts is contained in the forward curve prices and volatilities.

12.1.3 Jumps and seasonal patterns

Jumps can be a significant component of the behaviour of spot prices. This type of behaviour, where the price exhibits sudden, large changes, can be modelled by using jump processes. A simple and realistic model for a spot price, which is identical to the Black–Scholes model except for the addition of a jump process, is the jump-diffusion model introduced by Merton (1976). This model is described by the following SDE:

$$dS = \mu Sdt + \sigma Sdz + \kappa Sdq \qquad (12.2)$$

The annualized frequency of jumps is given by ϕ, the average number of jumps per year (ϕ is defined by prob($dq=1$)$=\phi dt$). The proportional jump size is κ, which is random and determined by the natural logarithm of the proportional jumps being normally distributed:

$$1n(1+\kappa) \sim N\left(1n(1+\bar{\kappa}) - \tfrac{1}{2}\gamma^2, \gamma^2\right) \qquad (12.3)$$

where $\bar{\kappa}$ is the mean jump size and γ is the standard deviation of the proportional jump size. The jump process (dq) is a discrete time process – jumps do not occur continuously but at specific instants of time. Therefore, for typical jump frequencies, most of the time $dq = 0$ and only takes the value 1 when a randomly timed jump occurs. When no jump occurs, the spot price behaviour is identical to GBM and is only different when a jump occurs. The proportional jumps (or equivalently jump returns) in equation (12.2) are normally distributed and therefore symmetrical. That is, the number of positive and negative jumps and the range of sizes of the proportional jumps will be equal on average.

12.1.4 Stochastic volatility

The assumption in the Black–Scholes model that volatility is constant is not always the case. The GARCH process is one representation of a stochastic volatility model. Many other models have been proposed for the behaviour of volatility. The Hull and White model (1988) became popular because of its realistic properties and computational tractability, and is described by the following processes for the spot price and the spot price return variance $V = \sigma^2$;

$$dS = \mu Sdt + Sdz \qquad (12.4)$$

$$dV = a(\bar{V} - V)dt + \xi\sqrt{V}\,dw \qquad (12.5)$$

Equation (12.4) is the GBM model but with a volatility, σ, which is no longer constant but which changes randomly. The behaviour of the volatility is determined by equation (12.5), which specifies the process followed by the variance – the square of the volatility. The variance mean reverts to a long-term level $\bar{V}$ at a rate given by a. The absolute volatility of the variance is $\xi\sqrt{V}$ which is proportional to the square root of the variance, that is, the volatility of the spot price. The source of randomness in the variance, dw, is different from the dz driving the spot price, although it may be correlated with correlation coefficient ρ.

12.2 FORWARD CURVE MODELS

Forwards and futures markets are often used by risk managers to hedge risk, with liquid forward prices providing a price discovery mechanism to determine the fair value for future delivery. Forward curves contain information about the prices an investor can lock into today to buy or sell at a certain time in the future. Forward curves are well known and understood in the debt markets. Forward rate agreements and exchange traded futures contracts are heavily traded and allow users to lock in borrowing and lending rates for future time periods.

In contrast to futures and forwards, price forecasts are predictions on the likely spot price for periods in the future, and can differ widely between market participants. Forward prices, however, depend on the relationship between traded instruments. Tradable prices today for future spot transactions can be locked in using forward prices, and as such capture the market reality. Therefore prices from forwards and futures markets are key inputs to many derivative pricing models, and are as essential in the pricing of derivatives as spot prices.

In the past the majority of work on modelling prices has focused on stochastic processes for the spot price and other key variables, such as the dividend yields, convenience yields and interest rates. This approach, however, can have some fundamental disadvantages. The first is that key state variables, such as the convenience yield, are unobservable and, second, the forward price curve is an endogenous function of the model parameters, and therefore will not necessarily be consistent with the market observable forward prices. As a result many industry practitioners require the forward curve to be an *input* into the derivative pricing model, rather than an *output* from it.

Term structure consistent models set out to model the dynamics of the entire term structure in a way that is consistent with the initial (observed) market data. These models can be further classified into those that fit the term structure of prices such as interest rates, and those that fit the term structure of prices and price volatilities. There are models in the interest rate world and recent developments in the energy and commodity markets that use term structure approaches. An approach based on modelling the entire forward price curve with multiple sources of uncertainty uses all the information contained in the term structure of futures prices in addition to the historical volatilities of futures returns for different maturities. The following discussion as applied to the energy markets is based on this approach and draws on material from Clewlow and Strickland (2000).

12.2.1 A single factor model for the forward curve

The expression 'forward curve models' is defined as models that explicitly model all the forward prices simultaneously rather than just the spot price. A simple single factor model of the forward curve can be represented by the following stochastic differential equation:

$$\frac{dF(t,T)}{F(t,T)} = \sigma e^{-\alpha(T-t)}dz(t) \tag{12.6}$$

The inputs to the model are the observed forward curve $F(t,T)$ which denotes the forward price at time t for maturity date T, and $\sigma e^{-\alpha(T-t)}$ which is the single 'factor' or volatility function associated with the source of risk $dz(t)$. Equation (12.6) also has no drift term. As futures and forward contracts have zero initial investment, their expected return in a risk-neutral world must be zero, implying that the process describing their evolution has zero drift. The volatility function of equation (12.6) has a very simple negative exponential form illustrated in Figure 12.3.

For this volatility function, short-dated forward returns are more volatile than long-dated forwards – information occurring in the market today has little effect on, say, the 5-year forward price but can have a significant effect on the 1-month forward price. The parameter values used for Figure 12.3 are $\alpha = 1.0$ and $\sigma = 0.40$. Here σ represents the 'overall' volatility of the forward curve, while α explains how fast the forward volatility curve attenuates with increasing maturity. With an α of 100% the 1-month forward has a volatility of about 37%, decreasing to approximately 2% for the 3-year forward.

The volatility function is not restricted to have the parameterized form of equation (12.6). The function can be generalized as:

$$\frac{dF(t,T)}{F(t,T)} = \sigma(t,T)dz(t) \tag{12.7}$$

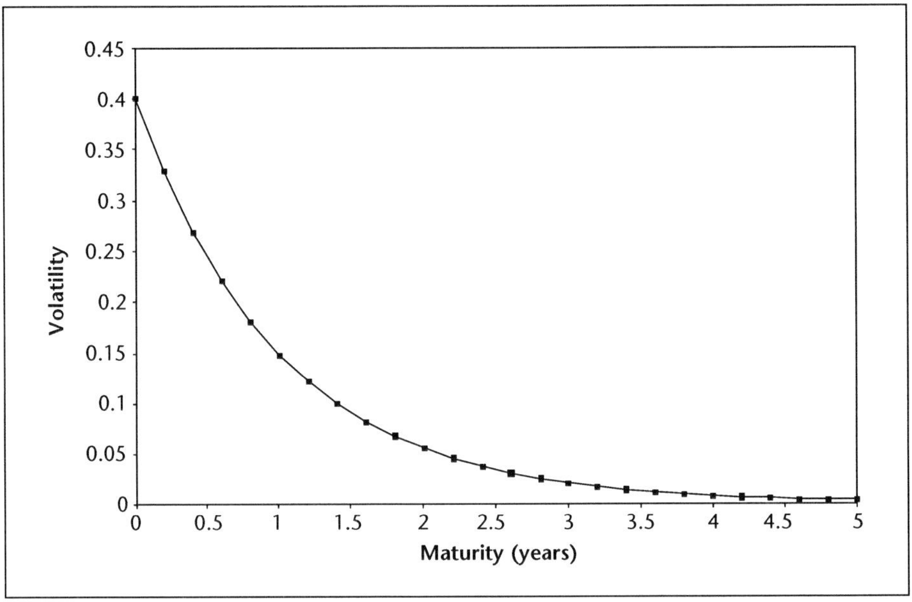

Figure 12.3 A negative exponential volatility function for forward prices

where $\sigma(t,T)$ would be read as 'the time t volatility of the T-maturity forward price return. The form of $\sigma(t,T)$ can be determined from market data.

12.2.2 The dynamics of the forward curve

An important observation is that forward prices of different maturities are not perfectly correlated. The curves generally move up and down together but they also change shape in apparently quite complex ways. One method that can be used to determine the set of common factors that drive the dynamics of the forward curve is principal components analysis (PCA) or eigenvector decomposition of the covariance matrix. This procedure can be utilized to simultaneously identify the number of important factors and estimate the volatility functions. The technique involves calculating the covariances between every pair of forward price returns in a historical time series to form a covariance matrix. The eigenvectors of the covariance matrix yield estimates of the factors driving the evolution of the forward curve.

The implication is that to effectively describe the evolution of the energy forward curve more than a single factor is required. The model described by equation (12.7) can be modified through the addition of sources of risk and volatility functions. For a general multifactor model the behaviour of the forward curve can be represented by the following equation:

$$\frac{dF(t,T)}{F(t,T)} = \sum_{i=1}^{n} \sigma_i(t,T)dz_i(t) \tag{12.8}$$

In this formulation there are n independent sources of uncertainty which drive the evolution of the forward curve. Each source of uncertainty has associated with it a volatility function which determines by how much, and in which direction, that random shock moves each point of the forward curve. Therefore $\sigma_i(t,T)$ are the n volatility functions associated with the independent sources of risk $dz_i(t)$. In practice n is usually set to $n = 1, 2,$ or 3.

12.2.3 Relationship between forward curve and spot price models

Intuitively, a model that describes the evolution of the whole forward curve is implicitly describing the front end of the curve, which is simply the spot energy price, and so the forward curve models must be related to spot price models. The defining stochastic differential equation (12.8) can be integrated to obtain the following solution:

$$F(t, T) = F(0, T)\exp\left[\sum_{i=1}^{n}\left\{-\frac{1}{2}\int_0^t \sigma_i(u, T)^2 du + \int_0^t \sigma_i(u, T)dz_i(u)\right\}\right] \tag{12.9}$$

This equation expresses the forward curve at time t in terms of its initially observed state (time 0) and integrals of the volatility functions. The spot price is just the forward contract for immediate delivery and so the process for the spot price can be obtained by setting $T = t$, that is:

$$S(t) = F(t, t) = F(0, t) \exp\left[\sum_{i=1}^{n}\left\{-\frac{1}{2}\int_0^t \sigma_i(u, t)^2 du + \int_0^t \sigma_i(u, t)dz_i(u)\right\}\right] \qquad (12.10)$$

Equation (12.10) can then be differentiated to yield the stochastic differential equation for the spot price:

$$\frac{dS(t)}{S(t)} = \left[\frac{\partial \ln F(0, t)}{\partial t} - \sum_{i=1}^{n}\left\{\int_0^t \sigma_i(u, t)\frac{\partial \sigma_i(u, t)}{\partial t}du + \int_0^t \frac{\partial \sigma_i(u, t)}{\partial t}dz_i(u)\right\}dt \right. \qquad (12.11)$$
$$\left. +\sum_{i=1}^{n}\sigma_i(t, t)dz_i(t)\right.$$

The term in square parentheses in the drift can be interpreted as being equivalent to the sum of the deterministic riskless rate of interest $r(t)$ and a convenience yield $\delta(t)$ which in general will be stochastic. Also, since the last component of the drift term involves the integration over the Brownian motions, the spot price process will, in general, be non-Markovian – that is, the evolution of the spot price will depend upon its past evolution.

One special case of the general model is the simple single factor model described by equation (12.6). For this model $n=1$ and $\sigma_1(t,T)=\sigma e^{-\alpha(T-t)}$. Clewlow and Strickland (2000) evaluate (12.11) with this volatility function and show that the resulting spot price process is given by:

$$\frac{dS(t)}{S(t)} = \left[\frac{\partial \ln F(0, t)}{\partial t} + \alpha\big(\ln F(0, t) - \ln S(t)\big) + \frac{\sigma^2}{4}\left(1 - e^{-2\alpha t}\right)\right]dt + \sigma dz(t) \qquad (12.12)$$

This implies:

$$\frac{dS(t)}{S(t)} = [\mu(t) - \alpha \ln S(t)]dt + \sigma dz(t) \qquad (12.13)$$

where

$$\mu(t) = \frac{\partial \ln F(0,t)}{\partial t} + \alpha \ln F(0,t) + \frac{\sigma^2}{4}\left(1 - e^{-2\alpha t}\right).$$

This single factor forward curve model is therefore just the single factor Schwartz (1997) model with a time dependent drift term. It is this term in the drift which allows the model to now fit the observed forward prices. Note also that this particular form of the forward curve volatility function results in a 'Markovian' spot price process – as the dependence in the drift on the path of the Brownian motion disappears.

The relationship between the forward curve model and the spot return model also shows that the mean reverting behaviour of the spot price is directly related to the attenuation of volatility of the forward curve. By setting $\alpha = 0$ the Black (1976) model is obtained. This is therefore a special case of the general model in equation (12.8) with $\sigma(t,T) = \sigma$ and $n = 1$. The main advantage of the forward curve modelling approach is the flexibility that the user has in choosing both the number and form of the volatility functions. These can be chosen in one of two general ways; historically, from time series analysis; or implied from the market prices of options.

12.3 ALTERNATIVE REAL OPTIONS METHODS

The contingent claims approach to valuing real options requires the spanning assumption to hold, that is, the financial markets are sufficiently complete in that there exists some traded asset, or portfolio of traded assets, that tracks the underlying asset or project. The spanning assumption should carry for most assets that are traded in spot and futures markets, and for prices that correlate with equity or portfolio values. There will however be some cases where the spanning assumption will not hold. In these situations, two methods, dynamic programming and decision analysis, offer approaches to solving real options problems where valuations based on financial markets are not possible.

12.3.1 Dynamic programming

Dynamic programming was developed as an approach to the optimal control problem found in an area of economics called dynamic optimization. Optimal decisions problems, where current decisions influence future payoffs, can be solved using dynamic programming, and it is particularly useful when dealing with uncertainty. The method derives possible values of the underlying asset by extrapolating out over the duration of the option, and then folding back the value of the optimal future value to the present. Dynamic programming can deal with complex decision structures that include constraints and complex relationships between the option value and the underlying asset. The binomial option pricing method is a form of dynamic programming.

Dynamic programming and contingent claims analysis are based on similar partial differential equations. There are similarities in the way the Bellman equation used in dynamic programming is interpreted in terms of an asset value and to what degree investors are prepared to retain that asset, while in contingent claims analysis boundary conditions define where investors decide the optimal exercise date that maximizes asset value. The differences lie in the definition of the rate of return. Dynamic programming specifies the discount rate exogenously, and is therefore considered a subjective valuation of risk. In contingent claims analysis, the rate of return on an asset is derived from assets traded in financial markets.

12.3.2 Decision analysis

12.3.2.1 Decision analysis terminology

Over the course of its development decision analysis (DA) has changed from focusing on finding solutions to decision problems to providing alternative perspectives and supporting innovation in decision making. DA is about analysis, which is defined as breaking something down into its constituent components. Therefore DA involves the decomposition of a decision problem into a set of smaller problems, which are addressed separately and then integrated so that a course of action can then be determined from the results. DA is also about making rational decisions. If a set of rules regarded as being rational by the majority is accepted then a decision maker will have a preference for a designated choice over its alternatives. It follows that the end results from the application of decision analysis will imply how rational decision makers would behave. DA can therefore be described as normative or prescriptive, and defines the choice among alternatives for decision makers when they are consistent with their stated preferences.

Even though decision problems are usually specific to an issue, they do share some common features. An *alternative* is a possible choice in solving a problem, and is assessed on the basis of the value added to various decision criteria. A decision problem's *criteria* reflect the different factors that are influenced by the alternatives and significant to the decision maker. A decision problem's states of nature define the future events that cannot be influenced by a decision maker. The outcomes for the alternative states of nature define the values for the different decision criteria under each alternative. Although a decision problem could consist of infinite possible states of nature, typically a manageable discrete set of states of nature is used in DA to encapsulate future possible events.

12.3.2.2 Decision analysis under uncertainty

The decision analysis techniques considered here are those where risk and uncertainty are central concerns of the decision maker. In these situations decision rules can be based on the probabilities of outcomes. Although probabilities can often be estimated from historical data, many decision problems represent one-off decisions where historical data may not be available. In these circumstances probabilities are often applied subjectively, either by experts or through structured interviews.

An expected value is obtained when a process is repeated a number of times, and the average is derived by multiplying each outcome by its probability of occurrence and summing the results. The expected monetary value (EMV) is the equivalent using monetary values. The EMV decision rule is the selection of the alternative with the largest EMV. The EMV of an alternative i in a decision problem is:

$$EMV = \sum_j r_{ij} p_j \tag{12.14}$$

where:

r_{ij} = the payoff for alternative i under the jth state of nature

p_j = the probability of the jth state of nature

The EMV for a decision alternative specifies the average payoff received if the identical decision problem is repeatedly encountered and the alternative always selected.

EMV does have some limitations. The decision alternative with the highest EMV may not always be the decision maker's preferred alternative. EMV focuses only on one attribute, which is money. Another problem is that EMV does not reflect the relative riskiness of an alternative.

Risk-neutral decision makers will typically make decisions that maximize the EMV. Risk-adverse decision makers tend to avoid risk, while risk seekers will typically search for risk. Determining a decision maker's risk and return profile in DA can be achieved through the use of utility theory. Decision makers in utility theory are assumed to use a utility function to interpret a decision problem's possible payoffs. A payoff's utility is a non-monetary measure that symbolizes the total value in a decision maker's decision alternative.

12.3.2.3 Decision trees

Decision problems can be represented and analysed effectively in a graphical form known as a decision tree. A decision tree is a collection of nodes, which are symbolized by circles and squares, which are linked by branches that are indicated by lines. A square node represents a decision and is therefore called a decision node. The alternatives for a particular decision are represented by branches, which extend out from the decision nodes. Event nodes are circular nodes in a decision tree that represent uncertain events. Event branches extend out from event nodes and relate to an uncertain event's possible states of nature or outcomes. The various branches in a decision tree end at terminal nodes, which are points where the decision problem can terminate. Probabilities are associated with the event branches that extend from each event node.

Decision trees are typically used to implement the EMV rule, which is to identify a decision's largest EMV. Creating a decision tree is usually an iterative process, with the initial structure being modified numerous times as the analysis of the problem develops. Large and complex trees that attempt to capture every possible scenario can be impractical, as the intention of a decision tree is to facilitate a decision maker's analysis of a problem. Decision trees are models that represent an abstraction of a problem. The strength in a decision tree lies in the simplification of a problem through the modelling process, as it facilitates the insights and inferences that can be drawn from the analysis that would otherwise be obscured by complexity and detail.

12.4 MODEL RISK

Over the last twenty years there has been a huge growth in the use of theoretical models for valuation and pricing in financial markets. A large body of the theory relates to derivatives, financial instruments where value is derived from underlying assets. These theories are being extended into real options, where models are being developed for options on real assets. Relying on models to analyse and quantify value and risk, however, carries its own risks. The term *model risk* has many connotations and is used in many different contexts. The following is based on Renardo's (2001) definition. Model risk is the risk, at some point in time, of a significant difference between the modelled value of a complex and/or illiquid asset and the realized value of that same asset.

In the physical sciences, where quantitative modelling originated, predictions can be made reasonably accurately. Variables in physical science models such as time, position, and mass exist regardless of the existence of humans. The fundamental unknown in financial markets, however, is certainty. Many financial and real assets only trade at certain discrete times, while financial variables also only symbolize human expectations. Risk and return refers to expected risk and return, variables that are unobserved and not realized. In most circumstances, however, models based on financial concepts and theory assume causation and stability between the values of these unobserved variables and asset values.

There a number of ways in which the development of a financial model can go wrong:

- The most fundamental risk is that modelling is just not appropriate. Modelling requires knowledge and content of a discipline. Mathematics is a representation or an abstraction of a discipline, and is a means to an end and is not the end itself.

- All the factors that affect valuation may not have been included in the model.

- Although a model may be theoretically correct, the model variables such as forward prices, interest rates, volatilities, correlations, and spreads may be poorly estimated. A model's variables, for example, may be based on historical data, which may be unstable and therefore not provide a good estimate of future value.

- Incorrect assumptions can be made about the properties of the asset values being modelled and the relationships between the variables in a model.

- A model may be inappropriate in the existing market environment, or some of the assumptions such as the distributions of variables may not be valid. Even if a model itself is satisfactory, the world it is predicting may be unstable.

Financial modelling draws on a multitude of disciplines, from business management practicalities and financial theory to mathematics and computer science, and is as much about art and content as it is about theory and quantitative techniques. An intimate knowledge of markets and how market participants think about valuation and risk are also part of the model practitioner's skill set. Derman (1996) provides some procedures for constructing financial valuation models:

- Identify and isolate the most important variables used by market participants to analyse value and risk, and decide which variables can be used in mathematical modelling.

- Separate the dependent variables and the independent variables.

- Determine which variables are directly measurable and those that are more in the nature of human expectations, and so are only indirectly measurable.

- Specify which variables can be treated as deterministic and those that must be considered as stochastic. Uncertainty will have little effect on the future values for some variables and these therefore can be approximated. For other variables, however, uncertainty will be a critical issue.

- Build a quantitative picture that characterizes how the dependent variables are influenced by the independent ones.

- Determine how to obtain the market values of independent observable variables, and how to derive the implied values of indirectly measurable ones.

- Create a mathematical picture of the problem, and determine which stochastic process best describes the evolution of the independent stochastic variables. Determine whether an analytical or numerical solution is appropriate.

- Deliberate the issues and difficulties in solving the model, and simplify it if necessary to make the solution as easy as possible. Only give up substance, however, for a relatively easy or elegant analytical solution when it is absolutely necessary.

- Finally, program the model, test it, and apply to the valuation problem.

Therefore the application of financial modelling draws from a palette that includes knowledge of the business, the applicability of the financial model, the relevance of the mathematics used to solve the problem, the systems and software used to implement and present it, and in the accurate communication and dissemination of the information and knowledge gained from the analysis. Drawing from these various disciplines can address the issues and reduce the risks associated with the application of financial modelling.

12.5 REAL OPTION PORTFOLIOS AND COMPLEX PAYOFFS

So far the quantitative material has focused on valuing individual options. Simple real options are projects or investments that are evaluated on an individual basis. Real options can exist, however, as portfolios of real options. A portfolio of real options such as options to defer, expand or abandon can exist as mutually exclusive alternatives, with each option valued independently. The portfolio in these cases is represented by the sum of the individual real options.

The options described in Chapter 8 are often defined as 'plain vanilla' or 'standard' derivatives. However, there will be many occasions when a real option's attributes will not be considered as vanilla or standard. Issues such as any interaction between real options, complex payoffs, multiple sources of uncertainty, path dependencies, sequential decisions, and the attributes of the underlying assets will all have an impact on the specification of a valuation method.

In the financial markets 'exotic' options are derivatives that have a more complicated payoff structure than standard derivatives. Some of these non-standard derivatives are basically combinations of vanilla calls and put options. Other non-standard option types, however, have payoffs and underlying assets that are much more complex to model. The complexity issue also applies to the modelling of many real options. Some examples of complex real options are compound options, exchange options, switching options and rainbow options.

12.5.1 Compound options

If there are interactions between the real options within a portfolio, it may not then be represented by the sum of the real options. This can be the case when the options are compound options, or options on options, where the payoff is another option. Compound options allow the holder to purchase or sell another option for a fixed price. There are four main compound option types, a call on a call, a put on a put, a call on a put and a put on a call. Projects and investments that are staged as a sequence are compound options, where the initial investment cost is the exercise price for the subsequent option on the next stage of the investment. Plant development, product development and research and development are examples of sequential compound options.

Compound options are useful for analysing the strategic impact of an investment on an organization. Many projects and strategic investments are not independent, as assumed in a DCF analysis, but are a series of interrelated cash flows where the initial investment is a prerequisite for the following outlays. Geske (1979) developed the original closed form solution for a compound option as a call option on a firm's equity, which itself is a European call option on the total value of the firm. The compounding in this specification occurs simultaneously, as both the firm's equity, a call option on the leveraged value of the firm, and the call option on the equity appear at the same time. Both simultaneous and sequential compound options can be solved in trees, although the valuation progressively more complicated as more options are added.

12.5.2 Exchange and switching options

Exchange options give the holder the right to exchange one asset for another. Examples of exchange options can be found in takeover bids, where a corporation offers its own shares in exchange for equity in the takeover target. An option to exchange in these situations is held by the owners of the stock in the takeover candidate. Another example of exchange options are spread options, where the payoff is the price differential between two underlying assets. Spread options are used to speculate on or hedge the comparative performance between two assets.

Other example of an exchange option is the option to switch. Switching options give the holder the right to switch between two means of operation for a fixed cost, and can be found in situations where the flexibility to switch inputs or outputs may optimize an operation or offer a competitive advantage. The flexibility to switch may exist in an organization's processes or products, for example switching between fuel inputs such as oil or gas, within products such as pharmaceuticals, cars and electronics, the exit and re-entry of an industry, and the starting and shutting down of a resource. The opportunity cost of the premium for the option to switch may be worth the flexibility provided to respond to volatile markets.

Switching options can be path-dependent derivatives. Path-dependent options have payoffs that depend on the path that the underlying asset follows before maturity (or some part of the options life), and not solely on the terminal asset value. In financial markets, Asian options, which are based on average asset values, and barrier options, which either cease to exist (knock-out) or only come into existence (knock-in) if the underlying price crosses a barrier, are examples of path-dependent options. In the case of a switching real option, the dependency could be on the price path of a product or commodity and the initial state of the operation, which could be either running or shut down. Switching options when defined as path-dependent options can be analysed using analytical models, Monte Carlo simulation and in binomial or trinomial trees.

12.5.3 Rainbow options

Rainbow options in the financial markets are options where the payoff depends on two or more assets. These payoffs can refer to the maximum or minimum of two or more assets, the better of two assets and cash, portfolio options and dual strike options. In the real options world, rainbow options derive value from multiple sources of uncertainty such as prices, quantities, technologies, regulation and interest rates. The real options may have not only multiple sources of uncertainty but also appear in multiple stages, in which case the real option is specified as a compound rainbow option (Copeland and Antikarov, 2001).

12.5.4 Quantifying complex real options

The valuation of complex real options can be performed with analytical models, trees or Monte Carlo simulation. In many situations, closed form solutions may not exist, in which case numerical procedures would be used for solving complex real options problems. Simulation is generally suited to European-type options, when the payoffs are complex and there may be several underlying state variables. The binomial and trinomial approaches are generally better suited to valuing American options and complex projects that have multiple options.

In financial markets over the last twenty-five years the innovations in derivative valuation methods have been almost limitless. Exotic options continue to be developed to meet the demand for the pricing and hedging of specific risks. Developments in valuing complex real options will continue as research and interest in this area continues to expand. As always the trade-off in any quantitative valuation will be the development of tractable, applicable, relevant and manageable models versus capturing the substance of the complexities that exist in real options.

REFERENCES

Black, F. The pricing of commodity contracts, *The Journal of Financial Economics*, **3**, (Jan–March): 167–79, 1976.

Briys, E., Bellalah, M., Minh, Mai, H. and De Varenne, F. *Options, Futures and Exotic Derivatives*, Wiley, 1998.

Clewlow, L. and Strickland, C. *Implementing Derivative Models*, Wiley, 1998.

Clewlow, L. and Strickland, C. *Energy Derivatives, Pricing and Risk Management*, Lacima, 2000.

Copeland, T. and Antikarov, V. *Real Options*, Texere, 2001.

Derman, E. *Quantitative Strategies, Research Notes: Model Risk*, Goldman Sachs, 1996.

Dixit, A. and Pindyck, R. *Investment Under Uncertainty*, Princeton University Press, 1994.

Geske, R. The valuation of compound options, *Journal of Financial Economics*, **7**: 63–81, 1979.

Haug, E.G. *The Complete Guide to Option Pricing Formulas*, McGraw Hill, 1998.

Hull, J. and White, A. An analysis of the bias in option pricing caused by stochastic volatility, *Advances in Futures and Options Research*, **3**: 29–61, 1988.

Merton, R. Option pricing when underlying stock returns are discontinuous, *Journal of Financial Economics*, **3**: 125–44, 1976.

Ragsdale, C.T. *Spreadsheet Modelling and Decision Analysis*, South-Western College, 1998.

Rebonato, R. Model risk: new challenges, new solutions, *Risk*, March 2001.

Schwartz, E. The stochastic behaviour of commodity prices: implications for valuation and hedging, *Journal of Finance*, **LII**(3): 923–73, 1997.

Vasicek, O. An equilibrium characterisation of the term structure, *Journal of Financial Economics*, (5): 177–88, 1977.

PART IV

Real Options Case Studies and Practical Implications

CHAPTER 13

Seven Strategic Real Options Case Studies

13.1 INTRODUCTION

The five initial case studies, the IT project, the power generator, the pharmaceutical company, firm growth and firm abandoment, and two additional case studies, the modularity concept and the sale of real estate assets are now analysed using a real options approach. The IT project is considered as an option to defer, the equivalent to a call option; the power generator as switching options which are represented as a series of call options on the plant; and the pharmaceutical company as a valuation that includes a growth option. The modularity case study explores the real options in modular design, and the sale of real estate assets analyses the put real option in deferring an office property sale.

13.2 SOFTWARE REAL OPTION EXAMPLE

13.2.1 Value and flexibility

The way in which an organization's software is structured can have a significant influence on value. Any flexibility that an IT manager has in making software modifications over time is determined by a system's structure. As the business environment becomes increasingly dynamic and uncertain, flexibility as a capability can have a significant impact on value, by offering protection from the downside risks while maintaining an exposure to any upside opportunities. For example, the capability to abandon a project at an early stage as new unfavourable information becomes available provides downside protection, while the flexibility to adapt to a evolving market or select from a range of developing technologies provides upside potential (Sullivan et al., 1999). An organization can hedge against adverse outcomes by staging IT investment and making decisions contingent on project risks and market demand, while capturing the upside benefits if market conditions turn out to be positive. The capabilities to make management decisions such as these more effectively has the potential for substantial economic payoffs in terms of value.

The software restructuring project is now analysed under the concept that there is value in the form of a real option. This option offers the flexibility to defer any software modifications until one time step into the future, at which point new information will become available. The focus in this relatively simple case study is more on demonstrating the concept of real options, rather than developing a market-based real option evaluation through arbitrage methods. However, the concepts can still provide capabilities in software management and therefore add value to an organization.

13.2.2 Software real options

The DCF software restructuring analysis in Section 4.2.3 factored risk into the analysis by using a discount rate to discount the cash flows. Another way to analyse the software restructuring is to recognize two possible scenarios that can result from the uncertainties associated with future conditions. One uncertainty could be the future requirements for software modifications, which could be either frequent or occasional. Another future scenario is the possible success of replacement software that is under development, which would limit any requirements for modifications to the existing legacy system. To illustrate these future uncertainties two possible scenarios for the restructuring of the software are assumed, one where numerous modifications are required, which implies the potential for outlays on restructuring, and the alternative where no or only a relatively small number of modifications are needed, in which case there would be no major outlays on restructuring.

A one step binomial tree is used to analyse the uncertainty associated with the restructuring decision. The payoff is now represented as three cash flows, with the restructuring costs at t_0 (the present) of $100,000, and two possible payoffs at t_1 (one step into the future) of $198,000 at one branch if the outcome is favourable, and $66,000 at the other branch if the outcome is unfavourable. Arbitrary probabilities of 0.5 are assigned to each branch, and the same discount rate of 10% is used. These are simplified parameters for the purpose of illustration. In option modelling a continuously compounded interest rate and risk-neutral probabilities would typically be used.

If the decision is made to invest immediately, the benefits are the asset S, the expected value of the profit stream from restructuring at time t_0. Over the time period Δt from t_0 to t_1, the asset value S can either go up to uS (favourable) or down to dS (unfavourable), with values at t_1 defined in this case study as:

$$uS = 198,000$$
$$dS = 66,000$$

Table 13.1 Software restructuring cash flows: invest immediately

Costs at t_0	=	(100,000)
Favourable savings at t_1	=	198,000
Unfavourable savings at t_1	=	66,000
NPV at t_0	=	20,000

$$NPV = -100,000 + 0.5 * \left(\frac{198,000}{1.10}\right) + 0.5 * \left(\frac{66,000}{1.10}\right)$$

$$= 20,000$$

With probabilities $p = 0.5$, the expected asset value is therefore:

$$S_0 = 0.5 * \left(\frac{198,000}{1.10}\right) + 0.5 * \left(\frac{66,000}{1.10}\right)$$

$$= 120,000$$

With the inclusion of the outlay of 100,000, or the strike K, the payoff from exercising at t_0 is $S_0 - K$, which equals 20,000. Table 13.1 illustrates the cash flows for the decision to invest immediately. The NPV at t_0 is still $20,000 as per the case in Table 4.1 of the DCF analysis, and again the restructuring project would then be accepted immediately based of this analysis. The same analysis appears below in Table 13.2 using a simple binomial tree.

The software restructuring project is now analysed as an option to defer, or a call option on the restructuring project at t_1, with a strike of $K = 100,000$ (the restructuring costs of $100,000 are assumed to be constant at t_0 and at t_1). At t_0 the payoff for the call option on the restructuring project is:

$$c = Max(S_T - K, 0) \tag{13.1}$$

Table 13.2 Software restructuring binomial tree cash flows (1)

T	p	r	df	K	uS	dS
1	0.5	10.00%	0.9091	(100,000)	198,000	66,000
	t_0		t_1			
	Key:					
	CFt					
	NPV					
			198,000			
	(100,000)					
	20,000					
			66,000			

where c is the value of the call option, and T is equal to t_1. The payoffs for the option at the up and down nodes at t_1 are:

$$c_u = Max(uS - K, 0) \qquad\qquad\qquad (13.2)$$

$$c_d = Max(dS - K, 0) \qquad\qquad\qquad (13.3)$$

The expected value of the call option at t_0 is:

$$c = P(t,T)\left[0.5 * Max(uS - K, 0) + (1 - 0.5) * Max(dS - K, 0)\right]$$

The expected cash flow payoff at t_0 is therefore:

$$c = P(t,T)\left[0.5 * Max(198,000 - 100,000, 0) + (1 - 0.5) * Max(66,000 - 100,000, 0)\right]$$

$$= 44,545$$

The same analysis appears in Table 13.3 using the simple binomial tree.

In this software restructuring example the alternative strategies are to either exercise at t_0 or to wait until t_1. The IT manager has the right to invest immediately in the restructuring at t_0, and a call option on the restructuring with exercise at t_1. The DCF analysis implies that the project should proceed immediately as the discounted cash flows are positive. The decision to proceed with the restructuring at time t_0, however, gives up the right to exercise the call option at t_1. Therefore the value of the decision to invest immediately at t_0 is 20,000 (the value of investing immediately) minus 44,545 (the value of the call option, or the option to defer) which equals –24,545.

Although the initial perception is that the best alternative based on the NPV analysis is to invest at t_0, it is clearly not the optimal decision for adding value to

Table 13.3 Software restructuring binomial tree cash flows (2)

T	p	r	df	K	uS	dS
1	0.5	10.00%	0.9091	(100,000)	198,000	66,000
	t_0		t_1			
	Key:					
	St					
	Call					
			198,000			
			98,000			
	120,000					
	44,545					
			66,000			
			0			

the organization when the option to defer is also considered. If the DCF analysis had given a negative NPV for the project at t_0, the right to defer the project may still have value due to the call option. Even though the project had a positive NPV at t_0, the organization may gain by delaying the project and proceeding with it in the future. In the DCF analysis this right is worthless and adds no value to the organization. When the right to delay the project is considered as a call option, however, this right does have value and should therefore be considered in the analysis.

13.3 ENERGY VALUATION CASE

13.3.1 Energy options

As the limitations of DCF techniques have become evident, the energy industries are adopting more sophisticated models that account for the optionality in strategic assets. The options in an energy company's electricity portfolio can exist in a range of assets, such as power plants, natural gas (commodity or pipeline capacity), oil (as a commodity and in storage) and emission credits (Challa, 2000). The new types of models are designed to capture the opportunity and risks associated with the volatility in the value of these assets, and can be readily used for valuations, capital allocation decisions, operations and risk management.

Electricity peaking plants can be valued as options on the spread between the fuel cost and the power price. The optionality in an individual peaking unit provides the owner, or option holder, with the right to operate the unit when electricity prices are higher than the cost of the fuel used to generate. A portfolio of peaking units can therefore increase marginal value significantly. The problem with the industry standard economic supply-demand dispatch models is that they take no account of volatility. Although the DCF model recognizes that a peaking plant has intrinsic value, that is, electricity prices can increase to a point where there is value in switching on the plant, it does not capture any value derived from the volatility in the spark spread.

The operating characteristics of the Sparkie Power Station (SPS) can be defined as the equivalent to a power spread option. As SPS is a peaking plant, Energy Corporation (EC) can choose to only run the power plant when the power price exceeds the marginal fuel cost. The real option for EC is the ability to choose whether to generate or not at a given power price. While the peaking plant may have available capacity, there is no obligation to generate regardless of the electricity price. In deregulated power markets, however, a rational generator operator would choose to generate when power prices are above the fuel cost and any start-up costs. These types of real options are switching options, defined in this case study as a series of European call options on the spark spread between power and natural gas prices. Valuing the power plant as a real option illustrates the value in the flexibility to call the plant when the energy spread is positive, which can be used to optimize operations and therefore value.

13.3.2 Pricing energy derivatives

There are a number of practical problems associated with derivative modelling in energy markets. Some of the important issues associated with energy derivative pricing that were often overlooked in early modelling approaches are:

- Energy prices tend to be drawn to production costs. The GBM assumption permits price series to drift to unrealistic levels when applied to energy markets. In the short run, divergence from the cost of production can be possible under abnormal market conditions; however, in the long run, supply will adjust to the anomaly and prices will move to the level determined by the cost of production. This property is described as *mean reversion*.

- Energy prices display *seasonality*. Seasonality in energy prices and volatility may correspond to the time of year, such as winter or summer, and also can result from regular demand patterns due to factors such as the weather.

- Energy commodities cannot be treated solely as financial assets, as energy commodities are inputs to production processes and/or consumption goods. Models based on an automatic extension of those developed for financial markets may therefore break down when applied to energy markets.

- Another problem with applying the GBM assumption to energy prices is that market price behaviour often does is consistent with the assumption of price continuity over time. Commodity and energy prices often display *jump behaviour*, determined in many cases by fluctuations in demand and supply. The frequency of these extreme values is often larger than the probability implied by GBM models.

In some markets such as energy the concept of being able to perfectly replicate options by continuously trading the underlying asset can be unrealistic. Many energy derivatives, however, actually rely on futures prices rather than the spot price, and therefore futures can be used to replicate options positions and permit the application of the risk-neutral pricing approach.

13.3.3 Energy spread options

The payoff in a spread option is derived from the price differential between two underlying assets. These types of exotic options can be used either to take a position on, or to hedge the risk associated with, the relative performance of two underlying assets. The payoff of a European spread call option at maturity T is:

$$c = \max[S_{1T} - S_{2T} - K, 0] \qquad (13.4)$$

where S_{1T} and S_{2T} are the spot prices of the two underlying assets, and K is the exercise price. Most option pricing models have the underlying assumption that the risk-neutral price distribution of the underlying asset is lognormal. A spread option is priced as the discounted double integral of the option payoffs over the risk-neutral distribution of the two underlying assets at maturity T (Pearson, 1997). Analytical Black–Scholes-type models for valuing spread call and put options that include a strike, however, are not known, and therefore numerical techniques have to be used.

If the futures contracts underlying the option are written on two separate energies, in this case natural gas and electricity, then the option is often referred to as a *crack spread option*. Organizations exposed to the price differences between two different energies often use options of this type. In this case of a natural gas-fired power generator, energy is an input into a process that produces another energy. If $F_a(t,T)$ represents the price of a T maturity futures contract on energy a, in this case power, $F_b(t,T)$ represents the price of a T maturity futures or forward contract on energy b, in this case natural gas (times the heat rate), and K represents the start-up costs, then the payoff for a European call option with maturity T and strike K on the spread between the two forward contracts is:

$$c = Max\left(F_a(t,T) - F_b(t,T) - K,\ 0\right) \tag{13.5}$$

and therefore the value of the call option at time t can be written generally as:

$$= P(t,\ T)E_t\left[Max(F_a(t,\ T) - F_b(t,\ T) - K,\ 0)\right] \tag{13.6}$$

where $P(t,T)$ is the continuously compounded discount factor.

Note: This section has largely been adapted from Clewlow and Strickland (2000).

13.3.4 The Schwartz single factor model

Energies such as electricity and natural gas exhibit the property of mean reversion. Modelling these price series using Black–Scholes-type models can produce unrealistic spreads between the two related energy commodities. Mean reversion can be captured in a more realistic single factor model introduced by Schwartz (1997), which assumes that the spot price follows a mean reverting process:

$$dS = \alpha(\mu - \lambda - \ln S)Sdt + \sigma Sdz \tag{13.7}$$

where α is the mean reversion rate, which is the speed of adjustment of the spot price back towards its long-term level μ, σ is the spot price volatility and λ is the market price of energy risk. By defining $x = \ln S$ and applying Itô's lemma to equation (13.7), the log price can be characterized by the Ornstein–Uhlenbeck process:

$$dx = \alpha(\hat{\mu} - x)dt + \sigma dz \tag{13.8}$$

where:

$$\mu = \hat{\mu} - \lambda - \frac{\sigma^2}{2\alpha}$$

This process leads to the following differential equation for all contingent claims where the payoff depends on the level of the energy spot price and time:

$$\frac{1}{2}\sigma^2 S^2 C_{SS} + \alpha(\mu - \lambda - \ln S)SC_S + C_t - rC = 0 \tag{13.9}$$

where C is the contingent claim price, and r is instantaneous continously compounded interest rate.

13.3.5 Forward curves

Capturing the significant features of the energy markets is important in applications of energy pricing models. Although a number of energy derivative models use forward curves for pricing, there are some associated problems. Energy forward curves are typically composed of discrete monthly futures contracts, and therefore are not continuous as assumed in the pricing model. Some energy markets can be in *backwardation* (where futures prices are lower than spot prices) while others might be in *contango* (where futures prices are higher than spot prices), which gives the spread its own forward curve. The spread can also become negative as a consequence of these properties. Another issue is that seasonality can also exist in the spreads. Figure 13.1 illustrates the forward curves used in the DCF and the real option example. The forward curves were derived for the case study, with annual seasonal patterns and negative spark spreads from January to March for each year.

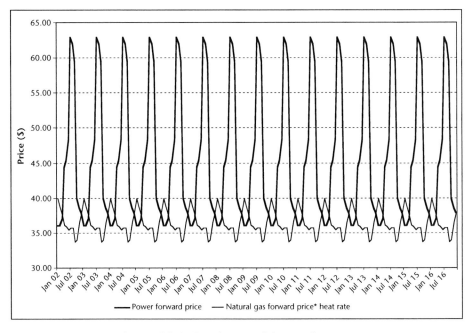

Figure 13.1 Spark spread forward curves

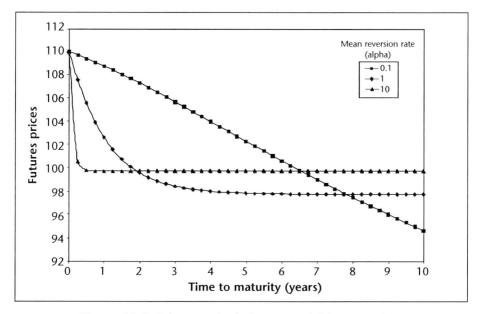

Figure 13.2 Schwartz single factor model futures prices
Source: Clewlow and Strickland (2000)

13.3.6 Schwartz single factor futures and forward pricing

Futures and forward prices with maturity s in the Schwartz single factor model are equal with the appropriate boundary conditions and are given by:

$$F(t, s) = \exp\left[e^{-\alpha(s-t)} \ln S + (1 - e^{-\alpha(s-t)})\left(\mu - \lambda - \frac{\sigma^2}{2\alpha}\right) + \frac{\sigma^2}{4\alpha}(1 - e^{-2\alpha(s-t)})\right] \quad (13.10)$$

The mean reversion rate α determines how quickly forward prices even out to the long-term level. Figure 13.2 illustrates the sensitivity of the futures price defined in equation (13.10) to the mean reversion parameter, or the speed of mean reversion. The parameters used in the illustration are $S=110$, $\sigma=0.3$, $\lambda=0$, $\mu=\ln(100)$ and $\alpha=0.1$, 1 and 10. The long-term level of the futures curve does not equal $\exp(\mu)$, as it is adjusted by an amount that depends on the relative size of α and σ:

$$F(t, \infty) = \exp\left[\mu - \lambda - \frac{\sigma^2}{4\alpha}\right] \quad (13.11)$$

13.3.7 Volatility

The volatility measure used in energy pricing models should be defined and estimated in the context of the specific stochastic price process, capturing the key features of the energy markets such as mean reversion. The constant volatility assumption used in the Black–Scholes model is not consistent with the empirical observation that long-dated energy forwards are less volatile then short-dated energy forwards. Figure 13.3 illustrates the shapes of the power and natural gas volatility term structures used in the generator real option case study.

Itô's lemma can be applied to equation (13.10) to provide the term structure of proportional futures volatilities in the single factor model:

$$\sigma_F(t, s) = \sigma e^{-\alpha(s-t)} \tag{13.12}$$

Figure 13.4 illustrates the effect of the speed of mean reversion, α in equation (13.12), on the term structure of volatility of futures prices. Volatility parameters of 0.3 and $\alpha = 0.1$, 1 and 10 are used in the illustration. Increasing the speed of mean reversion, for example, increases the attenuation of the volatility curve. As the maturity of the forward contract increases, the volatility of the contract also tends to zero.

While the volatility term structure based on the Schwartz single factor model is a more accurate representation than the Black–Scholes model, its shape is still relatively simple. Even though a volatility function of this type describes the attenuation of typical market forward volatility term structures, the volatility parameters tend to zero for longer dated maturities. While market volatilities of forward energy prices do decrease as maturities increase, they typically do not approach zero and therefore the Schwartz model has a problem when pricing options on long maturity forward contracts.

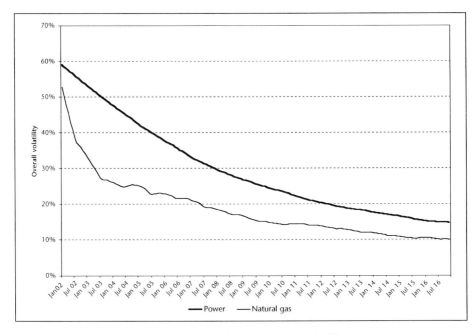

Figure 13.3 Power and natural gas volatility curves

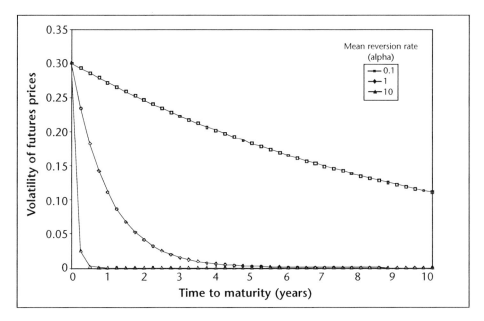

Figure 13.4 Volatility of futures prices in the Schwartz single factor model
Source: Clewlow and Stricland (2000)

13.3.8 Correlation

The volatility of a spread is less than the volatilities of the individual components, and should be considered in the pricing of spread options. Although there is typically a term structure of correlation similar to the term structures for forward prices and volatility, the correlation (or rho as it is typically called) between the volatilities is defined as a constant term in this case study. The correlation between two assets is captured by:

$$\xi_{1,t} = \varepsilon_{1,t} \tag{13.13}$$

$$\xi_{2,t} = \rho\varepsilon_{1,t} + \varepsilon_{2,t}\sqrt{1-\rho^2} \tag{13.14}$$

where $\xi_{1,t}$ and $\xi_{2,t}$ are two independent random numbers from a standard normal distribution, and ρ is the correlation between the two assets.

13.3.9 Simulating mean reversion

A Monte Carlo simulation simulates possible future values of an underlying asset using a stochastic process based on assumptions of the behaviour of the relevant market variables. The advantages of Monte Carlo simulation are that it can facilitate accuracy in the modelling of market price behaviour by including factors such as jumps, seasonality, stochastic volatility and possible future structural changes in the market. The disadvantages are its relative complexity in implementation and the resources required for computation.

The mean reverting spot price model in equation (11.1) can be specified in terms of the natural logarithm of the spot price, $x = \ln(S)$:

$$dx = \left[\alpha(\mu - x) - \tfrac{1}{2}\sigma^2\right]dt + \sigma dz \qquad (13.15)$$

which can be discretized as:

$$\Delta x_i = \left[\alpha(\mu - x_i) - \tfrac{1}{2}\sigma^2\right]\Delta t + \sigma\sqrt{\Delta t}\varepsilon_i \qquad (13.16)$$

In contrast to the GBM model the discretization in this specification is only correct in the limit of the time step tending to zero, as the drift term is dependent on the variable x. Time steps that are relatively small to the speed of mean reversion should therefore be chosen. To simulate the path of the spot price, the parameters α, μ, σ and Δt are chosen or estimated, normally distributed random numbers ε_i are repeatedly generated and new values of Δx are calculated, from which a new spot price at each time step is then derived.

13.3.10 Estimating the mean reversion rates

Two methods can be used to estimate the mean reversion rate α, either through linear regression using spot price data or by fitting the single factor volatility function to the empirical volatility term structure. The simple mean reverting process for the natural logarithm of the energy spot price:

$$dx = \alpha(\bar{x} - x)dt + \sigma dz \qquad (13.17)$$

is essentially the same as equation (13.15) but with the $-\tfrac{1}{2}\sigma^2$ included in $\bar{x}$. This can be discretized as:

$$\Delta x_t = \alpha_0 - \alpha_1 x_t + \sigma\varepsilon_t \qquad (13.18)$$

where $\alpha_0 = \alpha\bar{x}\Delta t$ and $\alpha_1 = \alpha\Delta t$. Observations of the spot price through time imply the linear relationship between Δx_t and x_t with the noise term $\sigma\varepsilon_t$. Regressing observations of Δx_t against x_t obtains $\alpha_0 = \alpha\bar{x}\Delta t$ and $\alpha_1 = \alpha\Delta t$ as estimates of the intercept and slope of this linear relationship. As the time interval between observations Δt is known, estimates of α and $\bar{x}$ can therefore be obtained.

An alternative is to estimate α, the mean reversion rate, from the term structure of volatility. Figure 13.3 compares the volatility of short-term energy forward contract versus long-term energy contracts, with short-term contracts being more volatile that long-term contracts, and the volatility declining as the maturity increases. Equation (13.19) represents this decline in the volatility as t gets large:

$$\sigma_1(t, T) = \sigma e^{-\alpha(T-t)} \tag{13.19}$$

where $n=1$. The mean reversion rate of the spot energy price can be estimated through the relationship between the spot price process and single factor model described in Section 11.9. The negative exponential function of equation (13.19) can be fitted to the volatility curves illustrated in Figure 13.3. The volatility function $\sigma e^{-\alpha(T-t)}$ is set as equal to the observed volatility $\sigma(t,T)$ by minimizing the square root of the squared differences between the two curves and solving for α.

Table 13.4 illustrates the alpha parameters derived from the complete power and natural gas volatility term structures. The volatility term structures for the actual data and the volatility functions are compared in Figures 13.5 and 13.6. While the power volatility term structures compare favourably, the natural gas term structures do not. The initial steeper attenuation in the short dated natural gas volatility term structure has a relatively stronger implied mean reversion. Reducing the volatility term structure sample size to one year will give a higher estimate of α, however, the volatility for longer dated forwards in the single factor model converges to zero too quickly (see 'Volatility function 2' in Figure 13.6). This implies that the single factor model can underestimate the volatility of longer dated natural gas forward contracts, and can therefore give a downward bias to options priced on these parts of the curve.

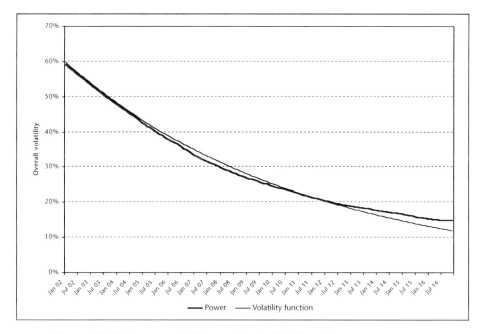

Figure 13.5 Power volatility and volatility function term structures

Table 13.4 Estimation of the power and natural gas alpha parameters

Month	Power			Natural gas			Natural gas: 1 year		
	Spot σ 60.00% α 0.1081 Σε 0.1613			Spot σ 53.00% α 0.1712 Σε 0.7723			Spot σ 53.00% α 0.5117 Σε 0.0334		
	Power %	Volatility function %	Difference %	NG %	Volatility function %	Difference %	NG %	Volatility function %	Difference %
Jan 02	59.08	59.73	−0.65	52.80	52.62	0.18	52.80	51.86	0.94
Feb 02	58.58	59.21	−0.63	50.30	51.89	−1.59	50.30	49.76	0.54
Mar 02	58.08	58.69	−0.61	47.90	51.18	−3.28	47.90	47.74	0.16
Apr 02	57.58	58.16	−0.58	45.50	50.45	−4.95	45.50	45.75	−0.25
May 02	57.08	57.64	−0.56	43.20	49.74	−6.54	43.20	43.83	−0.63
Jun 02	56.59	57.12	−0.53	40.90	49.03	−8.13	40.90	42.00	−1.10
Jul 02	56.09	56.61	−0.52	38.80	48.33	−9.53	38.80	40.24	−1.44
Aug 02	55.59	56.09	−0.50	37.20	47.63	−10.43	37.20	38.53	−1.33
Sep 02	55.10	55.59	−0.49	36.50	46.96	−10.46	36.50	36.91	−0.41
Oct 02	54.61	55.09	−0.48	36.00	46.29	−10.29	36.00	35.37	0.63
Nov 02	54.12	54.59	−0.47	35.00	45.63	−10.63	35.00	33.89	1.11
Dec 02	53.63	54.10	−0.47	34.10	44.98	−10.88	34.10	32.47	1.63
Jan 03	53.14	53.61	−0.47	33.10	44.33	−11.23			
Feb 03	52.66	53.14	−0.48	32.10	43.73	−11.63			
....	....		....	....		....			
Dec 16	14.67	11.90	2.77	10.00	4.08	5.92			

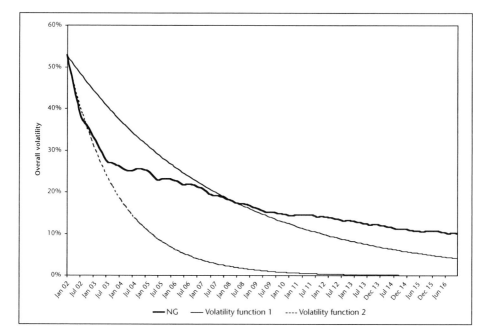

Figure 13.6 Natural gas and volatility function term structures

13.3.11 The half-life of a mean reverting process

A key property of a mean reverting process is the half-life. This is the time taken for the price to revert half way back to its long-term level from its current level if no more random shocks arrive. Ignoring the randomness allows a focus on the mean reverting behaviour alone. The half-life, denoted by $t_{1/2}$, can be derived as:

$$t_{1/2} = \ln(2)/\alpha \qquad\qquad (13.20)$$

The half-lives of power and natural gas are:

- *Power:* The value of 0.1081 for α_{power} implies a half-life for price shocks of 6.4 years.
- *Natural gas:* The value of 0.1712 for $\alpha_{n\ gas}$ implies a half-life for price shocks of 4 years.

These half-lives are averages over a long time period, representing the time shocks to the spot price take to decay to half their deviation from the long-term level. Table 13.5 illustrates the range of half-lives for various values of alpha.

Table 13.5 Mean reversion rates and the corresponding half-lives

α	$t_{1/2}$
1	8 months
10	25 days
100	2.53 days
1000	6 hours

Source: Clewlow and Strickland (2000)

13.3.12 Pricing the energy spread option

A sample of the results of the Monte Carlo simulation for the call spread options is illustrated in Table 13.6. The switching real options on SPS are priced as a series of European call spread options with payoffs as specified in equation (13.5). The pricing data consisted of the power and natural gas monthly forward and volatility curves, and the start-up costs as the strike K for each month. The power and natural gas forward prices for each month were used for the mean parameter μ, and the α parameters were derived in Section 13.2.10. The 10% correlation between the two assets, defined as rho, was estimated from spot price returns.

It was assumed that the generator would run continuously during the weekdays for the summer months of July, August and September, and be started up each weekday for the remaining months of the year. This is reflected in the per MWh start-up costs for each month. The middle of each month is used as the maturity or expiry date for each spread option. The interest rate used for each month was derived as a term structure of zero coupon rates from USD LIBOR, Eurodollar futures and interest rate swaps. Although in academic derivative valuations a risk-free interest rate such as a Treasury Bill rate is typically used in option pricing, most organizations borrow at interest rates that are much closer to LIBOR than Treasury Bill rates.

The price paths for the two assets, power and natural gas, were simulated from t_0 to T, the maturity or expiry for each European call spread option (in this case the middle of each month). Ten thousand simulations were used for each of the 180 European spread options. The payoff for the spread option at T, as defined in equation (13.5) is then derived for each simulation, and added to an incremental sum of the payoffs. The value of each call spread option is the expected value of the total payoffs simulated for each T, that is, the sum of the payoffs simulated for each month divided by the number of simulations.

The single factor model used in this case study is a relatively simple model for the forward curve. While the volatility structure under the Schwartz single factor model is more realistic than the Black–Scholes model, it still has a relatively simple shape, and the volatilities tend to zero for longer maturities. The single factor model can be generalized and modified, as illustrated in sections 11.7 and 11.8, to include multiple sources of uncertainty in the forward curves. Clewlow and Strickland (2000)

Table 13.8 Monte Carlo simulation of the two-asset energy spread option (as at 31 December 2001)

Month	Jan 02	Feb 02	Mar 02	Apr 02	May 02	......	Aug 16	Sep 16	Oct 16	Nov 16	Dec 16
Power curve	36.02	36.00	37.00	44.36	45.36	......	61.93	59.40	39.98	38.57	37.88
NG*Heat rate	40.00	38.80	37.50	36.10	35.90	......	35.80	33.70	34.00	36.50	37.80
Power σ	59.08%	58.58%	58.08%	57.58%	57.08%	......	14.83%	14.83%	14.83%	14.75%	14.67%
NG σ	52.80%	50.30%	47.90%	45.50%	43.20%	......	10.00%	10.10%	10.10%	10.10%	10.00%
Correlation (ρ)	10%	10%	10%	10%	10%	......	10%	10%	10%	10%	10%
Time to maturity (T)	0.04	0.12	0.20	0.29	0.37	......	14.63	14.72	14.80	14.88	14.97
Start-up costs	1.04	1.04	1.04	1.04	1.04	......	0.15	0.12	1.04	1.04	1.04
Strike (K)	1.04	1.04	1.04	1.04	1.04	......	0.15	0.12	1.04	1.04	1.04
Alpha (α) power	0.1081	0.1081	0.1081	0.1081	0.1081	......	0.1081	0.1081	0.1081	0.1081	0.1081
Mean (μ) power	3.58	3.58	3.61	3.79	3.81	......	4.13	4.08	3.69	3.65	3.63
Alpha (α) gas	0.1712	0.1712	0.1712	0.1712	0.1712	......	0.1712	0.1712	0.1712	0.1712	0.1712
Mean (μ) gas	3.69	3.66	3.62	3.59	3.58	......	3.58	3.52	3.53	3.60	3.63
Interest rate (ρ)	1.8419%	1.9251%	1.9052%	1.9318%	1.9521%	......	6.3681%	6.3724%	6.3767%	6.3809%	6.3850%
dt	0.0001	0.0002	0.0003	0.0005	0.0006	......	0.0244	0.0245	0.0247	0.0248	0.0249
Number of time steps	600	600	600	600	600	......	600	600	600	600	600
Number of simulations	10,000	10,000	10,000	10,000	10,000	......	10,000	10,000	10,000	10,000	10,000
MR spread option price	0.66	2.30	4.21	10.95	13.04	......	11.41	11.01	3.52	2.50	2.04
Energy – MWh	300	300	300	300	300	......	300	300	300	300	300
Total hours	384	336	352	352	384	......	552	552	352	368	368
Total option cash flows	76,513	232,082	444,185	1,156,524	1,502,223	......	1,889,564	1,823,780	371,295	275,497	224,802
O & M costs	1.50	1.50	1.50	1.50	1.50	......	1.50	1.50	1.50	1.50	1.50
Total O & M costs	172,800	151,200	158,400	158,400	172,800	......	248,400	248,400	158,400	165,600	165,600
df	0.9992	0.9976	0.9961	0.9945	0.9928	......	0.3938	0.3915	0.3891	0.3868	0.3845
PV O & M costs	172,665	150,842	157,785	157,522	171,552	......	97,819	97,238	61,638	64,058	63,678
Net present value	−96,152	81,240	286,399	999,002	1,330,671	......	1,791,745	1,726,542	309,657	211,440	161,124

Total value = $266,636,868

value energy options in a general multi-factor model for the forward curve, which can capture multiple sources of uncertainty. As spread options depend simultaneously on forwards related to separate energies, Clewlow and Strickland extend the multi-factor model to a specification that can simultaneously model a number of different energy forward curves, and therefore capture the multiple dynamics of the forward curves in the valuation of spread options.

13.3.13 Implications for energy analysis and valuation

The DCF valuation of SPS is $136,874,152, while the spread option valuation approach is $266,636,686 using the NG alpha of 0.1712. While the DCF method does capture the intrinsic value, it does not account for the value in the volatility in the spark spread. Figure 13.7 compares the spread option values and the DCF intrinsic values by month.

SPS is essentially an out-of the money option for at least part of the year. Although the spark spread can be negative, as is the case from January to March, the relatively large volatility associated with the energy markets implies that there is time value in the option, as there is some probability that the spark spread can be positive in these months. Consequently the DCF valuation of SPS is likely to understate the true long-term value that SPP will offer to EC.

EC can also maximize value by considering the natural gas power generator as an asset that can be traded through its option value. A number of factors can have an influence on the value of natural gas power generator. The 15-year life used for the power plant in this case study is arbitrary, and can feasibly be extended to value a new power plant. A benchmark for the cost of building a natural gas power plant is USD $500,000 per MW. For the 300 MW used for the generator in this case study the cost to build would be USD $150,000,000 million. The value captured by including the volatility in the valuation will therefore have a significant impact on management decisions such as whether to build, divest, or shut down a generator. Another driver of value that will influence decisions is the heat rate, the efficiency at which natural gas is converted into electricity. New natural gas generators will typically have lower heat rates that older plants, which will produce a relatively wider spark spread, and therefore have a competitive advantage over older generators.

13.4 PHARMACEUTICAL

13.4.1 Background

Much of the value in the early stages of a pharmaceutical drug is contained in the promise that a blockbuster drug will result. In the biotechnology industry in particular, many companies have significant valuations long before they earn any profits from selling their products. In the past ten to fifteen years, investors have bid up the stock prices of many biotech companies, and their prices have remained high

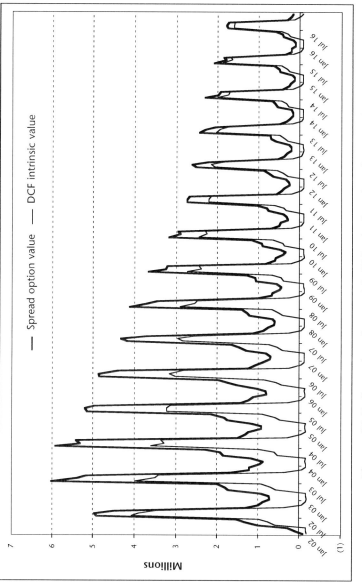

Figure 13.7 Spread option and DCF intrinsic values by month

relative to their discounted cash flow valuations. This phenomenon is surprising to many market observers because some authors (for example, Grabowski and Vernon, 1994) have suggested that pharmaceutical research has an (expected) net present value close to zero.

Real-options valuation methods can help to assess the value that investors are assigning to biotech companies. The value of the company is derived from the expected profits of the company's products and the potential for growth of the company into one with many profitable drugs. Real-options valuation methods can be applied to estimate the value of individual projects, but the challenge addressed here is how to use real options valuation models to assess the value of a company when it is viewed as a portfolio of projects.

The decision tree and binomial lattice methods are explained and the methods are used to compute the value of a biotechnology company, Agouron Pharmaceuticals, as the sum of the values of its current projects. Each project's value is found by using the decision tree and binomial lattice methods. The computed values of Agouron were then compared with actual market values at selected points in time during the development of Viracept, an Agouron drug used to treat HIV-positive patients.

The intention is to illustrate how real-options valuation methods can be used for financial analysis. Because the analysis uses data based on results from prior studies, the results here reflect the value of Agouron under the assumption that its situation matches that of a typical research-intensive pharmaceutical company in the 1980s and early 1990s. Some of the ways in which Agouron's situation differed from that assumed by this case study model are also discussed. A securities analyst with access to better information than that presented in this case study would be able to use these methods to improve these results.

The methods presented here provide stock analysts with a means to value biotechnology companies that have no current revenue. Financial analysts in pharmaceutical companies can use these methods to value projects and compare their relative worth for capital budgeting purposes. Executive managers of pharmaceutical companies can use these methods to increase their understanding of the value of their projects and convey that value to investors. Finally, for academic readers, this interesting case study provides empirical evidence of the usefulness of real-options valuation methodologies.

13.4.2 Valuation

The decision tree and binomial lattice methods that are used to value Agouron are now discussed.

13.4.3 Decision analysis method

In the first method a model was constructed with the purpose of calculating the expected net present value (ENPV) of that drug without taking into account growth options. ENPV is calculated as follows:

$$ENPV = \sum_{i=1}^{7} \rho_i \sum_{t=1}^{T} \frac{DCF_{i,t}}{(1+r_d)^t} + \rho_7 \sum_{j=1}^{5} q_j \sum_{t=1}^{T} \frac{CCF_{j,t}}{(1+r_c)^t} \tag{13.21}$$

Where:

- $i = 1, \ldots 7$ represents an index of the seven stages from discovery through post-approval described in Chapter 4

- ρ_i is the conditional probability that stage i is the end stage for a drug that has reached stage $i - 1$

- T is the time at which all future cash flows become zero

- DCF_{it} is the expected development stage cash flow at time t given that stage i is the end stage

- r_d is the discount rate for development cash flows

- $j = 1, \ldots 5$ is an index of quality for the drug (defined in Chapter 4)

- q_j is the probability that the drug is of quality j

- CCF_{jt} is the expected commercialization cash flow at time t for a drug of quality j

- r_c is the discount rate for commercialization cash flows.

The decision tree model is represented graphically in Figure 13.8.

The use of different discount rates for development cash flows and commercialization cash flows follows Myers and Howe (1997), who based their selection of rates partly on Myers and Shyam-Sunder (1996). Rates of 6% and 9% respectively were used for development cash flows and commercialization cash flows. The inflation estimate came from the average GDP deflator index over the five years prior to the date of the valuation. For example, in calculating the ENPV of an NME in 1994, the inflation estimate was 3.58%, resulting in nominal rates of r_d=9.8% and r_c=12.9%.

Table 13.7 shows the ENPV calculation of a discovery stage NME in spreadsheet form. The spreadsheet determines the present value of all possible end points and calculates the sum product of the present values and their respective probabilities. The values of each of the company's project ENPVs are adjusted according to the company's sharing agreements with partners and are then summed and divided by the shares and warrants outstanding to obtain a per-share value of the company. This method has several advantages. First, it is easy to construct and calculate because no NME will have more than 11 potential end points. Second, it is easy to communicate – through the use of either tables or decision trees. Third, it incorporates the notion of an abandonment option as well as the potential of five scenarios of successful outcomes. The decision tree method is limited, however, because continuous outcomes are discretized and, in this case, the growth options are ignored.

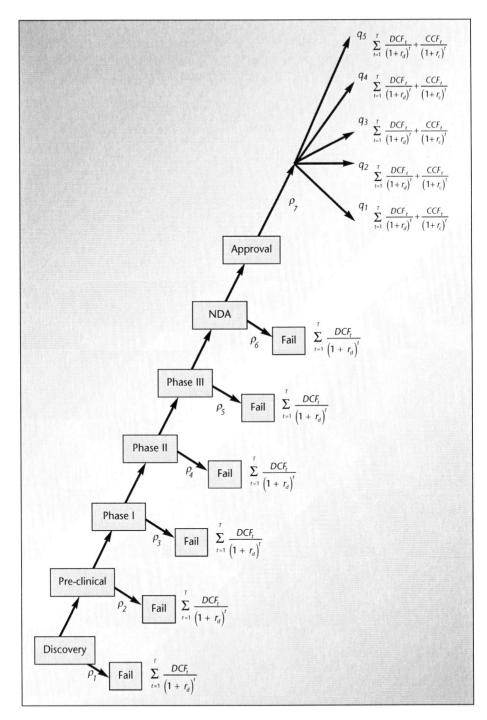

Figure 13.8 Decision tree for pharmaceutical development

Table 13.7 Expected net present value of a drug in the discovery stage in 1984 ($ in 000s)

End phase	i	j	(1) p_i	(2) q_i	(3) $\sum_{t=1}^{T} \dfrac{DCF_t}{(1+r_d)^t}$	(4) $\sum_{t=1}^{T} \dfrac{CCF_{it}}{(1+r_c)^t}$	[(4)–(3)]×(1)×(2)
Discovery	1		0.400		$2,004		–$802
Pre-clinical	2		0.060		13,203		–792
Clinical							
Phase I	3		0.135		15,223		–2,055
Phase II	4		0.203		19,455		–3,949
Phase III	5		0.030		29,810		–894
NDA submission	6		0.043		31,395		–1,350
Approval	7		0.129				
Quantity category							
Dog		1		0.10	31,395	$3,762	–356
Below average		2		0.10	31,395	4,230	–350
Average		3		0.60	31,395	33,011	125
Above average		4		0.10	31,395	315,819	3,669
Breakthrough		5		0.10	31,395	615,013	7,529
ENPV = $775							

13.4.4 Binomial method

Values for Agouron were found by using a binomial lattice with the addition of a growth option. The growth option is represented by a second binomial lattice for a research stage NME whose value at the time of the launch of the first NME is added to the last branch of the first NME's binomial tree. This approach takes into account Copeland's (1998) discussion of compound rainbow options and Amran and Kulatilaka's (1999) description of periodic revaluations of decisions through use of a binomial approach.

The key inputs to the binomial lattice are:

- the current value of the asset, A
- standard deviation of the asset value, σ
- risk-free rate, r
- amount and timing of the exercise prices
- probability of proceeding to the next stage of development.

The binomial lattice method takes the risk-neutral valuation approach advocated by Cox et al. (1979). Their key insight was that because the option values are independent of investor's risk preferences, the same valuations will be obtained even when everyone is assumed to be risk-neutral. This important assumption simplifies the calculations by eliminating the need to estimate the risk premium in the discount rate. Furthermore, as the focus is on the market (rather than a subjective or private) value of the project to Agouron, the use of risk-neutral pricing is justified by the same arguments made by Cox et al. for pricing financial assets that are traded directly in the market.

The value of Viracept at June 30 1994 is used to illustrate the calculation (all amounts are in millions). The current value of the asset, A, is found by discounting the value of the expected commercialization cash flows to time zero:

$$A = \sum_{j=1}^{5} q_i \sum_{i=1}^{T} \frac{CCF_{j,t}}{(1+r_c)^t} = \$\,123{,}921$$

An n – period binomial lattice of asset values is constructed period by period. In the first period there are two possible outcomes, Au and one of Ad. In the second period there are three possible outcomes, Au^{II}, Adu and Ad^{II}. The process of considering all possible combinations of up and down movements of the asset value for each period is continued until the nth period, which has end-branch values E_k, $k=1$, ... , $n+1$. Figure 13.9 illustrates a bionomial lattice that extends four periods.

Following Amran and Kulatilaka, u and d are set as $u=e^{\sigma}$ and $d=e^{-\sigma}$, where $e \equiv 2.718$ is the base of the natural logarithm. Because the goal is for the value of the NME to be able to grow from A to a maximum value of h after l years, $h = Au^l = Ae^{\sigma l}$ is required. The value h represents the present value of a breakthrough drug at the time of the launch. For $l = 12$ and $h = \$2{,}875{,}675$, $\sigma = (1/l)\ln(h/A) = 26\%$. Thus $u = 1.300$ and $d = 0.769$ for a 12-year binomial lattice with one price change a year.

The next step is to add in the value of the growth option. The idea is that engaging in the development of an initial NME is similar to purchasing a call option on the value of a subsequent NME. By engaging in development of the initial NME, the company earns the right but not the obligation to develop the subsequent NME. The assumptions for the growth option are identical to the first option. The value of the growth option at the time of the launch of the first NME is added to each of the E_k values of the first NME.

Once the binomial tree of asset values is completed, the next step is to calculate the possible payoffs and roll back the values using risk-neutral probabilities. The possible payoffs are calculated as:

$$P_k = Max\left[E_k(\theta_t - DCF_t, 0)\right] \tag{13.22}$$

where the value θ_t is the probability in year t of continuation to the next year t (in this case 75%), and DCF_t is the R&D payment that occurs in year t (in this case $1,619). Because the value at launch of the NME is large (even if the NME is a dog)

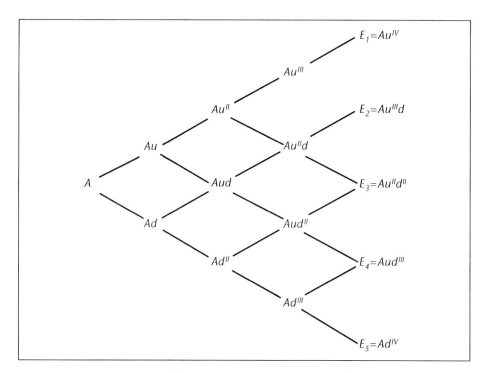

Figure 13.9 Four-period binomial lattice

relative to the last year's R&D payment (exercise price), the possible payoff is rarely going to be zero.

The P_k values are then rolled back by multiplying the adjacent values, such as P_1 and P_2 (denoted $V_{t+1,k}$ and $V_{t+1,k+1}$), by the respective risk-neutral probabilities p and $1-p$, the probability of continuation to the next year, and a discount factor $V_{t,k}$. The risk-neutral probabilities are computed as:

$$p = \frac{e^{r\Delta t} - d}{u - d} \tag{13.23}$$

where the risk-free rate, r, is the 10-year US T-bill rate, which was 7.09% in 1994. The result is $p = 0.573$. Table 13.8 shows the possible payoff values.

As the option values are rolled back, they are also adjusted for the probability of success at that stage of development and for the cost of development in that year. Thus the rollback option values are:

$$V_{t,k} = \max\left\{\left[V_{t+1,k}p + V_{t+1,k+1}(1-p)\right]e^{-r\sqrt{\Delta t}}\theta_t - DCF_t, 0\right\} \tag{13.24}$$

For a development stage having a duration of more than one year, θ_t is the probability of success for that stage in the final year of the stage and 1 for all other years.

Table 13.8 Possible payoff values for $DCF_t = \$1,619$, $\theta_t = 0.75$, and the value of growth option = $2,085

k	E_k	P_k
1	2,877,759	2,156,699
2	1,704,795	1,276,976
3	1,010,273	756,085
4	599,041	447,661
5	355,548	265,041
6	211,373	156,910
7	126,006	92,885
8	75,460	54,975
9	45,531	32,528
10	27,810	19,238
11	17,317	11,368
12	11,104	6,708
13	7,425	3,949

The amount DCF_t can be regarded as an annual exercise price. For example, $V_{12,1}$ is calculated as follows:

$$[\$2,156,669(0.573) + \$1,276,979(1 - 0.573)]0.9316(1) - 1,564 = \$1,657,654$$

This process is then continued until $V_{1,1}$ is reached, which is the value of the compound to the company.

13.4.5 Results

Kellogg and Charnes used the decision tree and binomial methods to calculate the values of Agouron for selected dates. Table 13.9 shows the values and, for comparison, the actual stock prices.

The dates were selected for their significance, as follows:

▨ June 1994 fiscal year end, Viracept was undergoing pre-clinical trials

▨ 20 October 1994, an announcement was made that Viracept would begin Phase I trials

▨ June 1995, fiscal year end

▨ June 1996, fiscal year end

▨ 23 December 1996, an announcement was made that Agouron was filing a new drug application for Viracept.

Table 13.9 Values of Agouron Pharmaceuticals computed from decision tree and binomial methods and actual stock prices, selected dates

Date	Actual stock price $	Method			
		Decision tree		Binomial	
		$	%	$	%
30/6/94	5.63	4.31	(−23.4)	4.51	(−19.8)
20/10/94	5.63	5.70	(+1.3)	5.87	(+4.3)
30/6/95	11.81	7.17	(−39.3)	8.51	(−27.9)
30/6/96	19.50	10.26	(−47.4)	10.44	(−46.5)
23/12/96	33.88	15.05	(−55.6)	15.45	(−54.4)

(Amount in parentheses is difference between actual stock price and method price)

During the period 30 June 1994 to 23 December 1996 Agouron had other projects in the discovery, pre-clinical or Phase I clinical trials stages of development, but Viracept was the only NME to make it to Phase II, III and new drug application submission during this period. The fiscal year end dates are helpful in assessing valuation because the 10-K reports filed with the US SEC indicate which projects were in the pipeline and their stages at the end of the fiscal year. Often the abandonment of a project is not announced. The result is that the potential of projects is included in a valuation when, in fact, those projects were not part of the product pipeline for valuations conducted on dates other than fiscal year ends.

Table 13.9 indicates that the methods valued Agouron relatively well when all the projects were in Phase I or earlier, but the calculated values deviated farther from the actual stock price as Viracept worked its way through the development process. Thus investors were apparently making different assumptions about the later development stages of this NME than they would have made for the typical NME specified in the model. If so, and if the model were adjusted for these assumptions, Kellogg and Charnes expect that the valuation given by the model would be much closer to the actual stock price.

Kellogg and Charnes believe that investors are making different assumptions for several reasons. First, these was (and remains) tremendous political pressure for the FDA to approve drugs for HIV-positive patients. Therefore, investors might have assumed that this drug would need less than eight years from beginning of Phase II to launch. And in fact, it took slightly less than two years. Second, an important assumption in the model is the probability distribution of the revenue stream. The model assumes an 80% probability that revenue will be under $100 million a year at peak. In fact sales of Viracept were more than $400 million during fiscal year 1998 (its first full year of sales) and were expected to be between $430 million and $440 million in fiscal year 1999. Again the market was likely to have assumed a different probability distribution for revenue. Finally the market is likely to have assumed a probability of approval for Viracept greater than that for a typical NME.

Kellogg and Charnes obtained decision tree valuations that were 19.1% higher and 15.9% lower than the stock price on 30 June 1996 and 23 December 1996 respectively by adjusting the assumptions in the decision tree model on those days:

- assuming a one-year duration for Phase III and one year for new drug application instead of three years each;
- assuming revenue distributions of 10% for dog, 10% for below average, 30% for average, 35% for above average, and 15% for breakthrough instead of 10%, 10%, 60%, 10% and 10% respectively;
- assuming a probability of success for Phase III of 90% instead of 85% and for new drug application 90% instead of 75%.

These adjustments are representative of what a securities analyst might have assumed in light of the target disease, political environment and competitive environment at the time. Making the same adjustments to the binomial model yielded similar results.

One other observation is that the inclusion of the growth option in the value of the initial option did not significantly increase the value of the initial option. The reason is that the value of a research project (assumed as the growth option) is low relative to the initial NME. This relatively low value is discounted more as a result of multiplying by the probabilities of success of the initial option.

13.4.6 Conclusion

The real options approach can be used to value a biotech company. Using average assumptions works well when the projects in the pipeline are in Phase I or earlier and little is known about the drug. As projects move into Phase II and later, more specific assumptions about time to launch, market size and probability of success will reflect the value of the company more accurately.

The Kellogg and Charnes Agouron example illustrates these conclusions. The methods used here to find the value of Agouron worked best in the early life of the Viracept project, when the use of industry averages for completion time and revenue streams was more easily justified. As Viracept progressed, the use of averages did not work as well. A financial analyst closely following the stock probably would have had better estimates of the important inputs for the later stages. Using the real options approach outlined here with better information could be a powerful addition to a security analyst's toolbox.

13.5 GROWTH, ADAPTION AND CONTINUITY

13.5.1 Industry evolution

Industry structures are dynamic and becoming increasingly so, driven by external factors such as demand, innovation and technology and internal factors such as competition and firm strategies. The result of these dynamics historically has been some firms adapting and thriving, while others decline and ultimately cease operations.

The fundamental capability for responding to external change is flexibility. Industry life cycles are not always predictable and are progressively shortening over time. The ability to recognize and adapt to external change is a source of competitive advantage and a critical success factor. The dynamics that establish a firm's competitive advantage can also be internal. Innovation generates internal change and can create a competitive advantage for a firm within an industry. While innovation is often defined in terms of new products or processes, it also includes new business models, management systems, organizations, value chains, processes, contractual relationships and investment approaches.

The ability to adapt to change implies that firms must compete concurrently within two time horizons. Firm value is a function of both managing operations in the short term while investing for the long term. An effective strategy maximizes value in the current environment through the productive use of existing resources and capabilities, while developing the resources and capabilities to adapt and compete in the future. These resources and capabilities are developed through investments in resource growth within or through acquisitions. Investments such as acquisitions have option like attributes, where downside losses can be limited to an initial outlay while creating an upside exposure. Internal investment in innovation such as research and development, new capacity and the development of technologies can also be structured as options on further investments.

The adaption option is a firm's capability to avoid adverse outcomes, and is a function of how a firm is structured and its ability to adapt, liquidate technologies and reinvent it's business model. A growth option is a firm's ability to adapt to positive outcomes. Adaption options limit a firm's downside risk, while growth options create potential upside opportunities for a firm. The growth option is the equivalent to the ability to place assets, or to grow net operating assets, and take advantage of new opportunities.

13.5.2 Industry evolution and climate change

Industrialization has had a significant influence on economic growth over the last two hundred years. A residual effect of the technologies and innovations that drove this growth has been the impact on climate. The same drivers of innovation also have the potential, however, to address the factors that contributed to climate change over the last two hundred years.

Schumpeter emphasized five industrial waves as innovations. The factory was an innovation that introduced scale, efficiency and standardization in production, and increased the output of many products. This increase in output intensified pressure on transportation infrastructure. Innovations in the steam engine produced the locomotive and steam driven ship, which along with the expansion of railways transformed the transportation of people and freight. The demand generated by railways resulted in the expansion of iron and then steel production. This created a surge in coal mining to supply the fuel for iron smelting and the developments in steam engines. Nineteenth-century railways also dramatically increased immigration, integrated markets and spurred other industries. This further created an enormous increase in the use of coal, iron, steel and petroleum based products.

Car manufacturing combined numerous innovations, including the internal combustion engine and new steel manufacturing methods. The mass production that followed in the early twentieth century led to lower prices and product access for the masses. Industry and agriculture also began using gasoline and diesel powered transportation and machinery.

The advent of electricity saw the development of long distance power transmission and the expansion of electricity utilities and grids. Electrical power became available for street lighting, residential use, public transport and industrial uses such as heat for the refining and manufacturing of copper and aluminum. Coal became the fuel source for electrical power with the development of coal fired electrical generating plants towards the end of the nineteenth century.

While industrialization has produced tremendous economic benefits, it has also generated significant burdens. Accompanying the Industrial Revolution was a massive growth in energy consumption, largely through the burning of coal, a fossil fuel. Since the onset of the Industrial Revolution societies have increased their use and dependence on fossil fuels such as oil, coal and gas, primarily to generate electricity and power transportation and industrial processes.

Fossil fuels when burned emit carbon dioxide (CO_2) and other gases. Many of these sources include direct emissions such as fossil fuel combustion and industrial process emissions, as well as indirect emissions such as electricity consumption. In the two hundred years since the start of the Industrial Revolution more than 2.3 trillion tons of CO_2 have been released into the atmosphere as a result of human activities. Of these emissions 50% have been released in the 30-year period from 1974 to 2004. Figure 13.10 illustrates the global carbon emissions trend from fossil fuel burning from 1751 to 2005.

Greenhouse gases (GHG) are atmospheric gases that are vital in moderating the Earth's temperature. CO_2 is the second most abundant greenhouse gas after water vapour. One influence of a gas on the greenhouse effect is its abundance. Carbon dioxide atmospheric concentrations have risen steeply since the start of the Industrial Revolution, with the largest increases coming after 1945. Figure 13.11 illustrates the rise in CO_2 concentration, which has increased from 280 parts per million (ppm) to 380 ppm since the start of the Industrial Revolution. Of this increase 50% occurred in over two hundred years from the start of the Industrial Revolution to around 1973. The remaining 50% increase took place in just over 30 years from 1973 to 2006. Other greenhouse gases include methane, which has increased 145% since the beginning of the Industrial Revolution, nitrous oxide, which has increased 15% over this period, and the man made gases such as CFCs, PFCs and HCFCs which did not exist in the atmosphere until the twentieth century.

Figure 13.12 illustrates a breakdown of the trends in global fossil fuel carbon dioxide emissions from human activity. Liquid and solid fuels accounted for 77.5% of the emissions from fossil fuel burning in 2004. Combustion of gas fuels such as natural gas accounted for 18.1%, or 1,434 million metric tons of carbon, of the total

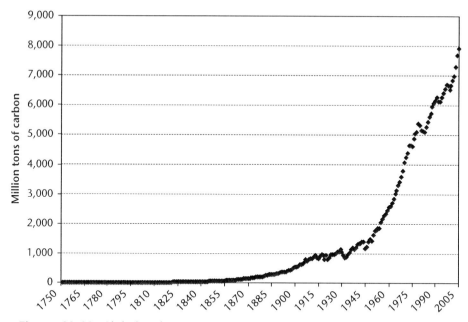

Figure 13.10 Global carbon emissions from fossil fuel burning, 1751–2005

Source: Compiled by the Earth Policy Institute from G. Marland, T.A. Boden and R.J. Andres, Global, Regional, and National Fossil Fuels CO_2 Emissions, in *Trends: A Compendium of Data on Global Change* (Oak Ridge, Tenn.: Carbon Dioxide Information Analysis Center (CDIAC), Oak Ridge National Laboratory, 2006), with 2004–05 data calculated using data from US Department of Energy, Energy Information Administration, International Energy Annual 2004 (Washington, DC: July 2006), BP Statistical Review of World Energy (London: 2006); CDIAC

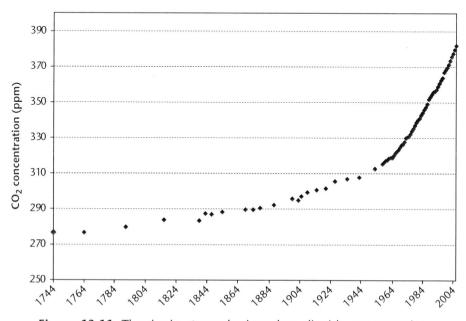

Figure 13.11 The rise in atmospheric carbon dioxide concentration from 1744 to 2004

Source: 1744–1953, historical CO_2 record from the Siple Station ice core, 1958–2005 Mauna Station

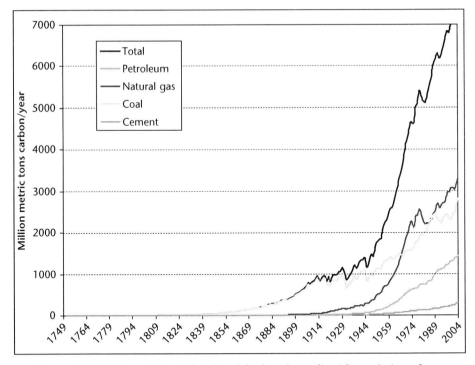

Figure 13.12 Trends in global fossil fuel carbon dioxide emissions from human activity, 1751–2004

Source: G. Marland, T.A. Boden and R.J. Andres, 2007, Global, Regional, and National CO_2 Emissions, in *Trends: A Compendium of Data on Global Change*. Carbon Dioxide Information Analysis Center, Oak Ridge National Laboratory, US Department of Energy, Oak Ridge, Tenn, USA.

emissions from fossil fuels in 2004, and reflects a gradually increasing global utilization of natural gas. Emissions from cement production, at 298 million metric tons of carbon in 2004, have more than doubled since the mid 1970s, and now represent 3.8% of global CO_2 releases from fossil fuel burning and cement production.

At the sector level the largest contributors to global emissions are electricity and heat (collectively 24.6%), land use change and forestry (18.2%), transport (13.5%) and agriculture (13.5%). The largest emissions by activity or end use come from road transport (9.9%), residential buildings (9.9%), oil and gas production (6.3%), agricultural soils (6.0%), commercial buildings (5.4%) and chemicals and petrochemicals (4.8%).

The influence of this change in atmospheric greenhouse gas concentrations is being reflected in the climate globally. Climate change refers to global warming, or the increase in average temperature in the contemporary climate. The consensus is that most of the increase in temperature since the middle of the twentieth century is associated with the rise in greenhouse gas concentrations from human activity. The impact of global warming is enormous, with its influences being felt on weather patterns, water resources, agriculture, disease rates, financial systems and national security. Projections based on current trends on average forecast that GHG emissions are expected to continue to increase by another 50% through to 2025.

13.5.3 Climate change and adaption

One of the great challenges of climate change today is that green house gas emissions result from almost every major function in society, including electricity production, transportation, agriculture and industry. Energy-related emissions account for about 60% of the world's total emissions. Fossil fuel combustion and transport are the major sources of the greenhouse effect and account for about half of global warming. Chemical products account for about 20%, which has been decreasing in recent years with regulation and the decline of halocarbons. Collectively the industry-related sectors spanning iron and steel and other industry comprise about 21% of global emissions.

Climate change and its associated issues generate systematic risks throughout the economy, and will have an influence on agriculture, energy, health, national income, regulation and reputations at the sector, industry and organizational levels. Sectors such as agriculture, fisheries, forestry, health care, insurance, real estate, tourism and the energy infrastructure will disproportionaly feel the effects of climate change. The consequence is that climate change is changing the competitive environment, with particular sectors, industries and organizations at risk more than others.

As there are uncertainties in regards to how climate change will impact future states of the world, any number of risk factors will have an impact on a firm. These include exposures to financial, commodity, legal, operational, strategic, technology, product, political and reputational risks. Climate change could include some or all of these risk factors depending on the nature of an organization's activities. Two specific risk categories can however be defined. Sector specific risk, the risk exposure to firms within a sector or industry, includes regulatory and physical risks, such as severe weather episodes directly effecting economic sectors such as insurance, agriculture, health care, real estate, water and tourism. Firm specific risk includes competitive, litigation and reputational risks, where a firm's operations could result in repercussions with consumers, shareholders and stakeholders.

Climate related events represent risks to all firms at some level. These can occur as events at regular frequencies and regionally, such as disruptions to agricultural or energy production, supply chains or infrastructure. Most firms have strategies and processes to manage the regular changes in climate. Firms in the future however cannot depend on climate conditions being consistent with those over the last century. Climate trends are anticipated to undermine the notion of continuity, with deviations both in general conditions and the number and severity of extreme weather events. Firms will therefore need to consider changes in the climate regime and factor them into their strategies and business models.

The Pew Center Global Climate Change Survey consensus is that the climate change issue is driving a major transition that will both alter existing markets and create new ones. As in any such transition there are risks and opportunities, with winners and losers. A growing number of firms in the Pew survey believe that inaction is no longer a viable option, with all firms affected in varying degrees and with some obligation to assess their business exposure and decide whether action is required. Some of the themes from the survey include strategic timing and the creation of business opportunities. There is general consensus among the surveyed firms that changes in the level of external awareness of climate risks, stronger government policy and consumer demand for cleaner and more efficient products make it essential to address the issue. Timing is therefore a critical issue for a firm in both responding to eventual regulation and identifying the options that provide the required flexibility. Firms that integrate climate change into their strategies and business models will be in the best position to take advantage of emerging opportunities and gain a competitive advantage in the changing market environment.

The climate change issue is persuading firms to take advantage of the opportunities that exist in providing the products, services and technologies needed to create a sustainable society. As a result firms are changing the way they design products and develop business models to reduce their exposure to environmental constraints and risks and maintain long-term competitiveness.

13.5.4 Growth options

Defining a firm's future growth investments as call options on real assets provides a framework for approximating the value of the firm's growth options. A firm's value (V) can be broken down into the current earnings stream, or the value of assets in place (VAIP), and the value within the firm's potential future investment choices, or the value of growth opportunities (VGO):

$$V = VAIP + VGO \tag{13.1}$$

The value of growth options VGO is a function of the value that is ultimately derived from a firm's investment choices, while the assets in place VAIP represents assets whose value is independent of these investments. This relationship can be extended by quantifying the firm's growth option value as the differential between its market value and capitalized current earnings stream. The capitalized current earnings stream symbolizes the firm's VAIP with no growth factored into value. The percentage of a firm's value that can be sourced to growth options, the growth option value (GOV), is therefore represented by:

$$GOV = VGO / V = [V - \text{current earnings/discount rate}] / V \tag{13.2}$$

This relationship can be extended through the use of the economic profit concept, which considers the firm's cost of capital. Earnings only take into account the cost of debt capital, whereas economic profit considers a firm's earnings or profit net of all capital costs, including the cost of equity:

$$EP = NOPAT - [CI * WACC] \tag{13.3}$$

where:

EP   =   economic profit
NOPAT =   net operating profits after tax
WACC   =   the weighted average cost of capital

The firm value (V) includes the book value of all equity, debt and other capital invested (CI) plus a residual factor over CI, the market value added (MVA):

$$V = CI + MVA \tag{13.4}$$

The firm's MVA represents the total NPV of all investments, which is the equivalent to the present value (PV) of the expected economic profit:

$$MVA = PV \text{ of expected EP} \tag{13.5}$$

Expected EP therefore is comprised of a current EP with no growth, plus a future residual factor that represents EP growth, that could be either positive or negative due to declining operations or unsuccessful investment outcomes.

$$PV \text{ of expected EP} = PV \text{ of current-level EP} + PV \text{ of EP growth} \tag{13.6}$$

The firm's value (V) can be redefined using the above equations:

$$V = CI + PV \text{ of current-level EP} + PV \text{ of EP growth} \tag{13.7}$$

Combining the first two terms CI and PV of current-level EP is the equivalent to the firm's value of assets in place VAIP in equation (13.1), while the firm's value of growth options is established through the PV of EP growth or VGO in equation (13.1). The firm's growth option value (GOV) is derived by solving equation (13.7) and then dividing the result with the firm value (V):

$$GOV = [V - CI - PV \text{ of current-level EP}]/V \tag{13.8}$$

where:

V   = the firm's market value
GOV   = the firm's growth option value as %
CI   = capital invested, the total book value of debt and equity
PV of current-level EP = EP perpetuity discounted by the firm's WACC

13.5.5 Wave Nouveau Materials case study

Wave Nouveau Materials Inc. operates in an industry and in markets where the climate change issue will have a significant influence. Government policy responses and consumer demand for more energy efficient products are creating an environment where new products and operational flexibility will define the winners and losers. Wave Nouveau's growth strategy is to develop products and expand into the environmental and alternative energy markets. The percentage of Wave Nouveau's value that can be sourced to growth options is examined using equation (13.8).

The market value of the firm (V) is derived using Geske's compound option model. The Geske model is specified as a call option on a stock which itself is an option on the firm's assets. The functional representation of this relationship is:

$$C = f(S,t) = f(g(V,t),t) \tag{13.9}$$

where C is the value of a call option, S is the firm's stock and V is the value of the firm. Transformations in the call option value are therefore defined as a function of transformations in firm value and time. The Geske model transforms the option's underlying state variable from the firm's stock to the firm's market value (V), or the total market value of the firm's equity and debt. The Geske specification therefore provides a measure of firm value when applied to listed options.

The Geske model is specified as:

$$C = VN_2 \left(h_1 + \sigma_V \sqrt{T_1 - t}, h_2 + \sigma_V \sqrt{T_2 - t}; p \right)$$
$$- Me^{-r_{F2}(T_2 - t)} N_2 \left(h_1, h_2; p \right) - Ke^{-r_{F1}(T_1 - t)} N_1 \left(h_1 \right) \tag{13.10}$$

where:

$$h_1 = \frac{\ln(V/V^*) + \left(r_{F1} - \frac{1}{2}\sigma_V^2 \right)(T_1 - t)}{\sigma_V \sqrt{T_1 - t}}$$

$$h_2 = \frac{\ln(V/M) + \left(r_{F2} - \frac{1}{2}\sigma_V^2 \right)(T_2 - t)}{\sigma_V \sqrt{T_2 - t}}$$

$$p = \sqrt{\frac{T_1 - t}{T_2 - t}}$$

V^* represents the firm's critical total market value where the firm's stock level S_{T1} is equal to the option strike K. S_{T1} is derived using Merton's definition of the Black–Scholes model where a firm's stock is the equivalent to an option:

$$S = VN_1 \left(h_2 + \sigma_V \sqrt{T_2 - t} \right) - Me^{-r_{F2}(T_2 - t)} N_1 \left(h_2 \right) \tag{13.11}$$

therefore, at $t = T_1$ when $S_{T1} = K$

$$S_{T1} = V^*_{T1} N_1 \left(h_2 + \sigma_V \sqrt{T_2 - T_1} \right) - Me^{-r_{F2}(T_2 - t)} N_1 \left(h_2 \right) = K \tag{13.12}$$

where h_2 is defined above. The variable M is the face value of a firm's debt, while T_2 represents the debt's duration. The addition of the M term to the Black–Scholes model reflects the effects of leverage, where leverage changes the firm's equity volatility. The Black–Scholes model assumes that a firm's equity volatility is not a function of the level of equity. The Geske model however considers that a firm's equity volatility has an inverse relationship with a firm's stock level. As a firm's stock level increases, the firm's leverage and stock volatility will fall, and the inverse of this relationship also holds. The Geske model also implies the volatility of a firm's total market value, conforms to Miller and Modigliani, and is the equivalent to the Black–Scholes model when the firm has no debt.

A summary of the Geske model variables follows:

C	=	current market value of a firm's stock call option
S	=	current market value of the a firm's stock
V	=	current market value of the firm's securities (debt + equity)
V^*	=	the critical total firm market value where $V >\ = V^*$ which implies $S >\ = K$
M	=	face value of market debt (debt outstanding for the firm)
K	=	strike price of the option
r_{Ft}	=	the risk-free rate of interest to date t
σ_V	=	the instantaneous volatility of the firm market value return
σ_S	=	the instantaneous volatility of the equity return
t	=	current time
T_1	=	expiration date of the option
T_2	=	duration of the market debt
$N_1\ (.)$	=	univariate cumulative normal distribution function
$N_2\ (...)$	=	bivariate cumulative normal distribution function
ρ	=	the correlation between the two option exercise opportunities at T_1 and T_2

Refer to Geske and Zhou (2007a) for further details of the application of the Geske model to firm value. Geske and Zhou (2007a) also provide details on calculating M, the firm notional debt.

The firm value (V) is found by solving the three equations (13.10), (13.11) and (13.12) simultaneously for three variables, the total firm market value (V), the total instantaneous volatility of V, σ_V, and V*, the value of (V) at a specific time in the future (T_1) where S_{T1} is equal to the strike price K of an option expiring at t_1. The option price C represents a quoted bid/ask average, near term at-the-money option price. At-the-money options are usually the deepest and most liquid.

The value for the firm market value (V) was solved using the following Wave Nouveau variables:

S	=	400 million, the total market capitalization
M	=	220 million, weighted duration of total debt

$$K = S_T$$
$$t_1 = \text{option expiry (1 month)}$$
$$T_2 = \text{debt duration (5 years)}$$
$$S = \$80.00$$
$$K = \$80.33$$
$$r = 5\%$$
$$\sigma_S = 15\%$$
$$C = \$1.38$$

Wave Nouveau Materials has 5 million shares outstanding, and as the firm's current stock price (S) per share is $80 the total market capitalization is $400 million. The firm's market value (V) was derived using equations (13.10), (13.11) and (13.12) as $571 million. The capital invested (CI) for Wave Nouveau is equal to the sum of the book value of debt ($220 million) and the book value of equity ($308 million) which equals $528 million. Table 13.10 summarizes the compound variables.

The total value of a firm is equivalent to the sum of the original investment, or the book value of debt and equity, and the MVA, or the NPV of the economic profit cash flows discounted at the weighted cost of capital. This is the equivalent to the total value of the firm as the sum of the original investment and the NPV of the sum of the residual earnings discounted at the cost of equity.

The residual earnings number in 4.5.3 is substituted for the economic profit parameter to arrive at Wave Nouveau materials growth option value. A WACC of 5% is used for illustration. The perpetuity for the PV of current-level EP is derived as the 2008 residual earnings of 12,000 divided by the WACC of 5%, which equals 316,800.

Wave Nouveau materials growth option value, or the firm's growth option value as a percentage of firm value is therefore:

$$GOV = [571 - 528 - 0.317]/571$$
$$= 7.48\%$$

Table 13.10 New Wave compound option variables for firm market value (V) (in $millions)

Compound option model variable	Description	Variable
Asset price (S)	total market capitalization	400
Strike underlying option (X₁)	face value of debt (M)	220
Strike option on option (X₂)	ATM option price × total equity	402
Time to maturity – option on option (t₁)	option maturity	0.08
Time to maturity – underlying option (T₂)	duration of M	5.00
Discount rate (r)	interest rate	5.00%
Volatility (σᵥ)	volatility	10.50%

13.6   THE FIRM ABANDONMENT OPTION

13.6.1   Overview

Economies are continually responding to the dynamics of competition, comparative prices and innovations in technology. Structural change results from shifts in the relative significance of the various technologies, economic factors and production processes that create economic output. Economic structural change inevitably creates successes and failures as certain industries grow while others decline.

The economic waves in Schumpeter's analysis are distinctive and determined by totally dissimilar industry clusters. Creative destruction is a function of market dynamics, where capital markets eliminate firms if their operations are not competitive or they operate within a discontinuous or declining industry. Discontinuities are the limits to durable firm operations that result from the inevitable transformations within an economy, and result from changes in the competitive environment, technology, consumer behaviour or government policy.

The waves that result from the dynamics of creative destruction will probably continue with increasingly shorter economic cycles, creating an external environment to which firms will need to adapt. A firm's assets will provide value if the going-concern value is greater than the firm's liquidation value. The continuity of organizations however over the twentieth century has changed considerably, with the firm life average in the S&P 90 Index declining from 65 to 10 years. Liquidation becomes the final alternative in the event where a firm is ultimately no longer competitive, and is the ultimate breakup of a going-concern.

If the capital markets believe that a firm's management is performing in the shareholders interest, the firm's market value should represent fair value. In the case where a firm is not performing well and the firm's equity does not reflect fair value, then the firm's investors may campaign for the breakup of the firm and the realized value returned to investors.

13.6.2   Investor valuation of the abandonment option

The value to investors in a firm's liquidation can be defined as an option to abandon the firm for its exit value. This option can be valued as an American put on a dividend-paying stock, where the stock price is the equivalent to a firm's cash flows and the strike is an uncertain exit value. The value of this option increases along with the firm's exit value. Structural change within an industry may therefore persuade investors to value and even exercise this option. The data in a firm's balance sheet can be used to value the option to abandon the firm for the exit value of its assets.

Berger, Ofck and Swary (BOS) (1996) present a method for assessing the value of the abandonment option. The following equation defines the relationship between firm value and those attributes that determine the value of the abandonment option:

$$\text{VALUE} = \text{PVCF} + P(\text{PVCF, EXIT, SDEV}) \qquad (13.13)$$

where:

VALUE = the firm's market value, or market capitalization
PVCF = the firm's present value of expected operating cash flows
P = American put option
EXIT = the firm's assets exit value
SDEV = standard deviation of the PVCF/EXIT ratio

The investors' decision to sell the firm is illustrated by equation (13.13), where firm market value is equal to the total of the value of expected operating cash flows and the abandonment option value. Equation (13.13) can be redefined as a function of the option's parameters, where the value of the abandonment option is expressed as the percentage by which firm value exceeds PVCF:

$$(VALUE/PVCF - 1) = P(1, EXIT/PVCF, SDEV) \tag{13.14}$$

The value of the abandonment option is now the percentage by which the value of equity is greater than the after-interest cash flows for a firm as a going-concern. There is no closed form solution available for the abandonment option, however the relationships in equation (13.13) can be used to determine the option payoff. This option value is a function of the EXIT/PVCF ratio, which is defined as the excess exit value. The excess exit value in equation (13.14) is a put option's stochastic strike with the underlying stock value normalized to one.

The abandonment option value is at-the-money when the excess exit value is equal to one, in which case a firm's exit value is equal to its expected cash flows. The option moves into-the-money with an increase in the exit value, and out-of-the-money with an increase in the value of the expected cash flows. There is therefore a positive relationship between a firm's excess value and the value of the abandonment option.

Observable exit values for the assets of firms as going-concerns are typically unavailable. The focus however is on the relationship between balance sheet data and the value of the abandonment option. BOS derive estimates for the relationships between the book value of assets and the exit value, and find on average exit values of $0.72 for receivables, $0.55 for inventory and $0.54 for fixed assets.

BOS derive the cash flow present value (PVCF) proxy through analysts' earnings forecasts. The use of earnings forecasts instead of cash flows has advantages and disadvantages. Earnings are measured for firms as going-concerns, and therefore a PVCF proxy based on earnings forecasts does not include the value of the abandonment option. Forecasts of distributed cash flows would include the expected cash flows from occurrences outside the going-concern assumption such as a firm's exit.

The disadvantage however is that earnings are not the same as cash flows, and therefore the present value of earnings from a going-concern should be modified to arrive at the PVCF as a going-concern. These adjustments are required as capital expenditures may not match depreciation and working capital growth is not deducted from earnings. No adjustments are made for changes in the capital structure as these are unknown.

The specification of the PVCF proxy is:

$$PVCF = \sum_{t=1}^{n} \frac{EARN_t}{(1+r)^t} + \sum_{t=n+1}^{10} \frac{EARN_2 * (1+gr)^{t-2}}{(1+r)^t} + \frac{EARN_2 * (1+gr)^9}{(r-tg)} *$$

$$\frac{1}{(1+r)^{10}} - CAPEX\ ADJUST - WC\ ADJUST \qquad (13.15)$$

where:

PVCF	= present value of analysts' forecasted going-concern cash flows.
$EARN_t$	= the forecast at year t of the analyst's after-interest earnings
r	= the expected CAPM return
gr	= five year earnings growth consensus forecast
tg	= the terminal growth rate for earnings
n	= number of years for the earnings forecast
t	= year index
CAPEX ADJUST	= present value of analysts' earnings forecasts adjustment down for the capital expenditures and depreciation difference
WC ADJUST	= present value of analysts' earnings forecast adjustment down for working capital growth

The *CAPEX ADJUST* is specified as:

$$CAPEX\ ADJUST = \frac{(CAPEX_0 - DEPN_0) / (r-g)}{EQUITY_0}$$

$CAPEX_0$	= the year 0 capital expenditures
$DEPN_0$	= the year 0 depreciation expense
$EQUITY_0$	= the year 0 market value of equity
g	= the growth rate of excess capital expenditures

The *WC ADJUST* is specified as:

$$WC\ ADJUST = \frac{([0.5(gr) + 0.5(tg)] * 0.5[NETWC_0]) / r}{EQUITY_0}$$

13.6.3 Sunset Examiner case study

The estimates in 4.6.4 provided the Sunset Examiner's exit value. The BOS dollar book exit value estimates for receivables, inventory and fixed assets were used for each book value component and the book values of debt and payables were deducted. A ratio of one was used for cash and short-term marketable securities in non-inventory current assets. The exit value is therefore equal to the sum $29.44 million.

The BOS PVCF equation as specified in equation (13.15) has five components. The first is the sum of the analysts' discounted expected earnings forecasts out to two years. The second term represents the sum of the discounted earnings forecasts from three to ten years based on analysts' long-term five-year earnings growth projections. The third variable is the present value of a perpetuity for earnings greater than ten years, with the assumption of a constant nominal terminal growth rate (tg).

The fourth component deducts an adjustment for the net present value of future capital expenditure excesses after subtracting future depreciation. Earnings forecasts are not cash flows that can be distributed, and growth in earnings usually requires capital investments that are greater than depreciation. BOS arrive at a value of 12% for the capital expenditure adjustment. The fifth item, the working capital adjustment, is a similar adjustment representing the present value of the growth in working capital. BOS derive a value of 5.5% for the working capital adjustment.

Table 13.11 illustrates Sunset Inc.'s condensed income statements. The decline in circulation has created a downward trend in net income, while advertising has held up due to Sunset Inc.'s online venture.

Table 13.11 Condensed income statements for Sunset Inc. ($000)

	2005	2006	2007	2008
Revenues:				
Advertising	120,000	120,000	120,000	120,000
Circulation	35,000	33,000	32,000	30,000
Total revenue	155,000	153,000	152,000	150,000
Total operating costs	140,000	140,000	140,000	140,000
Net income	15,000	13,000	12,000	10,000

The following table illustrates the calculation of the first two terms in equation (13.15) using an earnings forecast of $9 million, which is based on a decline in circulation revenues from $30 million to $29 million for 2009. The earnings forecast to ten years and perpetuity for earnings from year eleven assume a constant 2% nominal terminal growth rate. The present value of future cash flows is then derived by adjusting the present value of future earnings with the deduction of the present value of future capital expenditures minus future depreciation and working capital growth. A CAPM discount rate of 5% is used for illustration.

The total of the sum for each of the first two terms, $16.7 million and $113.9 million, and the third term perpetuity of $17.5 million results in the unadjusted PVCF of $148.1 million. Deducting the capital expenditure adjustment of $17.8 million and the working capital adjustment of $8.2 million provides an adjusted PVCF of $122.2 million.

Table 13.12 PVCF earnings projections

Year	1st term	df	2nd term	gr
2009	8,571,429	0.9524	–	1.0200
2010	8,163,265	0.9070	–	1.0404
2011	–	0.8638	11,056,328	1.0612
2012	–	0.8227	11,841,328	1.0824
2013	–	0.7835	12,682,062	1.1041
2014	–	0.7462	13,582,488	1.1262
2015	–	0.7107	14,546,845	1.1487
2016	–	0.6768	15,579,671	1.1717
2017	–	0.6446	16,685,827	1.1951
2018	–	0.6139	17,870,521	1.2190
2019	–	0.5847	–	1.2434

Note: The 3rd term in equation (13.15) is the perpetuity which is derived as $17,520,119.

   BOS's research provides results for the variables in the valuation of the abandonment option. The median sample value of the abandonment option is 11.5% with an excess exit value of −0.761. Using the Sunset Inc. example, the market capitalization value of the firm is $136.2 million and the excess exit value is −0.759. As the exit value of $29.4 million is less than the PVCF of $122.2 million, the value of the abandonment option is out-of-the-money for investors.

   The factors that can influence the value of the abandonment option include the degree of specialization in a firm's assets. The option has greater value when the assets are less specialized. Current assets are less specialized than fixed assets and therefore provide greater option value, while land is less specialized than other fixed assets and also provides greater option value.

   The model in equation (13.15) was stressed to identify the sensitivity of the model variables. The at-the-money value of the abandonment option was derived by adjusting the advertising revenue forecast, the discount rate and growth rate forecast. The earnings forecast for 2009 is adjusted down to $2.2 million based on a decline in 2009 advertising revenues of approximately 5.7%. The discount rate was increased to 8% and the growth forecast lowered to minus 1%. Table 13.13 illustrates the calculation of the stressed first two terms in equation (13.15) using an earnings forecast of $2.2 million, the 8% discount rate and growth forecast of minus 1%.

   The sum of the first two terms, $3.9 million and $27.4 million, and the third term perpetuity of $4.3 million resulted in an unadjusted PVCF of $35.6 million. Subtracting the $4.3 million capital expenditure adjustment and $2 million working capital adjustment resulted in an adjusted PVCF of $29.4 million. As the exit value is $29.4 million the stressed abandonment option is therefore at-the-money. The PVCF was found to be most sensitive to declines in advertising revenue and therefore had a significant influence on the value of the abandonment option.

Table 13.13 At-the-money abandonment option PVCF earnings projections

Year	1st term	df	2nd term	gr
1	2,027,778	0.9259	–	0.9900
2	1,877,572	0.8573	–	0.9801
3	–	0.7938	2,676,831	0.9703
4	–	0.7350	2,862,068	0.9606
5	–	0.6806	3,060,123	0.9510
6	–	0.6302	3,271,883	0.9415
7	–	0.5835	3,498,298	0.9321
8	–	0.5403	3,740,380	0.9227
9	–	0.5002	3,999,214	0.9135
10	–	0.4632	4,275,960	0.9044
11	–	0.4289	–	0.8953

Note: The 3rd term perpetuity value from equation (13.15) is $4,319,151.

13.7   MODULARITY

13.7.1   A modular design

Baldwin and Clark (2000) defined modularity as modularity in design, or the creation of a modular system, modularity in production, which refers to separating complex production tasks into simpler processes, and modularity in use, which relates to the potential to organize elements to arrive at a design configuration that reflects consumer requirements.

A design is defined as a complete description of a product, and consists of a set of parameters and their physical or logical interdependencies. A module is a unit that has strong interrelated parameters between itself while having a relatively weaker interconnection to parameters in other units. A modular design consists of a hierarchical set of modules that are bound by specific design rules. The tasks of design connect the input and outputs to a design process.

These design rules are organizational principles that each module follows to preserve compatibility with other modules and the system itself. The individual modules sit within a hierarchical framework and are assigned structural functions according to their location within the framework. Hierarchical modules are located at the top level of a modular design, and establish a set of design rules, or visible information, for hidden dependent and connected modules that are located at a lower level in the hierarchy.

Figure 13.13 illustrates a simplified modular design. The size of a module's set of implied design rules imposed on lower modules in the hierarchy is a function of its position within the modular structure, with those modules higher up imposing a larger set of design rules. The hidden modules can change within the specific design

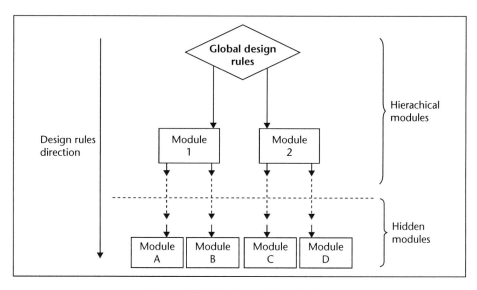

Figure 13.13 A modular design
Source: Gamba and Fusari (working paper)

rules imposed by the higher modules. More than one hierarchical level of modules can also exist within a complex design.

Modularity in design creates options in development, while modularity as a process facilitates design specialization. These attributes create the capabilities to manage complexity, as modularity breaks down a system into a set of modules while the design rules combine the modules into a hierarchical structure. This capability distributes the design and implementation of each specific unit, allowing specialization and independence within the design rules that bind the modules to a hierarchical structure while facilitating the aggregation of the modules into a system.

13.7.2   Design and value

Value within the context of modular design is defined as a measure the worth of an artifact within a specific social context. Artifacts and design can be framed in terms of a search for value, where value flows from designers' ideas to product markets and capital markets. Value is the underlying driver of designers endeavouring to create new artifacts, which collectively represent innovation and the dynamics within an economic system. This search for value is framed by valuation, contracting and guidance technologies. Valuation identifies, transfers and determines wealth. Contracting facilitates the formation and continuation of firms, while guidance provides the means to organize collectives of people toward specific goals. Value is the catalyst for design choices, and these choices are also consistent with maximizing value.

A single module project is an interconnected structure, with linked parameters that cannot be changed without influencing the others, and with limited design information on the relationships between them. As a result the project can only be considered and improved upon in its entirety. This single module project with an interconnected structure is a non–modular system, with the value of its interconnected structure defined as:

$$V_1 = S_0 + E\left(X_N^+\right) \tag{13.16}$$

where V_1 is the value of the one module design that has N tasks, S_0 is the system which for illustration equals zero, and X is a random normally distributed variable with a mean of zero and a variance equal to $\sigma^2 N$. Equation (13.16) defines the value of a new design when it adds value to the existing design, which is represented by the superscript $+$. This single module project can also be valued using NPV techniques, where project redesign adds value if it has a positive NPV, which is the new marginal value minus the research, development and implementation costs over the NPV of the existing design.

The functional design of a non-modular system is the result of information on interdependencies being discovered during the design, which in most cases results in a design that lacks flexibility. An alternative is to initially identify design rules and separate the design tasks between independent modules. The modular system that ultimately results from this alternative creates flexibility through the ability to further modify and enhance the underlying module designs. If a design process is divided into j independent modules, with N the number of tasks staying constant, then the expected value of the modular design V_j is:

$$V_j = S_0 + E(X_1^+) + E(X_2^+) + \ldots + E(X_j^+) \tag{13.17}$$

where X_i is the marginal added value of the i-th module to the complete system. Each module in equation (13.17) can be evaluated against a benchmark, where a value greater than zero will add value, or the existing design can be retained if the value is equal to or less than zero.

The design decision can therefore be framed as value choices between a modular versus a pre-determined design. A modular design can offer customization at a point in time or selective upgrading over a period of time. An interconnected design process generally offers a single option while a modular design offers multiple options. Modularity generates design options, and in doing so offers value alternatives for a given set of designs.

13.7.3 The operators

A structure adapts over time through the progressive transformation of that structure. In due course this process of consecutive structural modifications identifies a fundamental set of modifiers or operators. The recurring action of these operators generates recognizable modification sequences, and therefore a structure's evolution can be described by the action of these operators on the structure itself.

The dynamics within a modular design are identified by six modular operators, which generate development paths for a design structure and differentiate a modular from a non–modular system design. These six operators describe the evolution from an interrelated design to a modular design structure. The operators are classified as splitting a design and tasks into two or more modules, the substitution of modules, augmenting a system through the addition of modules, the exclusion of modules from a system, inversion which generates new design rules, and the porting of modules into other systems.

The splitting and substitution operators are applicable to modular and non–modular designs. The splitting operator is the hub of modularity, as it generates a set of independent modules from an interrelated design. The other four modular operators however are applicable only to modular systems. The dynamics of a modular system are achieved through the application of the six operators, with each having the potential to be utilized locally without affecting the remaining structure.

The valuation of a modular system is achieved through the six operators. A feature of modularity is that the value of each operator can be aggregated to value a modular structure or process. A modular operator can also be defined as an option to add value to a design. The operator value alternatives are the equivalent to random payoffs that can be transformed into single-point values. If the function of these operators is the creation of value, then the modularity concept can be applied to investment decisions and extended using real options theory.

The six operators conceptually are options in the design of a modular system, and identifying the operators within real options theory provides a value framework for the modularization process. This is achieved by specifying specific option models for the six modular operators. The following describes a modular real options framework proposed by Gamba and Fusari that specifies an option valuation approach for each operator, which when combined can evaluate a modular design valuation and also describe the interactions among the operators.

13.7.3.1   The splitting operator

A system or a module can be divided into two or more modules when the appropriate design rules are available and parameters are independent. The splitting operator serves the function of creating a modular design from an interconnected system, or splitting a module into two or more modules within a modular design where each module has independence from the other modules. At least two types of splitting operators can be defined. The first concerns an initial design that is interconnected such that the challenge is isolating independent components to convert into modules. The second involves an interconnected design structure in which a designer can identify the parameter links, in which case the design has been rationalized such that the modules that can be split from the interconnected system can be identified. In the second case the current design value also serves as a benchmark for decisions on new module versions.

Figure 13.14 illustrates the application of the first splitting operator to an interconnected design that is split into two modules. The design is split at $t = \sigma_{spl}$, where the designer has identified the design rules and the modules within a modular structure. The components are illustrated above the time line and the design evolution below the time line. Figure 13.15 illustrates the splitting operator applied to a rationalized design, where potential modules are defined at the start of the modularization process. Splitting a rationalized design requires the creation of design rules at $t = \tau_{spl}$. Research then starts on each module to improve the system at $t = \tau_{sub1}$ and $t = \tau_{sub2}$.

The valuation of an interconnected structure consists of two state variables, the total system value W_t before the redesign, and W_t^* after the redesign. Assuming the system design can be split into J modules, W_t^* represents the sum of the individual module values W_t^{*j} for $j = 1, 2, \ldots, J$. The marginal value of redesigning the system is therefore $V_t = W_t^* - W_t$, or the modularized redesign value minus the costs associated with the redesign being greater than the existing value of the interconnected project.

The value of the first splitting operator type is:

$$F_{spl}(t, V_t, J) = \sup_{\tau_s \in H(t,T)} \left\{ E_t \left[e^{-r(\tau_s - t)} \Pi_{spl}(\tau_s, V_{\tau_s}, J) \right] \right\} \tag{13.18}$$

with a payoff function equal to:

$$\Pi_{spl}(t, V_t, J) = \max \left\{ V_t - \sum_{j=1}^{J} C_j - C_s(J), 0 \right\} \tag{13.19}$$

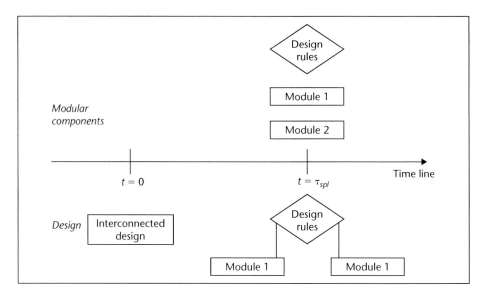

Figure 13.14 A splitting operator
Source: Gamba and Fusari (working paper)

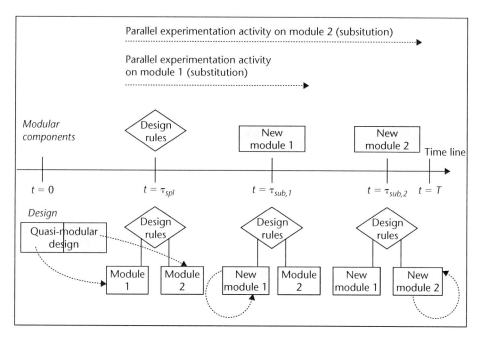

Figure 13.15 A splitting operator in a rationalized system
Source: Gamba and Fusari (working paper)

where C_j is defined as the cost of the j-th module, and $C_S(J)$ represents the design rule costs for the modularized design as a function of J modules in the redesign. Equation (13.19) is the equivalent to a call option with a payoff on V_t, with the assumptions that the existing system has not been rationalized and only one new module version is being taken into account.

The splitting operator can be generalized to the second splitting operator type by relaxing these two assumptions. This splitting operator is defined as rationalized, where each individual J-th module that can result from splitting the interconnected system can be valued in isolation. The marginal value of a modular project is therefore the sum of the marginal module values.

In this second case the marginal value of redesigning the system is $V_t^j = W_t^{*j} - W_t^j$, where W_t^j is the total value before the redesign, and W_t^{*j} the total value after the redesign. The total marginal value from splitting the interconnected system is:

$$V_t = \sum_{j=1}^{J} V_t^j \tag{13.20}$$

The option to split a rationalized interconnected system would result from an improvement in at least one module. Therefore the payoff from the splitting operator in equation (13.19) is:

$$\Pi_{spl}(t, V_t, J) = \max\left\{ \sum_{j=1}^{J} F_{sub}(t, V_t^j) - C_s(J), 0 \right\}, \tag{13.21}$$

where F_{sub} is defined in section 13.7.3.2 below. The splitting operator F_{spl} in the second case is a complex compound American option on the maximum of multiple marginal call options, and therefore F_{spl} is an option on a portfolio of options.

13.7.3.2 The substitution operator

The substitution operator has the primary role of improving the system, and can function in both interconnected and modular structures. The operator when applied to an interconnected system creates a new interconnected project, while within a modular structure the operator influences the individual modules. The substitution operator facilitates the ability to exchange a module that is an improvement for the same module type. This ability to enhance an existing module without redesigning the whole structure is a primary incentive for modularizing a system.

Figure 13.16 illustrates the substitution operator. The operator provides the ability for a new module to replace an existing one by performing K experiments over a given timeframe. At $t =$ zero different versions of potential replacement modules are explored, until ultimately at $t = \tau_{sub}$ the most suitable alternative module is substituted for the existing module. Again the components are illustrated above the time line and the design evolution below the time line.

Given a time horizon T to replace a module or interconnected design over a predetermined number of trials K, and W_t^k the total value after the redesign for the k-th implementation, then $V_t^k = W_t^{*k} - W_t$ is the marginal value from the k-th trial.

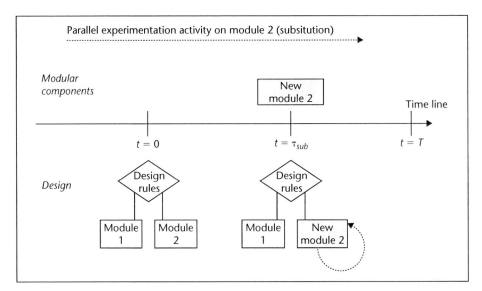

Figure 13.16 A substitution operator
Source: Gamba and Fusari (working paper)

For the vector of marginal module values $V_t = (V_t^1, \ldots, V_t^K)$, the substitution operator value is:

$$F_{sub}(t, V_t, K) = \sup_{(k,\tau)} \left\{ E_t \left[e^{-r(\tau - t)} \Pi_{sub}(\tau, V_\tau^k, K) \right] \right\} \tag{13.22}$$

where the control is (k, τ), k denotes the trial version selected, and $\tau \in H(t, T)$ is the decision stopping time.

The payoff for the substitution operator is:

$$\Pi_{sub}(t, V_t^k, K) = \max \left\{ V_t^k - Q - \sum_{k=1}^{K} I_k - C_k, 0 \right\} \tag{13.23}$$

where Q is defined as the visibility cost which can equal zero when the module is hidden, C_k is the marginal cost of implementing the selected new module version, and I_k represents the cost to run experiments on the k-th module versions. The substitution operator value reduces to a simple call option when $K = 1$.

If the number of K trials is chosen optimally ex ante then the substitution operator value becomes:

$$F_{sub}(t, V_t) = \max_{K \in N} \left\{ \sup_{(k,\tau)} \left\{ E_t \left[e^{-r(\tau - t)} \Pi_{sub}(\tau, V_t^k, K) \right] \right\} \right\} \tag{13.24}$$

13.7.3.3 The augmenting operator

The augmenting operator enhances a design through the addition of modules. In contrast to the splitting and substitution operators, the augmenting operator only applies to modular systems. Modular systems have pre-existing design rules and a modular structure, and therefore the addition of modules through the augmenting operator does not change the existing design rules for that structure. Figure 13.17

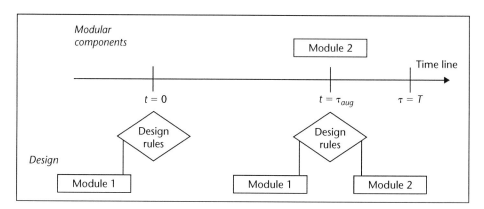

Figure 13.17 An augmenting operator
Source: Gamba and Fusari (working paper)

illustrates the augmenting operator, where a modular design is augmented at t equals τ_{aug} with the formation of a new module, module 2, that expands the total design's functionality.

Under the assumptions of a finite time horizon T for a module addition and a single version of the $(J+1)$-th module, the marginal value of the $(J+1)$-th module to the system is $V_t^{J+1} = W_t^{J+1} - W_t^J$, where W_t^J is the total design value before the addition of a module, and W_t^{J+1} is the total design value after the addition of a module, The augmenting operator value from an additional module is:

$$F_{aug}(t, V_t^{J+1}) = \sup_{\tau \in H(t,T)}\left\{E_t\left[e^{-r(\tau-t)}\Pi_{aug}(\tau, V_\tau^{J+1})\right]\right\} \tag{13.25}$$

where $\Pi_{aug}(\tau, V_\tau^{J+1}) = \max(V_\tau^{J+1} - C_{J+1}, 0)$, and C_{J+1} represents the research and development cost for the $(J+1)$-th module. The augmenting operator payoff is the equivalent to a call option on V_t^{J+1} with the strike price of C_{J+1}.

13.7.3.4   The excluding operator

The excluding operator allows the creation of a minimal design with the potential to increase a modular system through the augmenting operator if the initial design proves to be successful at a later stage. The augmenting and excluding operators are therefore frequently combined. As in the case of the augmenting operator, the excluding operator is applied only to modular systems and not interconnected systems. As a modular structure and its design rules are set initially, the excluding operator involves the specification of new design rules in contrast to the augmenting operator. The excluding and augmenting operators offer both strategic and financial capabilities. The excluding operator reduces the potential impact of failure for a modular design, while the initial exclusion of modules from the modular system facilitates the subsequent funding of an expansion through the cash flows generated by the initial operating design.

Figure 13.18 illustrates the excluding operator. The operator permits the implementation at $t = \tau_{excl}$ of an initial minimal design that has an option to augment the modular system at a later stage if market conditions turn favourable. The whole modular structure is established, although not implemented, at $t = $ zero. Module two is designed at $t = $ zero, however its implementation within the modular structure is delayed until $t = \tau_{aug}$.

The value of the excluding operator is the equivalent to a compound American option. The excluding operator is valued recursively using the assumptions of T_o representing the time horizon for the application of the set of design rules, and T_ω the time horizon to finish the design. The option to add a second module is derived by applying the augmenting operator:

$$F_{aug}(t, V_t) = \sup_{\tau \in H(t,T_\omega)}\left\{E_t\left[e^{-r(\tau-t)}\Pi(\tau, V_\tau)\right]\right\} \tag{13.26}$$

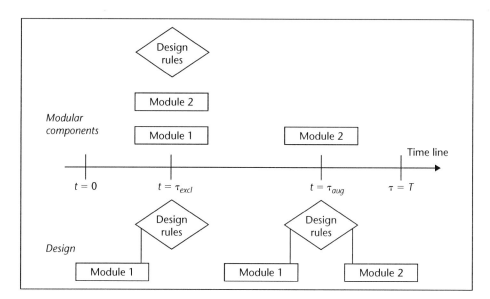

Figure 13.18 An excluding operator
Source: Gamba and Fusari (working paper)

where $\Pi(\tau, V_\tau) = \max(V_\tau - C, 0)$, and C represents the realized cost of an additional module. The value of the excluding operator is therefore:

$$F_{excl}(t, W_t, V_t) = \sup_{\tau \in H(t,T_\alpha)} \left\{ E_t \left[e^{-r(\tau-t)} \Pi_{excl}(\tau, W_\tau, V_\tau) \right] \right\} \qquad (13.27)$$

where

$$\Pi_{excl}(\tau, W_\tau, V_\tau) = \max \left\{ W_t - C_w - C_s + F_{aug}(\tau, V_\tau), 0 \right\}.$$

C_w represents the realized costs for the minimal system, and C_s the cost associated with the design rules for the whole system.

13.7.3.5 The inversion operator

The inversion operator describes the rationalization of a design through the consolidation of common functions distributed across a structure into a single module. Figure 13.19 illustrates the inversion operator. In the left panel the comparable components are identified, while in the second panel the splitting operator is used to isolate the identified components, and finally in the right panel a new module is created which is connected to other common modules.

A module can be located at a higher hierarchical level by inverting its rank within the original design hierarchy. The tradeoffs with the inversion operator are reduced flexibility due to the additional of a new hierarchical level, while on the other hand economies of scale can be achieved.

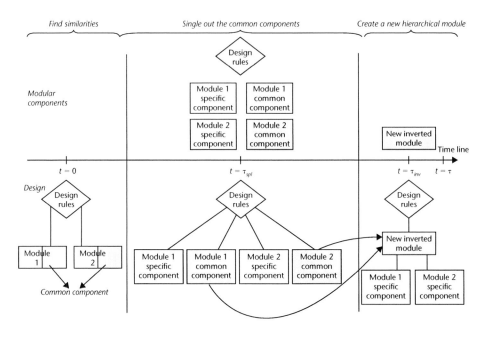

Figure 13.19 An inversion operator
Source: Gamba and Fusari (working paper)

The value of the inversion operator is derived as:

$$F_{inv}(t, V_t) = \sup_{\tau \in H(t,T)} \left\{ E_t \left[e^{-r(t-t)} \Pi_{inv}(\tau, V_\tau) \right] \right\} \tag{13.28}$$

where

$$\Pi_{inv}(t, V_t) = \max \left\{ V_t^{\hat{i}} - C_{\hat{i}} - Q - \sum_{j=1}^{J} F_{sub}(t, V_t^j), 0 \right\} \tag{13.29}$$

13.7.3.6 The porting operator

The porting operator is used in situations where a module's functionality can be applied to a different structure. The module in this case has a set of independent parameters that can function outside the existing design rules, and can therefore be attached to other designs.

Figure 13.20 illustrates the porting operator. The porting process has three steps, the discovery of the module, the splitting of that module into one that is independent of the current design and one connected to the current design, and finally the porting of the identified module to an outside structure.

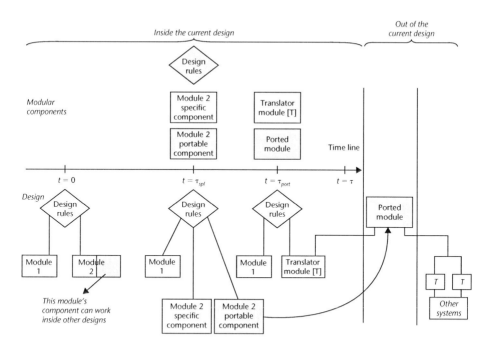

Figure 13.20 A porting operator
Source: Gamba and Fusari (working paper)

The value of the porting operator, which takes into account the marginal value of all the systems for which the module can be used, is:

$$F_{port}(t, V_t) = \sup_{\tau_p \in H(t,T)} \left\{ E_t \left[e^{-r(\tau_p - t)} \Pi_{port}(\tau_p, V_{\tau_p}) \right] \right\}$$

where

$$\Pi_{port}(t, V_t) = \max \left\{ V_t^{\hat{P}} - C_{\hat{P}} - Q - \sum_{i=1}^{M} R_i - \sum_{i=1}^{M} F_{sub}(t, V_t^i), 0 \right\}. \tag{13.30}$$

$V_t^{\hat{P}}$ in equation (13.30) is the marginal value associated with the realization of the ported module, and represents the difference between the new design value $W_t^{\hat{P}}$, and the initial value of the modules in the porting process, $W_t = \sum_{i=1}^{M} W_t^i$. $C_{\hat{P}}$ represents the associated research and realization cost, $-\sum_{i=1}^{M} F_{sub}(t, V_t^i)$ is the opportunity cost associated with the decision of avoiding the independent improvement for each system which reduces the flexibility within the modular structure, $\sum_{i=1}^{M} R_i$ is the related cost of creating the translator modules for the external systems, and Q is the visibility cost from a redesign of the interface for the internal translator module.

13.7.4   The least-squares Monte Carlo numerical method

Numerical methods are used for the valuation of the modular operators due to their optimal stopping characteristics and the complexities within a modular design. The operator valuations in section 13.7.3 are addressed by solving the following stochastic optimal control in the form of:

$$F(t, V_t) = \sup_{\tau, u}\left\{ E_t\left[e^{-r(\tau - t)}\Pi(\tau, V_\tau, u)\right]\right\} \tag{13.31}$$

where V_t represents the dimension n, $\Pi(t, V_t)$ the immediate exercise payoff for the operator, $\tau \in H(t,T)$, $H(t,T)$ is the set of stopping times within $[t,T]$, and $u \in U(\tau, V_\tau)$ is a control selected at τ.

Dynamic programming is used for solutions to these types of problems, by working recursively from the end date T to the current date to solve the Bellman equation for all decision dates. The function F is estimated by dividing the time interval $[t,T]$ for a given number of steps of length equal to dt. The Bellman equation is specified as:

$$F(t, V_t) = \max\left\{ \max_{u \in U(t,V_t)} \Pi(t, V_t, u), \Phi(t, V_t)\right\}$$

where $\Phi(t, V_t)$ represents the value associated with continuation, which is the equivalent to the conditional expectation under the EMM of the operator value for the following step discounted to time t at the risk-free rate:

$$\Phi(t, V_t) = E_t\left[e^{-rdt}F(t + dt, V_{t+dt})\right].$$

The continuation value is derived using the least-squares Monte Carlo (LSM) numerical method, which allows for multivariate state variables. Paths for the relevant state variables are generated using a Monte Carlo simulation procedure for all decision dates to estimate the value of continuing. This is achieved through a least-squares regression on the discounted future payoffs for a linear combination of a set of functions representing the simulated state variables at time t:

$$\Phi(t, V_t) \approx \sum_{\ell=1}^{L} \hat{\beta}_\ell \varphi_\ell(V_t)$$

where L represents the number of functions in the regression, $\hat{\beta}_\ell$ the estimated coefficient relative to the ℓ-th function, and φ_ℓ a specific function for the state variables. Dimensional problems are mitigated through a complete set of polynomials of degree p in n variables, which defines the functions $\varphi_\ell(\cdot)$. The number of coefficients β_ℓ estimates required therefore increases polynomially with the state space dimension n.

13.7.5   Testing the LSM method for individual modular operators

In the numerical experiments the alternative power, Chebyshev, Hermite and Legendre polynomials up to degree $p = 3$ are used, with no substantial difference in the numerical results obtained with each choice. Furthermore the simplifying assumption was adopted that the state variables of the valuation problem are the incremental values V_t, instead of the actual state variables W_t and W_t^* to keep dimensionality low and to be able to assess the reliability of the algorithm, that is, to assess the convergence to numerical results obtained using a binomial lattice in this first set of experiments.

The benchmark value estimates were obtained using the Cox et al. (1979) approximation for the valuation of the augmenting operator, which is a one dimensional problem, while for the remaining operators which are essentially multivariate problems the adjusted generalized log-transformed (AGLT) binomial method by Gamba and Trigeorgis (2007) was adopted. This required the assumption that the state variable V_t, instead of W_t^* and W_t, follows the correlated geometric Brownian motion (GBM):

$$dV_t^j = \alpha_j V_t^j dt + \sigma_j V_t^j dB_t^j,$$

where α_j is the risk-neutral drift of the process, σ_j is the standard deviation and dB_t^j is the increment of a Brownian motion under the EMM.

Monte Carlo sample paths were generated using an Euler discretization of the stochastic equation defining the GBM. These experiments were intended to illustrate the consistency of the proposed numerical methods with an accurate valuation method based on binomial lattices in conjunction with a two point Richardson extrapolation.

Five paradigmatic problems related to splitting, substitution, augmenting, exclusion, and porting were analysed. In the following the inversion operator was omitted, as the mathematical structure of the problem is similar to the porting operator.

Table 13.14 illustrates the parameters used to test the consistency of the numerical routines based on the LSM method. V_0 is the initial value of the state variables, C in splitting and substitution is the vector of incremental realization costs relative to the experimental activity, while for the other operators it represents the vector of research and realization costs for the modules involved in the modularization process. The parameters α and σ are the drifts and volatilities, respectively, of the state variables process under the EMM, while ρ represents the correlation coefficients.

For porting the correlation parameters are $(\rho_{1;2}, \rho_{1;3}, \rho_{1;4}, \rho_{2;3}, \rho_{2;4}, \rho_{3;4})$. C_s is the splitting cost; Q is the visibility cost; R is the vector of realization costs for the translator modules in the porting operator and I is the vector of research and development cost implied by the substitution operator, which is also embedded in the splitting operator. In all the cases the constant risk-free rate r is equal to 5%.

Table 13.14 Parameters used to test consistency of the numerical routines based on LSM method

Parameter	Splitting	Substitution	Augmenting	Excluding	Porting
V_0	(7, 9)	(6, 10)	10	(7, 9)	(13.3, 10, 4, 4)
C	(5, 8)	(5, 8)	(5, 8)	(5, 8)	(9, 11, 5, 4)
α	(0.04, 0.06)	(0.04, 0.02)	0.03	(0.04, 0.06)	(0.07, 0.04, 0.04, 0.02)
σ	(0.25, 0.17)	(0.25, 0.17)	0.15	(0.25, 0.17)	(0.1, 0.03, 0.04, 0.02)
$\rho_{i,j}$	0.3	0.3	–	0.3	(−0.1, 0.3, 0.5, 0.1, 0.6, 0.2)
C_s	3	–	–	0	–
Q	–	0	–	–	1
R	–	–	–	–	(1, 1, 1)
I	–	0	–	–	–
T	1	1	1	(0,5,1)	0.5

The splitting operator allows the creation of a project composed of two modules, as illustrated in Figure 13.14. There are two state variables with initial values $V_0 = (7, 9)$, drifts $\alpha = (0.04, 0.06)$, volatilities $\sigma = (0.25, 0.17)$ and correlation $\rho = 0.3$ that need to be realized subject to the research and realization cost, $C = (5, 8)$, and the cost of splitting $C_s = 3$.

The substitution operator provides the option to select the best of two competing versions of the module before $T = 1$, as depicted in Figure 13.16. There are therefore two state variables with current values $V_0 = (6, 10)$, and the parameters for these processes are $\alpha = (0.04, 0.02)$ and $\sigma = (0.25, 0.17)$ with a correlation $\rho = 0.3$. The incremental realization costs are $C = (5, 8)$ and zero research and development and visibility costs, that is, $I_{j,k} = 0$ for all $k = 1, \ldots, K$ and $Q_j = 0$ were assumed in the equation of substitution payoff.

For the augmenting operator a designer's option to expand the existing system by adding a new module was considered as in Figure 13.17. The parameters of the incremental value process are the initial values $V_0 = 10$, drift $\alpha = 0.03$ and volatility $\sigma = 0.15$. The realization cost is equal to 8.

For the excluding operator the opportunity to launch a minimal system was examined, with initial values $W_0 = 7$, drift $\alpha = 0.04$, volatility $\sigma = 0.25$, research and realization costs $C_W = 5$ and maturity $T_\alpha = 0.5$, with the subsequent option to expand by adding a new module with initial values $V_0 = 9$, drift $\alpha = 0.06$, volatility $\sigma = 0.17$ research and realization costs $C = 8$ and maturity $T_\omega = 1$ to the design as described in Figure 13.18. For simplicity while not reducing generality a zero cost was assumed for defining the design rules. The problem therefore has a two-dimensional state space.

Finally for the porting operator the case was considered where a portable module could be identified that fits within three different external systems. This also requires the realization of the translator modules. The valuation problem therefore

Table 13.15 Accuracy of the estimates obtained using the least-squares Monte Carlo method

	LSM	s.d.	accurate
Splitting	1.485	0.013	1.478
Substitution	2.504	0.011	2.526
Augmenting	2.219	0.002	2.217
Excluding	3.642	0.012	3.678
Porting	2.418	0.004	2.391

has four state variables, one set for the portable module (initial values of $V_0^{\hat{P}}=13.3$, drift $\alpha = 0.07$, volatility $\sigma = 0.1$ and realization costs $C^{\hat{P}} =9$) and three to model the dynamics of the potential values from the research activity in the three different systems, with initial values $V_0 = (10, 4, 4)$, drifts $\alpha = (0.04, 0.04, 0.02)$, volatilities $\sigma = (0.03, 0.04, 0.02)$ and realization costs $C = (11, 5, 4)$. The realization of the translator modules implies the cost $R = (1, 1, 1)$, and the visibility cost is set to $Q = 1$.

Table 13.15 illustrates the estimates obtained from the least-squares Monte Carlo method and the accurate values from a lattice method. LSM is the sample mean value obtained from 30 experiments for the splitting, substitution, augmenting and excluding operators; from 10 experiments for the splitting operator; from 20 experiments for porting. The corresponding standard deviation of the sample mean is s.d.

Each of the Monte Carlo experiments is based on 8,000 paths and 100 steps for substitution, 8,000 paths and 120 steps for porting, 10,000 and 100 for splitting, 15,000 and 100 for augmenting, and 10,000 and 400 for excluding. The simulated paths are obtained using the Euler discretization of the continuous time dynamics and the antithetic variates technique. These results are compared to the accurate values obtained using a lattice method together with a two point Richardson extrapolation. For the augmenting operator the approximation by Cox et al. (1979) was used with (100, 200) steps respectively. For the remaining operators the AGLT approximation by Gamba and Trigeorgis (2007) was used with 75,150 steps for the substitution, excluding and splitting operators, and with 10,200 steps for the porting operators.

In Table 13.15 it can be seen that the numerical method is reasonably accurate for the purposes of capital budgeting. While these basic examples allow a comparison to a numerical solution based on binomial lattices, the Monte Carlo simulation method allows the generalization of the number of modules and state variables involved in the decision process.

13.7.6 An automotive merger example

A merger between two car manufacturers is used to illustrate the Gamba and Fusari modularity real options valuation method. The two manufacturers, A and B produce comparable cars, and the merger strategy is to retain the brands while consolidating the design and production of the car frame. This process consists of two stages, isolating the car frame production line by splitting the existing production processes, and then applying the inverting operator to consolidate the car frame production.

The value of the initial combined manufacturing system is estimated for the application of the splitting operator, with $W_t = W_t^A + W_t^B$ representing the combined value of the current production for the two car manufacturers A and B. The splitting operator is then applied, which creates four modules, the specific modules $W_t^{A,s}$ and $W_t^{B,s}$ that produce all the brand-specific parts, and the car frame production modules $W_t^{A,c}$ and $W_t^{B,c}$. The system value after splitting is therefore $W_t^* = W_t^{A,c} + W_t^{A,s} + W_t^{B,c} + W_t^{B,s}$.

A new centralized module I is created to apply the inversion operator. Under the assumption that the original design is rationalized, the inversion can be applied at the start of the trial period while the original version is retained. The assumption is that three experiments are performed on the new version of the inverted module $\hat{I}$ with the optimal result selected at the end of the trials. The value $W_t^{I,k}$ is the version from the k-th experiment, and the related cost is $K_{\hat{I},k} = C_k + \sum_{k=1}^{3} I_k$ for $k = 1,2,3$ using the notation in equation (13.23). The associated visibility costs Q are required to ensure the compatibility of the specific car components with the new joint car frame. The value of the inverted module from equation (13.22) is therefore $F_{sub}(V_t^I)$ where the vector V_t^I has components $V_t^{I,k} = W_t^{I-k} - (W_t^{A,c} + W_t^{B,c})$ for $k = 1,2,3$. $V_t^{I,k} > 0$ should result from the scale economies generated by the inversion.

The production lines of the two car manufacturers are combined into one common manufacturing line using the inversion operator. The new common manufacturing line generates economies of scale by lowering total production costs, and therefore increases total cash flow assuming total combined revenues stay constant after the inversion.

The decision to invert is based on not only the direct costs but also the design opportunity costs of avoiding the independent upgrading of the individual common modules. Assuming that only one new version is considered, $\hat{W}_t^{A,c}$ and $\hat{W}_t^{B,c}$ are defined as the values for the two new module versions, and $C_{A,c}$ and $C_{B,c}$ as the costs associated with improving the two common production lines.

Based on the substitution operator valuation formula in equation (13.22), the opportunity costs are $F_{sub}(V_t^{A,c}) \geq 0$, where $V_t^{A,c} = \hat{W}_t^{A,c} - W_t^{A,c}$, and $F_{sub}(V_t^{B,c}) \geq 0$ where $V_t^{B,c} = \hat{W}_t^{B,c} - W_t^{B,c}$. It is assumed that there are no planned improvements for the brand specific production lines.

Given the assumptions, the payoff of the inversion operator is:

$$\prod_{inv}(t, V_t^I, V_t^A, V_t^B) = \max\left\{F_{sub}(V_t^I) - F_{sub}(V_t^A) - F_{sub}(V_t^B), 0\right\} \tag{13.32}$$

and the value is $F_{inv}(t, V_t^I, V_t^A, V_t^B)$. The payoff for the splitting operator, which includes the value of the inversion operator, is:

$$\prod_{spl}(t) = \max\left\{W_t^* - W_t - K_{A,c} - K_{A,s} - K_{B,c} - K_{B,s} - C_s + F_{inv}(t), 0\right\} \tag{13.33}$$

where $W_t^*-W^t$ is the incremental value for the split design, K_j represents the R&D and realization costs for each module, C_s is the splitting cost, and $F_{inv}(t) \geq 0$ is the value of the option to invert the common components. The solution of the problem involves the simulation of the following 11-dimensional Markov process:

$$W_t = (W_t^A, W_t^B, W_t^{A,s}, W_t^{B,s}, W_t^{A,c}, W_t^{B,c}, W_t^{I,1}, W_t^{I,2}, W_t^{I,3}, \hat{W}_t^{A,c}, \hat{W}_t^{B,c}),$$

For valuation purposes it is assumed that the values of the modules are correlated geometric Brownian motion (GBM) under the equivalent martingale measure (EMM). The parameters describing the stochastic process of the state variable and the costs are in Table 13.16.

The choice of the base case parameters was based on the following. The initial values of the two current systems is such that $W_0^A = W_0^{A,s} + W_0^{A,c}$, and $W_0^B = W_0^{B,s} + W_0^{B,c}$, that is, it is assumed that splitting the two systems does not change their current value. The current value of the inverted module is assumed to be higher than the sum of the current values of the two common modules for all three possible versions of the inverted module $W_0^{I,k} > W_0^{A,c} + W_0^{B,c}$, for $k = 1,2,3$. The new versions of the common modules, assuming they are chosen independently, improve the current versions but not the inverted module $W_0^{A,c} + W_0^{B,c} < W_t^{A,c} + \hat{W}_t^{B,c} < W_0^{I,k}$ for $k = 1,2,3$.

The cost of creating new modules is assumed to be the same for all modules. The only exception is the inverted module, as the design, test and realization costs are combined into one figure $K_{i,k}$. For simplicity it is assumed that the cost of the inverted module is the same for all possible versions. The visibility cost, Q, is relatively higher than the other costs to account for the changes that the brand-specific modules may require for compatibility with the new inverted module. These changes do not affect the value since they do not influence the cash flows, and are only required to make the modules work together. Finally the splitting cost, C_s, is relatively low as the initial system is almost modular.

The drift for the stochastic processes specified for the module values is assumed to coincide with the risk-free rate, or equivalently, the module values do not account for a convenience yield. The variance of W_t^A, W_t^B is approximately maintained by the processes $W_t^{A,s} + W_t^{A,c}$, and $W_t^{B,s} + W_t^{B,c}$ respectively. This illustrates that the value of splitting is positive when the overall uncertainty of the system is unchanged.

The following was observed for the correlations. It was assumed that the common component values are strongly and positively correlated, and are also positively correlated with the values of the three possible versions of the inverted module. The common component values are also positively correlated with the new versions of the common modules where the inversion does not take place. The values of the existing system are assumed to be weakly correlated with all other modules. Finally the two brand-specific modules have almost no correlation with the other modules. The time horizon for the option to split is set at $T_1 = 1$ year, and for the option to invert at $T_2 = 2$ years.

Table 13.16 Valuation of a complex design. Base case parameters.

Variable	Description	Initial value	Standard deviation
W_0^A	value of module A in the initial design	29	0.05
W_0^B	value of module B in the initial design	35	0.05
$W_0^{A,s}$	value of specific component of module A	10	0.06
$W_0^{B,s}$	value of specific component of module B	15	0.04
$W_0^{A,c}$	value of common component of module A	19	0.05
$W_0^{B,c}$	value of common component of module B	20	0.05
$W_0^{I,1}$	value of the first version of the inverted module	50	0.08
$W_0^{I,2}$	value of the second version of the inverted module	50	0.05
$W_0^{I,3}$	value of the third version of the inverted module	50	0.06
$\widehat{W}_0^{A,c}$	value of the alternative version of the common module of A	22	0.0405
$\widehat{W}_0^{B,c}$	value of the alternative version of the common module of B	23	0.0361
$K_{A,c}$	R&D cost of the common module of A	0.5	–
$K_{A,s}$	R&D cost of the specific module of A	0.5	–
$K_{B,c}$	R&D cost of the common module of B	0.5	–
$K_{B,s}$	R&D cost of the specific module of B	0.5	–
$K_{i,1}$	R&D cost of the first version of the inverted module	1.5	–
$K_{i,2}$	R&D cost of the second version of the inverted module	1.5	–
$K_{i,3}$	R&D cost of the third version of the inverted module	1.5	–
$C_{A,c}$	R&D cost of the alternative version of the common module of A	0.5	–
$C_{B,c}$	R&D cost of the alternative version of the common module of B	0.5	–
C_s	splitting cost	0.5	–
Q	visibility cost	2	–
T_1	time horizon of the splitting operator	1	–
T_2	time horizon of the inverting operator	2	–

The numerical analysis of the complex modularization decisions is illustrated in Table 13.17. The value of the inverting operator is estimated as the sample average of the values derived from 40 independent simulations using the LSM method. Each experiment is based on 10,000 paths and 100 time steps. An estimate of the probability of the application of the inversion operator was also derived as the sample average of the exercise probability. For a specific Monte Carlo experiment this is the number of paths where an operator is exercised over the total number of paths. To capture the timing of the inversion decision the average exercise time is also

Table 13.17 The auto modular parameters

	Value	Exercise probability	Average time
Base Case	3.9935 (0.0049)	0.0851 (0.0007)	1.6603 (0.0040)
Splitting & inversion triple test, no opp. cost	9.0545 (0.0068)	0.1187 (0.0016)	1.5378 (0.0123)
Splitting & inversion single test, no opp. cost	5.8324 (0.0050)	0.3114 (0.0180)	0.7726 (0.0376)
Splitting & inversion single test opp. cost	2.3447 (0.0052)	0.1116 (0.0008)	1.6673 (0.0026)
Splitting only	0.2782 (0.0013)	–	–

estimated conditional on such a decision being made. This is derived as the average of the exercise time for the paths where a decision is made for each Monte Carlo experiment. The exercise probability and the average time provide data for the analysis of the degree of flexibility on the decision policy. The standard deviations, which are in parentheses, for the sample estimates are also illustrated in Table 13.17.

The analysis of the value and the optimal policy for the project is based on the breakdown of the multiple sources of flexibility. Other problems were therefore solved where some of the base case model attributes were excluded.

The splitting only statistics in Table 13.17 illustrate the first sub-case where the value of the problem treated above is considered with the inversion operator omitted. This is equivalent to removing $F_{inv}(t)$ from equation (13.33), which allows the incremental value of the inverting operator to be determined over the value of splitting. In this case the dimension of the state space of the problem is reduced to six as the state variable is $W_t = (W_t^A, W_t^B, W_t^{A,s}, W_t^{B,s}, W_t^{A,c}, W_t^{B,c})$.

Restricting the inversion operator to the case where only one version of the inverted module is tested provides a second variation of interest. This is illustrated in Table 13.15, splitting and inversion, with a single test and with opportunity costs. This changes the payoff in equation (13.32) to:

$$\Pi_{inv}(t) = \max\left\{ F_{sub}(V_t^I) - F_{sub}(V_t^A) - F_{sub}(V_t^B), 0 \right\}$$

where V_t^I is one-dimensional and provides the testing of values for several versions of the inverted module for comparison to the base case. In this case the dimension of the state space for the problem is nine, as the state variable is $W_t = (W_t^A, W_t^B, W_t^{A,s}, W_t^{B,s}, W_t^{A,c}, W_t^{B,c}, W_t^I, \hat{W}_t^{A,c}, \hat{W}_t^{B,c})$.

A third sub-case is illustrated in Table 13.17, splitting and inversion, with a triple test and no opportunity costs. This involves the inversion of the common module without the opportunity cost of an independent development of the two common modules in equation (13.32), $F_{sub}(V_t^A) = 0 = F_{sub}(V_t^B)$, which reduces to $\Pi_{inv}(t) = F_{sub}(V_t^I)$. In this case the role of the independent substitution opportunities is captured and how their value changes the exercise policy of the inversion operator.

The state variable in this case is $W_t = (W_t^A, W_t^B, W_t^{A,s}, W_t^{B,s}, W_t^{A,c}, W_t^{B,c}, W_t^{I,1}, W_t^{I,2}, W_t^{I,3})$ with nine dimensions.

The final variation sub-case, as illustrated in Table 13.15, splitting and inversion, with a single test and no opportunity costs, is provided by considering the restriction to one version of the inverted module and the absence of opportunity costs simultaneously. This changes the payoff of the inverting operator to $\Pi_{inv}(t) = F_{sub}(V_t^I)$, and provides the value of the opportunity to invert the module without the derivation of any other form of flexibility.

The results in Table 13.17 allow a breakdown of the values for the different operators involved in the design problem. By comparing the case of the splitting operator only to the base case, it can be seen that significant value is provided by the possibility of inverting the module ($3.99 - 0.28 = 3.71$). The value of the splitting operator is composed of at least two components, the value of the substitution operator on the inverted module, and the opportunity cost due to the reduced flexibility.

Unfortunately there is no easy way to decompose the values of these two operators as they tend to interact. As a first approximation the possibility of conducting three tests as opposed to only one has a positive value of $3.99 - 2.34 = 1.65$, and the impact of the opportunity costs is $9.05 - 3.99 = 5.06$. When the base case is compared to the case with only one test and no opportunity costs however, it can be seen that the combined effect is significantly lower ($5.83 - 3.99 = 1.84$).

A second important aspect of the design problem is the optimal exercise policy for the inversion operator. Table 13.17 illustrates the exercise probability and the average time of exercise in the case where inversion actually takes place under the EMM. It can be seen that positive opportunity costs reduce the exercise probability and increase the average time of exercise for the inversion operator regardless of the number of tests on the inverted module. A less obvious observation is the effect of a higher number of tests. While it is certain that this increases the value, it also reduces the probability of inverting, as seen if, aside from the interaction effect with the opportunity costs, the case with three tests (approximately 11.9%) is compared to the case with one test (approximately 31.1%). The average time of inversion is also longer with three tests (1.54 years) than with one test (0.77 of a year).

The above also holds true, although at a reduced size, if the interaction with the opportunity cost is considered. This effect is due to the fact that the growth rate of the substitution operator for the inverted module with three tests is, given the current parameters, significantly higher than the one with one test. Since the option to invert is American, this induces an optimal delay due to a reduced convenience yield for the case with three tests.

13.8   THE SALE OF CORPORATE REAL ESTATE ASSETS

13.8.1   Overview

In this article, the authors analyze a downtown corporate office property that the corporate owner considered for a sale. They extend the conventional discounted cash flow analysis by valuing the embedded real put option held by the owner of the property to defer the sale until some optimal time in the future.

The use of such options, while increasingly commonplace in some industries, have yet to be widely adopted by commercial real estate investors and owners. Interestingly, embedded optionality – either explicit in the form of contractual rights, or implicit in the ability of an owner or lessor to exercise their ownership rights – is a feature common to many familiar real estate asset management decisions. The deferral option in our example is shown to depend upon both the future market value of the property, as well as the intrinsic value of the building to the corporate owner as an asset that contributes to production. The gap between these two values may differ significantly, however, since the implied discounted cash flows from the building treated as a market asset are not identical to those when the building is valued as a productive asset. The effects of this difference are clearly reflected in the options analysis; by contrast the conventional DCF approach does not make use of this gap and as a result, may lead to erroneous decisions. Our analysis both values the deferral option and via the calculation of the option's early exercise boundary, identifies the conditions under which a sale is optimally triggered.

13.8.2   Real options analysis

Real options analysis has made significant inroads into the resource allocation decisions of many capital intensive industries, such as energy and power generation, high technology, pharmaceuticals, mining, and telecommunications. Interestingly, the real estate industry, especially commercial real estate, has been a notable exception to this trend. (In the discussion that follows, we refer to the decisions of the owners or renters of the property asset itself, and not the owners of a derivative security.) Though a handful of academic papers have applied real options in the analysis of real estate problems, such as Schwartz and Torous (2003), Bulan, Mayer, and Sommerville (2002), Quigg (1993), Williams (1991), and Titman (1985), the commercial real estate industry has to date been somewhat resistant to adopting formal options methodologies. This is somewhat surprising for several reasons.

First, modern real estate capital markets routinely trade financial instruments which are characterized by significant optionality. For instance, commercial mortgage-backed securities are priced with respect to probability of loan default, which can be modeled as an exercise of an embedded default option by the borrower, e.g., Merton (1974), Fabozzi and Jacob (1996), Childs, Ott, and Riddiough (2003), and L'Heureux and Coleman (2003a). In a similar fashion, residential mortgage-backed securities are valued with respect to borrower prepayments which again, are typically represented as a rational option by the borrower to paydown the mortgage debt at a rate faster than the contractual amortization schedule.

Second, property investors are already quite familiar with contractual real estate option rights, such as lease extensions, redevelopment rights, future repurchases, and so on, and attempt to value such rights as part of their ongoing investment activities.

Third, as several authors have noted, e.g., Trigeorgis (1996), commercial real estate provides an excellent backdrop for real options analysis. Many property investment and leasing decisions are characterized by high fixed costs, long decision cycles, and are exposed to significant demand, supply, and price uncertainty over time. As a result, option premia should be quite large with respect to the underlying project NPV.

Finally, it is relatively straightforward to show that many of the most common commercial real estate asset decisions – purchases, sales, leasing, relocation, development and redevelopment, sale-leasebacks, etc. – are indeed characterized in a fundamental way by embedded optionality. Following methods outlined in the seminal work by Dixit and Pindyck (1994), this optionality can be effectively modeled and we argue, has both significant economic value to the decision maker and offers insights into the capital investment decision that may be far less obvious if only the traditional 'static' net present value rule is used.

This article presents a real-world example of modeling an extremely common real estate decision – a sale – as a deferral option. Specifically we explore the recent decision by a large US telecommunications firm to sell a corporate headquarters property in downtown San Francisco as part of the ongoing consolidation of its national real estate portfolio. The company conducted a conventional analysis using standard net present value techniques and determined that the sale of the property to a third-party at prevailing market prices met its financial objectives. Using the same underlying assumptions and data, we extend their analysis to consider the optimal timing of the sale, modeling the decision as an American put option. This deferral option is shown to depend upon both the future market value of the property, as well as the intrinsic value (or 'value in use') of the building to the corporate owner as an asset that contributes to production or earnings.

The gap between these two values may differ significantly, however, since the implied discounted cash flows from the building treated as a market asset are not identical to those when the building is valued as a productive asset. The effects of this difference are clearly reflected in the options analysis; by contrast the conventional DCF approach used by the company does not fully reflect the strategic value of this asset. Once the put option is modeled, we conduct a sensitivity analysis to show how the option value varies with real estate market valuations.

We also calculate the early exercise boundary, which we then map onto a forecast of future market values. This allows us to identify the market conditions under which a sale is optimally triggered and when such conditions might occur given a prediction of future property values.

In practice, this approach is generalized by the authors as a set of 'exchange options' from the current form of ownership to various alternatives (sell for cash, structured sale leasebacks, 1031 and other like kind exchanges, and synthetic leases with forward sale of the residual equity position).

While we are firm believers in the 'law of one price,' the real estate ownership and rental markets are highly segmented and have a microstructure which suggests that the 'best owner' and 'highest and best use' of an asset will change from time to time. This is particularly true during times when the direction of heavy capital flows are weakly correlated with rental market fundamentals. The result is that transactions may often occur at prices which appear at odds with the NPVs implied from discounting current building cash flows. Under such conditions, real options provide a useful framework to help an investor decide if it is best to sell now or wait.

13.8.3 The conventional decision to sell

Acquisitions and dispositions are among the most common commercial real estate decisions. The conventional discounted cash flow analysis of these transactions has been extensively researched and is now the fundamental method used for property valuation, see, e.g., Brueggeman and Fisher (1996) for a detailed discussion of the method in the context of commercial real estate analysis. For the present case, we consider the prospective sale of an office property owned by a large, publicly traded US telecommunications company. The company recently conducted an extensive review of its corporate real estate holdings across the United States, with an eye towards disposing of underutilized or obsolete facilities and reducing leasing and building maintenance expenses. As a result of this analysis, several properties, including the one presented here, were identified as likely candidates for sale. Once identified, a more extensive financial analysis was conducted, including a discounted cash flow analysis of a prospective sale to a third party at a price consistent with prevailing office market conditions in San Francisco.

The subject property is a 350,000 square foot (sf) building located in downtown San Francisco. The property currently houses several hundred employees, who would be relocated to other company owned or leased facilities in the event of a sale. The building, constructed in the 1920s, was flagged for sale in part because it had become increasingly functionally obsolete and expensive to maintain to current standards. Occupancy costs, including capital improvements, were rising sharply. The building is wholly owned by the company and unencumbered by debt. The company has owned and occupied the property for several decades, and it has been fully depreciated. A recent appraisal put the value of the property (and the surrounding parcel of land) at $53 million, a figure consistent with the company's internal analysis.

Based upon the current and projected costs of maintaining the property at its current level of occupancy and intensity of use, the company determined that the present value of keeping the property was $6.932 million. To determine the effects of a sale, the company assumed the property would sell for its appraised value and employees would be relocated to another company-owned facility. After factoring in operating, relocation and capital equipment expenses, brokerage fees, and taxes (note: under California state law, utilities are required to return 50% of any gain on land sales to ratepayers), the NPV was calculated to be $21.981 million. Note that these calculations were performed assuming a 10-year horizon. We summarize the results in Table 13.18 (note: all figures are in $millions). Based upon these results, the decision was made to sell the subject property.

Table 13.18 Preliminary sales analysis

Decision	Cost/Proceeds	PV/NPV
Keep property		$6,932
Sell and relocate		
Operating expenses	$1,485	
Expense to vacate	$3,334	
Capital to vacate	$3,854	
Sales price	$53,000	
Less commissions	(1,690)	
Less 50% gain on land	($8,927)	
Net sale proceeds	$42,383	$21,981
Difference		$15,049

13.8.4 Real options model of deferred sale

As is well known, the real options approach offers two strong advantages compared to traditional NPV. First, it correctly recognizes the inherent uncertainty and flexibility of many capital investment decisions. Second, it compels the analyst to establish a more rigorous link between the strategic or business value of an asset as a factor of production and it's value in the market to a third-party buyer. This latter requirement is particularly interesting in the case of commercial real estate since most firms tend to view their property holdings as static expenses, rather than as productive assets that can be optimally managed to contribute to earnings. That is, corporate real estate tends to be managed in a cost-minimizing fashion, i.e., firms work to keep operating and maintenance costs at a minimum, regardless of the impact such actions may have on the ability of real estate to contribute to earnings when augmenting other factors, such as labour. By contrast, many other types of assets, such as capital equipment, research and development expenditures, intellectual property, inventories, etc., are increasingly perceived and managed in a more dynamic fashion with an eye towards increasing earnings, and not simply 'cutting costs'.

As noted above, many common commercial real estate decision problems can be modeled as options. In actual practice, a building owner would identify a number of competing strategies for the asset, e.g., outright sale, subletting vacant space, sale-leaseback, or some combination of these, etc. Which of these alternatives are ultimately feasible depends on many factors – strategic business considerations, legal and tax restrictions, operational uses, market conditions, and company-specific financial requirements. The specific option models that must be evaluated will reflect this feasible set. For the subject property, the company considered several competing alternatives before opting on an outright sale. To keep our exposition

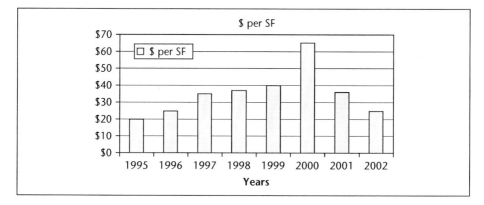

Figure 13.21 Asking rents in San Francisco office market

simple, we will present the real options modeling of the sale alternative only. This has the added benefit of being one the simpler options technically to model, interpret, and solve. Part of the motivation for selling the subject property has been the perceived imbalance recently between prices in the San Francisco office market and rental conditions.

Figure 13.21 depicts the path of office rents in the subject property's submarket. The unprecedented run-up in rents from 1999–2000, at the peak of the 'dot.com' boom stands out. Since 2000, however, office rents have declined 53% from their peak, as a combination of the bursting Internet stock bubble, the retrenchment of the high-tech sector, and the broader decline in the national economy have caused a precipitous decline in the demand for office space. At the same time, office vacancy rates, which stood at a scant 3.3% in 2003, are now over 18%. As a result, occupancy-adjusted cash flows from office properties have declined significantly. Interestingly, however, the prices investors will pay for real estate have for the most part remained firm. Much of this has to do with the amount of capital that institutional investors have allocated towards real estate in the past. Due to diminished equity returns, many large investors have increased their capital allocations to commercial property. As a result, capitalization rates (the discount factor that real estate investors apply to building cash flows for valuation purposes) have not risen nearly as sharply as the deterioration in rental rates and occupancies would have implied. Under these circumstances, many corporate property owners have recognized that they can sell property at favorable prices and simultaneously relocate to far cheaper leased space.

Given the dramatic softening of the office market in the past three years, and the sizable gap between the demand and supply for space, the office outlook not unexpectedly calls only for a very modest recovery in the next several years (see Figure 13.22). Rents are projected to stabilize in 2004, and then rise slowly thereafter. Vacancy rates, which generally follow rental changes with a short lag, should peak within two years, before moving downward again. The downward correction in property prices should gain momentum, as investors move back towards equity

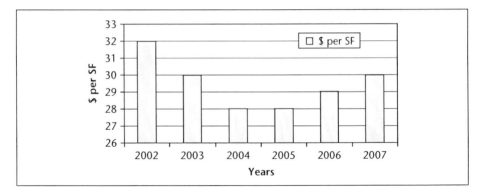

Figure 13.22 San Francisco office market – rent forecast

markets, and as the unfavorable rental market conditions further depress building cash flows.

We extend the company's preliminary analysis by formally introducing the idea that the decision to sell can be modeled as a deferral put option. That is, rather than simply sell today, as the NPV analysis implies, the company can choose the optimal point to sell any time within some future interval by putting the subject property to a buyer at the market price which prevails at the time the option is exercised. Since the buyer can choose to exercise this option at any time, this option is treated as an American put. In general, however, even a simple cash sale real options model introduces some complications.

First, many properties are income-producing, thus it would be reasonable to liken them to (perhaps stochastic) dividend paying stocks. In addition, the put option is not exercised at a fixed, pre-determined strike price; instead the sale occurs at an unknown stochastic future price. At a minimum some sort of one-factor model should be used to reflect the distribution of future building values. Further, equilibrium real estate prices are typically represented as the present discounted value of future rents, which as we note above, are imperfectly correlated with prices. As a result, a multifactor model should be used to capture the interaction between prices and rents. We recognize the importance of these requirements in developing a rigorous real options model for real estate. For the sake of expository clarity, however, we make a number of simplifying assumptions and use a standard American put option with no dividends (note: as many corporate owned buildings are fully owner-occupied and hence not earning rental income, the assumption of no dividend payments is not untenable). One of the challenges in using real options models centers on the difficulties of developing the necessary model input parameters. Our deferral option formulation uses two distinct prices. The first is the market value of the property, i.e., the sales price the building would command in a pure, arms-length transaction.

The second is an estimate of the 'value-in-use,' or the marginal revenue (or earnings) value of the property to the current corporate owner. This latter price reflects in some sense the value of the building as a factor of production, which has a certain

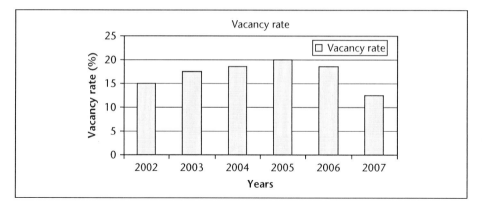

Figure 13.23 San Francisco office market – vacancy forecast

productivity or marginal revenue product. Given these prices, the put option is in-the-money when the market value of the property is greater than the marginal revenue product of the building as an operating asset. As the value-in-use of the property is closely tied to its operational functionality, this helps underscore the link between capital investment and business strategies that real options emphasize. To estimate this pair of prices, we begin by specifying a way to tie building value to market rents and capitalization rates (the main drivers of discounted cash flow pricing). For this, we adopt a relatively common 'mark-to-market' approach that capitalizes a market-based estimate of building rents, then makes an allowance for market vacancy rates. The basic idea is to identify an appropriate submarket or peer group of buildings, and then use the average rents and occupancy rates of this sample to create an estimate of net operating income (NOI), which in turn is used to value the property. This is very similar to the procedure that debt rating agencies use to underwrite pools of commercial mortgages when rating real estate securities and is the approach that many prospective buyers would take in valuing a property. The NOI calculation is detailed in Table 13.19.

To calculate the market value, the per square foot NOI is divided by a capitalization rate (or cap rate for short). This yields, on a per square foot basis, the discounted value of the building's net income stream, which when multiplied by the total size of the property produces an estimate of market value (see Table 13.20). Note that the market value estimate also includes the land value associated with the subject property.

Next, we need an estimate of the price of the subject property as a factor of production, which we denote value-in-use. The estimation of value-in-use ties closely to the nature and intensity of the business activities which the property supports. In many instances, establishing the 'earnings' generated by a specific property may be relatively straightforward. Retail properties are easily tied to the sales they support. The value of a warehouse building can be related to the dollar volume of goods shipped through the facility. Manufacturing plants can be linked to the value of the goods produced, while hotels have easily observed revenue streams. Office properties, however, are more problematic, since office space tends to be largely an augmenting

Table 13.19 Estimated property NOI

Factor	Value(psf)	Notes and sources
Asking rent	$25.00	Historical figures, quoted rents
Effective rent	$20.00	Historical figures, asking rents less free rent, concession, TI's
(−) Operating expenses	$4.11	Ongoing maintenance, insurance
(−) Capital expenses	$3.33	Company data; costs of maintaining building quality
Net rent	$12.55	Rents after expenses
Vacancy	18.0%	Historical figures, sub market vacancy rate
NOI	$10.30	Net rent* (1-Vacancy)

Table 13.20 Value calculations

	Market value	Value-in-use	Notes
Price	$53,080,144	$63,000,000	GLA × price (psf)
Gross leasable area (sf)	350,000	350,000	Building size
Price (psf)	$123.09	$180.00	NOI/discount factor
NOI (psf)	$10.29	$45.00	Estimated by authors
Discount factors			
Cap rate	8.36%		Source: Real Capital Analytics
Return on equity		25.0%	ROE target provided by company
Land value	$10,000,000		

Notes: Market value includes land. Cap rate is based on last 12 months of transactions in submarket, adjusted by authors.

factor, facilitating the productivity of labour, and there is no 'natural' way to directly assign a revenue value to a square foot of office space.

Moreover, regardless of the apparent ease of value-in-use estimation for any given property, there is the more complicating need to assess the potential strategic value of an asset. For instance, a retail property has value not just from supporting sales, but from preempting competition, generating branding for a company, or providing a platform for additional growth in the local trade area. These strategic factors are more difficult to estimate and often require very specific knowledge of a company, its competitors, and nature of its end markets, and so on.

For our example, the authors worked with company analysts to develop an estimate of value-in-use for the subject property. As a general rule, we have found that a large part of value-in-use is subjective. As this is a key component of the option's

Table 13.21 Benchmark option model inputs (per square foot basis)

Input	Value	Notes
Value-in-use	$180.00	Capitalized income to company from property
Strike price	$151.66	Current market value of asset (includes land)
Risk-free rate	4%	5-year treasuries
Annualized volatility	30%	Correlation of capitalized earnings and office values
Expiration (years)	5	Exercise time

moniness, sensitivity analysis should be performed across the value-in-use parameters when pricing this form of deferral option. As shown in Table 13.20, a point estimate of the value-in-use of the subject property was calculated to be $63,000,000, or about $10,000,000 more than the estimated market value.

The final step before solving the deferral option model is to specify the remaining model inputs (Table 13.21). We assume a five-year expiration for the put option, and use a 4% risk-free rate. As the option value depends on both the market value and value-in-use, we estimate a compound volatility that reflects the (imperfect) correlation between the volatility of capitalized company earnings and office real estate values.

13.8.5   The results

We utilize a standard binomial tree-based American option model to price the deferral. Using the baseline parameters in Table 13.21, the value to the company to put the subject property at the current strike price over the next five years is $17.71 per square foot, or $6.2 million in total. This represents 11.7% of the current appraised value, a substantial amount in the context of a commercial real estate transaction. We next conduct a sensitivity analysis with respect to current cap rates. The results are summarized in Table 13.22. The cap rate was allowed to vary from 6% to 12%, a range that is reflective of the historical volatility of San Francisco office market transaction prices. Table 13.22 indicates the resulting put option value and the put value's share of the corresponding market value of the property. Even for very high cap rates, the put value remains a significant share of the market value, implying that the flexibility associated with the ability to defer a sale is valuable. Even if the value of the surrounding land is factored out (we held this value constant in the analysis), the put retains a value sufficiently large to warrant the attention of management.

As noted above, a powerful dimension of real options methodology is the ability to show under what conditions the option may be exercised. For this, we calculated the early exercise boundary of the deferral put, using the benchmark parameters shown in Table 13.21. The result is shown in Figure 13.24. The boundary shows the minimum market price at which the put owner should optimally exercise, given the estimated value-in-use of the property. For this specific example, it would take historically low cap rates – under 5% – to trigger an optimal exercise.

Table 13.22 Sensitivity analysis-capitalization rates

Cap rate	6%	7%	8%	9%	10%	11%	12%
Market value ($)	$70,042,222	$61,464,762	$55,031,667	$46,025,333	$42,750,303	$42,750,303	$40,021,111
Put value per square foot	$37.51	$26.68	$19.64	$14.87	$11.53	$9.12	$7.35
Total put ($mil)	$13,128,500	$9,338,000	$6,874,000	$5,204,500	$4,035,500	$3,192,000	$2,572,500
% of value	18.7%	15.2%	12.5%	10.4%	8.8%	7.5%	6.4%
% w/o land	14.6%	11.0%	8.4%	6.4%	5.0%	3.9%	3.1%

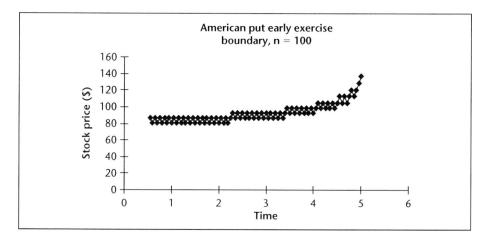

Figure 13.24 Early exercise boundary

13.8.6 Summary

There are two fundamental conclusions from our example: there is value in waiting to execute asset sale strategies and what a company does has a great impact on this value. Given a reasonable characterization of conditions and uncertainties in the real estate markets and corporate business environment, the real options approach provides a way to determine when and under what conditions (price being one) it is optimal to sell. This is a critical step for companies seeking to coordinate their real estate policies with the optimal investment decisions for the firm. What a company does in its commercial space and the optimal way it contracts to use that space are largely determined by the business opportunities and tax considerations of the corporation. As discussed in L'Heureux and Coleman (2003b), the revenue potential business opportunities of a company determine 'the size of the pie' while the competitive dynamics of the rental market (relative to other factor markets) determine the size of the slice paid as rent. As a result, the value-in-use of a real estate asset (or any fixed asset) for a corporate user is determined by the profitability considerations of their business.

As the corporate tenant can either decline to lease space (the option to lease) or sub-lease currently held space at market rates, this value will be greater than or equal to the rental rate for the space or the firm will sell. We are currently extending this approach in several directions. The conceptual framework above can be used to measure the impact of 'hidden assets' in commercial properties, e.g., L'Heureux and Coleman (2003c). These assets typically produce non-traditional real estate revenue streams. Examples include the ability to develop and lease a carrier hotel or central office in the basement of an office building, or construct and rent an 'antenna farm' on the roof. While these assets (or options to develop these assets) may or may not be reflected in the market value of the property, certain types of hidden assets provide non-transferable rights or facilities-specific services to the owners/users.

In the telecommunications industry, such options could entail the right to expand or upgrade critical links in the carrier's network. These rights to develop future business could explain why it may be optimal for the carrier to retain an empty building. As a result, the real options approach to formulating corporate real estate policies aligns the interests and efforts of a company's real estate department with the business objectives of the Treasury and operational units.

Acknowledgement – this article is reprinted from the *Real Estate Finance Journal* with permission of Thomson Reuters/West.

REFERENCES

Amran, M. and Kulatilaka, N. *Real Options: Managing Strategic Investment in an Uncertain World*, Harvard Business School Press, 1999.

Baldwin, C. Y. and Clark, K. B. *Design Rules: The Power of Modularity*. MIT Press, Cambridge, MA, 2000.

Baumert, K., Herzog, T. and Pershing, J. *Navigating the Numbers – Greenhouse Gas Data and International Climate Policy*, World Resources Institute, 2005.

Berger, P., Ofck, E. and Swary, I. Investor valuation of the abandonment option, *Journal of Financial Economics*, **42**: 257–87 1996.

Brueggeman, W. and Fisher, J. D. *Real Estate Finance and Investments*, 10th edn, Irwin Publishing 1996.

Bulan, L., Mayer, C. and Sommerville, C. *Irreversible Investment, Real Options*, and *Competition: Evidence from Real Estate Development*, unpublished manuscript, Faculty of Commerce, UBC, Vancouver, 2002.

Challa, R. Discovering multiple interacting options, *Energy and Power Risk Management*, July 2000.

Childs, P., Ott, H. and Riddiough, T. Effects of noise on optimal exercise decisions: The case of risky debt secured by renewable lease income, *Journal of Real Estate Finance and Economics*, **28**: 109–21, 2004, 2003.

Clewlow, L. and Strickland, C. *Implementing Derivative Models*, Wiley, 1998.

Clewlow, L. and Strickland, C. *Energy Derivatives, Pricing and Risk Management*, Lacima, 2000.

Coleman, M., L'Heureux, S. and Friedman, D. Modeling the sale of corporate real estate assets: A case study using real options, *The Real Estate Finance Journal*, Spring 2004.

Copeland, T. *A Practitioners View of Applications of Real Options*, Second Annual Conference on Real Options, Chicago, IL, June 1998.

Cox, J., Ross, A., and Rubinstein, M. Option pricing: a simplified approach. *Journal of Financial Economics*, **7**: 229–63, 1979.

DiMasi, J., Hansen, R., Grabowski, H. and Lasagne, L. Cost of innovation in the pharmaceutical industry, *Journal of Health Economics*, **10**(2): 107–42, 1991.

Dixit, A. and Pindyck, R. *Investment Under Uncertainty*, Princeton University Press, 1994.

Fabozzi, F. and Jacob, D. (eds). *The Handbook of Commercial Mortgage-Backed Securities*, John Wiley & Sons, 1996.

Foster, R. and Kaplan, S. *Creative Destruction*, Doubleday, 2001.

Gamba, A. and Fusari, N. *Valuing modularity as a Real Option*, working paper.

Gamba, A. and Trigeorgis, L. An improved binomial lattice method for multi-dimensional options. *Applied Mathematical Finance*, **14**(5): 453–75, 2007.

Geske, R. The valuation of compound options, *Journal of Financial Economics*, 1978.

Geske, R. and Zhou, Y. *Capital Structure Effects on Prices of Firm Stock Options: Tests Using Implied Market Values of Corporate Debt*, UCLA Working Paper, 2007a.

Geske, R. and Zhou, Y. *Predicting Risk and Return of the S&P 500: Evidence from Index Options*, UCLA Working Paper, 2007.

Grabowski, H.C. and Vernon, J.M. Returns to R&D on new drug introductions in the 1980s, *Journal of Health Economics*, **13**: 383–406, 1994.

Grant, R. *Contemporary Strategy Analysis*, Blackwell, 2006.

Haug, E.G. *The Complete Guide to Option Pricing Formulas*, McGraw-Hill, 1998.

Kasanen, E. and Trigeorgis, L. A. Market utility approach to investment valuations, *European Journal of Operational Research*, **74**: 294–309, 1994.

Kellogg, D. and Charnes, J.M. Real options valuation for a biotechnology company, *Financial Analysts Journal*, May/June 2000.

Kulatilaka, N., Balasubramanian, P. and Storck, J. Using real options to frame the IT investment problem, in Trigeorgis, L. (ed.) *Real Options and Business Strategy*, Risk Books, 1999.

L'Heureux, S. and Coleman, M. *Efficient Management of Corporate-Owned Real Estate Assets: A Real-Options Based Model*, unpublished manuscript, 2003a.

L'Heureux, S. and Coleman, M. *The Determination of Real Rental Rates*, unpublished manuscript, 2003b.

L'Heureux, S. and Coleman, M. *The Real Options Valuation of a Hidden Real Estate Asset: The Case of a Carrier Hotel*, unpublished manuscript, 2003c.

Mason, S.P. and Merton, R.C. The role of contingent claims analysis in corporate finance, in Altman, E. (ed.) *Recent Advances in Corporate Finance*, Irwin, 1985.

Mbanefo, A. *Co-movement Term Structure and the Valuation of Energy Spread Options, Mathematics of Derivative Securities*, Cambridge University Press, 1997.

McCraw, T. *Prophet of Innovation*, Belknap Harvard, 2007.

Merton, R. On the pricing of corporate debt: The risk structure of interest rates, *Journal of Finance*, **29**(2): 449–70, 1974.

Myers, S. and Howe, C.A. *Life Cycle Financial Model of the Pharmaceutical R&D Program on the Pharmaceutical Industry*, Massachusetts Institute of Technology, 1997.

Myers, S. and Shyam-Sunder, L. Measuring pharmaceutical industry risk and the cost of capital, in Helms, R.B. (ed.) *Competitive Strategies in the Pharmaceutical Industry*, Washington, DC, American Enterprise Institute Press, 1996.

Pearson, N. An efficient approach for pricing spread options, *The Journal of Derivatives*, Fall, 1997.

Penman, S. *Financial Statement Analysis and Security Valuation*, McGraw Hill/Irwin, 2004.

Pew Center on Global Climate Change, *Getting Ahead of the Curve: Corporate Strategies That Address Climate Change*, October 2006.

Quigg, L. Empirical testing of real option-pricing models, *Journal of Finance*, **48**: 621–40, 1993.

Ravindran, K. *Low-fat Spreads, Over the Rainbow*, Risk Publications, 1993.

Schwartz, E.S. The stochastic behaviour of commodity price: implications for valuation and hedging, *The Journal of Finance*, **LII**(3): 923–73, 1997.

Schwartz, E. and Walter, N. *Commercial Office Space: Tests of a Real Options Model with Competitive Interactions*, working paper, The Anderson School, UCLA, 2003.

Stearns, P. *The Industrial Revolution in World History,* Westview Press, 2007.

Sullivan, K., Chalasani, P., Jha, S. and Sazawal, V. Software design as an investment activity: a real options perspective, in Trigeorgis, L. (ed.) *Real Options and Business Strategy,* Risk Books, 1999.

Titman, S. Urban land prices under uncertainty, *American Economic Review,* **75**: 505–14, 1985.

Tong, T. and Reuer, J. *Corporate Investment Decisions and the Value of Growth Options,* 2004.

Trigeorgis, L. *Real Options: Managerial Flexibility and Strategy in Resource Allocation,* MIT Press, 1996.

US Congress, Office of Technology Assessment, *Pharmaceutical R&D: Costs Risks and Rewards,* OTA-M-522, Washington, DC: US Government Printing Office, February 1993.

Wellington, F. and Sauer, A. *Framing Climate Risk in Portfolio Management,* World Resources Institute, 2005.

Williams, J. Real estate development as an option, *Journal of Real Estate Finance and Economics,* **4**, 1991–2008.

Zhou, Y. *Pricing Individual Stock Options on Firms with Leverage,* Anderson School of Management at UCLA, 2007.

CHAPTER 14

Conclusion and Practical Implications

Organizations today are confronted with a number of developments that are likely to profoundly influence strategy. These include the commoditization of products and services, the effect of creative destruction and the breakdown of industry barriers, the impact of disruptive technologies, changes in demographics and demand patterns and the increasing dynamics and instability of markets generally. Achieving sustainable competitive advantage and value creation using management processes based on the notions of continuity and incremental improvement is becoming a difficult proposition. Static long-term strategies based on these management values will become increasingly harder to execute.

Corporate strategy is essentially about making choices and trade-offs in the allocation of resources. Over the twentieth century, however, corporate finance and corporate strategy evolved as complementary but nevertheless distinct disciplines for managerial decision making. Analysis in corporate finance has developed into a focus on DCF techniques for individual projects, which does not account for any flexibility to defer, abandon or change a project after a decision has been made. As a result DCF methods are not prominent in the strategy disciplines, where the principal themes are concepts such as competitive advantage, market leadership and industry structure.

Creating sustainable competitive advantage and value in the future will require capabilities in managing both an organization's current portfolio and the manoeuvring of the organization through an increasingly turbulent and dynamic environment. Organizations will need to focus on maintaining a strategic portfolio, by managing both the identified and the uncertain as they position themselves for the future. This will require new capabilities in strategy, the management of innovation, resource allocation, management processes and organizational structure. An organization's capabilities will therefore not only consist of the ability to manage sustainable technologies through incremental improvements, but also the value opportunities created through innovation, the disruptive technologies that are options on the future.

Established valuation methods such as DCF analysis will be sufficient for the current portfolio where there is little uncertainty. Real options analysis, however, will be essential in situations where there is a contingent investment decision, where there is value in future growth options rather than current cash flows, when it is better to wait for more information when the risks are significant, and when there is the potential to include flexibility in projects and strategy generally. To sustain value creation organizations will need capabilities in managing portfolios of real options, which will provide the link between value analysis and the issues of resource allocation, discontinuity, uncertainty, management flexibility, managing innovation and communicating strategy to stakeholders and financial markets.

There are, however, a number of potential issues that may need to be addressed with applying real options analysis. One of the fundamental principles of option theory is that a replicating portfolio can be created with an underlying asset and risk-free borrowing. This is extended to real option theory such that there exists a security or set of securities whose cash flows are correlated with those of the real asset. If, however, the spanning assumption will not hold, then dynamic programming and decision analysis offer alternative valuation methods to solving real options problems when traded values are not available.

The application of financial market models such as Black–Scholes to value real options can present problems. The financial markets are littered with experiences where financial models were applied that were not suited to the market environment and with assumptions that were not valid. A large component of the value in applying real options lies in the insights gained from the actual process of an analysis. Quantitative models and methods are tools that facilitate the analytical process and provide an abstraction of the problem. They are not black boxes that just produce a number, and are certainly not some enchanted device that provides instant and perfect solutions.

Another issue is that while a real option analysis may be theoretically correct, it may not have any significant influence on an organization's management decisions. A real options analysis has to consider an organization's culture, decision and management processes. This not only includes how an organization is managed and how decisions are made, but also how on occasions mistakes can be made. Increasing the effectiveness of a real options analysis within an organization includes identifying and communicating any limitations, and also seeking any potential interactions with other management disciplines such as industry analysis and competitor analysis.

What a real options framework does offer is the potential to combine strategic and financial analysis, and integrate investment decisions with corporate strategy and value. Real options can clarify management decisions by supporting strategic opportunities with values that are aligned with the financial markets, and provide the means to communicate these values to the financial markets. The real options concept also has the potential to enhance the aggregation of an organization's project values and the management of its risk exposures. Real option techniques will become a powerful component of an organization's strategic analysis, valuation, decision and risk management processes. As the business environment becomes more unpredictable and the implications of making incorrect business decisions continue to rise, the demand for sophisticated analytical disciplines such as real options is likely to grow rapidly.

Index